Researching Education

D0162603

Researching Education:
Perspectives and Techniques

Gajendra K. Verma
and Kanka Mallick

FALMER PRESS
Taylor & Francis Group

UK   Falmer Press, 1 Gunpowder Square, London, EC4A 3DE
USA   Falmer Press, Taylor & Francis Inc., 325 Chestnut Street, 8th Floor,
          Philadelphia, PA 19106

© G.K. Verma and K. Mallick, 1999

First published in 1999

A catalogue record for this book is available from the British Library

ISBN 0 7507 0530 2 cased
ISBN 0 7507 0531 0 paper

**Library of Congress Cataloging-in-Publication Data are available on
request**

Jacket design by Caroline Archer

Typeset in 10/12pt Times by
Graphicraft Limited, Hong Kong

*Printed in Great Britain by Biddles Ltd., Guildford and King's Lynn on
paper which has a specified pH value on final paper manufacture of not
less than 7.5 and is therefore 'acid free'.*

*Every effort has been made to contact copyright holders for their
permission to reprint material in this book. The publishers would be
grateful to hear from any copyright holder who is not here acknowledged
and will undertake to rectify any errors or omissions in future editions of
this book.*

Contents

Contents

List of Figures and Tables

Preface

When Falmer Press approached me with the suggestion that I might revise the book that Ruth Beard and I wrote on Educational Research, my immediate impulse was to agree. It was, after all, nearly 20 years ago that it first appeared and the worlds of both education and research had moved on. I imagined that it would be very much a case of up-dating the original text by inserting new references and mapping the changes that had occurred over the intervening years without having to engage in much re-writing.

However, when Kanka Mallick joined me in this enterprise, and we started to re-read the book with a critical eye, we soon came to the conclusion that we wanted to attempt something more radical than simply up-dating the original text. Not only had research and education changed over the years, I had changed, my co-author had changed, and so had the book's potential readers. Indeed, looking at the first edition, we became less and less certain about who it had been intended for. The more we thought about it, the more convinced we became that some fundamental restructuring was the only answer. The result of all this may be found in the following pages.

The influence of the first book upon the present one is unmistakable, and perhaps inevitable: what still holds true and is useful has been retained. The major differences arise, we think, because this time we had a clearer idea of the audience for which it was intended. Whereas the first research book was, subconsciously perhaps, intended for students who had already made up their minds to undertake research and were looking for a kind of guide which would conduct them on the journey on which they had already embarked; this one made no such assumption. Whilst we would hope — and do believe — that the first book will still be of help to them, this new book *Researching Education* is intended for people — you the readers — who may be standing, anxiously perhaps, outside a door marked 'EDU-CATIONAL RESEARCH' and wondering whether to knock on it, push it open and see what is on the other side. What this book seeks to do is to encourage you to push that door open, enter that world beyond it and explore.

Like any traveller in unknown territory, the process can be very arduous but the rewards for discovering something new can be great. For some, one voyage of exploration is enough. The explorer returns home and takes up his or her life, enriched by the experience. For others, perhaps you, it is the beginning of a lifetime of intellectual adventure as one quest leads, inevitably it seems, to the next.

If this little book arouses your interest, encourages you to book your passage on that journey, it will have succeeded in its aim. Good luck! Bring back treasure with which to enrich the world of education.

G.K.V.
K.M.

Acknowledgments

We would like to take the opportunity to thank colleagues who have helped in writing this book. First, we must mention Douglas Darby who has helped greatly in organizing the materials, both old and new, and providing very valuable suggestions and comments; and Tony Neasham, for his perceptive and valuable comments and suggestions at all stages from inception to completion. One chapter in particular, Chapter 8: 'Statistical Concepts and Educational Research', seemed particularly difficult to get right. In its original form, it seemed mathematically daunting to the readers for whom it was intended. The attempt to reduce the mathematical content and to focus on the concepts which underlay it was a particular challenge. We would like to thank Peter Pumfrey and Nicholas Boreham who read successive drafts of Chapter 8 and were, as always, generous with their time and helpful with their comments. Preparing a manuscript for publication is an arduous business which never gets any easier, however many times it has been done before. Janet Grimshaw, who was responsible for this (as well as for many earlier ones), has again been invaluable in the care and attention to detail that she has brought to the task.

Gajendra K. Verma
Kanka Mallick

Chapter 1

Introduction to Research

The term 'research' is often defined in terms of 'systematic inquiry'. Simply expressed, research involves finding out something which was previously not known, or shedding fresh light on an issue or problem. People often seem to regard research as something mystifying which is only conducted by professional researchers. In practice, we are all engaged in one form of research or another in our everyday lives without being necessarily conscious that we are doing it. Many attempts have been made to provide formal definitions of the activity of which the following are but a few.

The Encyclopaedia of the Social Sciences (1934) defined research as being the:

> ... manipulation of things, concepts or symbols for the purpose of generalising and to extend, correct or verify knowledge, whether that knowledge aids in the construction of a theory or in the practice of an art. The mechanic or physician is a research worker only when he attempts to generalise about all automobiles or all patients in a given class. (pp. 330–4)

A rather broader meaning of research was proposed by Wise, Nordberg and Reitz (1967):

> ... it is characteristically and inevitably a systematic inquiry for verified knowledge. In that simple description is implied the whole syntax of research.

This description clearly suggests that the purpose of research is to gain new, or to verify existing knowledge.

The Penguin English Dictionary (1965) defined research as 'scholarly investigation and study aiming at adding to the sum of knowledge of a specific branch.'

According to the Collins Cobuild English Language Dictionary (1987), research means the 'detailed study of a subject'. It further suggests: 'when you do research you collect and analyse facts and information and try to gain new knowledge or new understanding.'

Kerlinger (1983) defined research as the 'systematic, controlled, empirical and critical investigation of hypothetical propositions about the presumed relations among natural phenomena'. Similar views were expressed by Best (1970) who suggested that 'Research is a more systematic activity directed toward discovery and the development of an organised body of knowledge.' These characteristics obviously apply in the main to the natural sciences, and not to the social sciences within which education falls. In social science research, it is difficult, though by no means impossible, to establish cause and effect relations (see, for example, Lawrence, 1973). The main differences in the nature of research between the natural sciences and the social sciences may lie in the conduct and methods of research rather than its rationale which is the acquisition of knowledge/information.

Earlier views on the purpose of research focus on its use of systematic enquiry. This raises the question whether systematic enquiry is the main process of research, both in the natural and in the social sciences. For example, social research refers to both the collection and analysis of information on the social world, in order to understand and explain it better. Educational research refers to both the collection and analysis of information on the world of education (see Chapters 2 and 3 for further discussion). Classroom research refers to the kind of research that not only professional researchers but practising teachers are able to conduct within the context of their professional lives. This type of research attempts to utilize the insights and procedures of social and educational research in schools. The concept of research does not have the same meaning in all academic disciplines because of the diverse natures of activity. Thus, there is no universally accepted meaning of research. In one instance, research may appear to be a simple activity while, in another, an extremely complex one. It may take place in the laboratory, library, classroom or in the community. It may be local, national or international. Research may be conducted by a single researcher, or by a group of researchers. Whatever the research framework, the one thing common to all research activities is that they are supposed to be a thorough and systematic search for trustworthy and meaningful knowledge.

If the research is of an applied nature, its goal is to provide us with sound information for making decisions. There are, of course, theoretically oriented studies which may not have immediate practical application.

Cronbach and Suppes (1969), for example, have drawn a distinction between 'decision-oriented' studies and 'conclusion-oriented' studies. According to them, the goal of 'decision-oriented' research is to provide information for decision-makers, and 'conclusion-oriented' research follows the interests of the researcher. Thus, in decision-oriented research theory would be less important than conclusion-oriented research in which the goal may range from development of basic theory to applied and non-theoretical research, depending upon the interests of the researcher.

Whatever the orientation of their work, researchers should have the necessary skills and training to identify the precise research issues/problems, design a sound research framework, use appropriate techniques to collect information and present the findings clearly and concisely for relevant audiences to understand the message and, if appropriate, make decisions. The modern use of the term 'research' is broader than the traditional one, allowing it to be applied to the acquisition of any form of knowledge or information (Travers, 1978).

Opinions about the nature and purpose of research in most disciplines have changed over the last 40 years because of technological progress. Research as a human endeavour is often characterized by its persistent and organized effort to extend our knowledge and understanding about the world in which we live. The scope of research and its impact on our everyday life has now become wider than before because of the fact that we live in a global village. Whether research is conducted in a controlled situation or in a natural setting, its impact can be felt in seconds because of the faster communication system.

It is clear from the foregoing brief discussion that the quest for knowledge is an essential aspect of any form of research. Sometimes, information obtained from research may be inconclusive, unclear or apparently illogical, not helping us to reduce the areas of our ignorance. However, in the last 40 or 50 years, research has attained a great deal of respectability amongst educators, politicians, business people and others who often turn to researchers in the quest for reliable and valid information for making decisions. Today, every aspect of human life is affected by research technology. In fact, most advanced societies have evolved a research-oriented culture, or are in the process of moving in that direction.

What, then, are the characteristics of research? Some of its essential characteristics may be summarized as follows:

- Research is an organized and deliberate effort to collect new information or to utilize existing knowledge for a new purpose.
- Research seeks to answer worthwhile and fundamental questions, by utilizing valid and reliable techniques.
- Research is logical and objective, using the most appropriate test/s to justify the methods employed, data collected, and the conclusions drawn.
- The final outcome of research contributes to the gaining of new knowledge and a better appreciation of the issues involved.

Methods of Research

Considerable changes have occurred over the last few decades in the ways that researchers have sought to pursue plausible and objective explanations of problems or to address issues of concern. Those ways are properly referred to as methodology, that is, the particular methods or techniques employed in the conduct of the research. The selection of the most appropriate methods and techniques, whether in sampling, data collection or analysis, is part of the art of the researcher who must find the best way of tackling the topic under study and providing answers that are reliable and valid (Silverman, 1993). The tools and procedures for gathering and analysing data have also been refined in the last 30 years or so, not least because of technological progress in the field of computing. It also seems to be the case that research in the physical and biological sciences has developed faster than research in the social sciences because of the fact that external factors are less amenable to controlled scrutiny in the social sciences than in the natural sciences.

Research methods do not seem to be isolated; they overlap. Investigators need to reflect on their own understanding and thinking when using any systematic research method for obtaining reliable knowledge or for getting at what some writers describe as the 'truth'. In the early 1930s, Dewey gave an impetus of major importance to the so-called scientific method. He described the five main stages of thought or conceptualization when researchers attempt to acquire new knowledge:

1   Recognition and definition of the problem;
2   Observations, collection and classification of data considered relevant to the problem;
3   Formulation of a tentative hypothesis concerning these observations or the phenomena;
4   Verification of this hypothesis against all the obtained facts. This might involve the collection of additional/new data and the modification of the original hypothesis;
5   Formulation of conclusion/conclusions in terms of general principles concerning the problem or the phenomena. (Dewey, 1933)

While the above stages are a useful general guide in the construction and implementation of research, the researchers do not always need to follow these steps in a rigid way. In a practical situation, their thinking frequently moves to and fro across these basic steps. The exact formulation of a research strategy varies according to the nature and purpose of the research. The method of acquiring knowledge needs to be more flexible than is often the case.

It is also true that what has been broadly called in the literature the 'scientific method' has proved valuable in the study of the natural sciences, and has also helped social scientists to gain insight into many problems/issues. This method provides result which are quantifiable. The researcher is able to say, for example, that a particular technique of teaching reading applied to a group of children resulted in their having a reading age 7 months in advance of a similar group who were taught by another method. The apparent precision of the results obtained in quantitative studies makes the approach very attractive. However, the quantitative is not the only knowledge of reality, and all things do not exist in quantities that lend themselves readily to measurement (see Chapter 5). There are other research techniques to explore reality, such as those used by Piaget (1926; 1932) in his investigations of the beginnings of a child's concepts. Further, there are many qualities, behaviours and events that cannot yet be measured — because no instrument, tool or technique has been devised which can, by general consent, accurately and repeatedly be applied to measure them. An example of this might be beauty: no way of measuring this exists though the writer recollects listening to a radio game in which the members of the panel were asked to devise a new and useful unit of measurement. Denis Norden proposed the 'millihelen' which he defined as 'the quantity of beauty required to launch one ship'.

The research methods in the social sciences in particular have become closely bound up with the values, attitudes and perceptions of the researcher. This is not the same as suggesting that research is subjective. Inevitably, no researcher can claim to be value-neutral, free from assumptions, unbiased and objective in viewing the world. Scientific knowledge exists within a particular framework of expectation; the work of Kuhn challenged the existing belief that science is a rational and objective enquiry (Kuhn, 1970, 1972). Another point to remember is that there are many questions, particularly in the social sciences, which cannot be answered by the controlled method of enquiry which is often described as the scientific method. The planning of a research programme may include a great deal of exploratory work which is often intuitive or speculative, and at times fragmented. Although the investigator has to define the problem/issue in a precise manner at some stage, concepts and ideas might initially be vague and ill-defined. It may be necessary to observe and study the situations and even collect some preliminary data in order to establish the relevance of vaguely conceived ideas. In this process, reading around the field of study, intuition, speculation, hunch or intelligent guess becomes necessary for the formulation of a clearly defined problem. It should also be emphasized that problem recognition is one of the most difficult as well as the crucial part of the research process. Thus, research should not be regarded as a rigid activity.

A clearly defined problem may generate one or several hypotheses or research questions. The hypothesis/research question must be stated clearly in order to test its logical or empirical consequences. The use of hypothesis or research question may prevent an investigation from becoming too broad in scope or disorderly in the construction of the research design. Writing about the need for carefully formulated hypotheses, Van Dalen (1966) stated that 'No scientific undertaking can proceed effectively without well-conceived hypotheses. . . . Without hypotheses, research is unfocused, haphazard and accidental' (p. 457). Hypotheses, according to Van Dalen, are important because they tell the researcher what should be done to get an answer, and how it should be done. Thus, the focusing of research towards testing specific hypotheses or seeking the answer to questions guides the researcher to arrive at valid conclusions.

Another reason for establishing carefully formulated hypotheses or research questions is that at some stage the investigator might need to examine relationships and trends between the variables. Kerlinger (1983) remarks, 'The scientist cannot tell positive from negative evidence unless he uses hypotheses.' Hypotheses/questions are at the core of research activity and should, consequently, not be based on wild speculation. Moreover, they should be framed in such a way that they are capable of standing up to the rigours of testing in the course of the research.

It should be noted that many hypotheses, particularly in behavioural research, cannot be tested directly because they may deal with abstractions. The investigator therefore must choose a sample of behaviour, thought or feeling that can be tested or observed directly either by the researcher or the research subject. The sample of observable behaviours and feelings and their correlates may then be evaluated in terms of their consistency or inconsistency with the formulated hypothesis. On the basis of obtained evidence, the researcher may deduce the logical consequences of the hypothesis. For example, a research worker might formulate a hypothesis that mixed ability teaching provides greater intellectual stimulation for less able children than if taught in a streamed class. Two classes can be carefully selected — one containing mixed ability pupils and the other with less able pupils. A test of scholastic achievement can be administered at the end of the school academic year to both the groups. If the hypothesis were true, less able children in the mixed ability group would show significantly higher achievement scores as compared with those less able children who were taught in a segregated class. Thus, the researcher draws the consequences of the hypothesis. Some research studies may require the formulation of research questions rather than a specific hypothesis if there is very little previous knowledge about aspects of the issue to be researched. In some qualitative studies, there is no specific hypothesis at the outset but hypotheses are generated during the early stages of research (Silverman, 1993).

Theory, Construct and Model

At this point in mapping the domain of research, a brief description of the concepts of theory, construct and model would seem appropriate. The term 'theory' has a multiplicity of meanings (Snow, 1973). Its main role is to help guide the investigator/researcher. In the social sciences, it usually implies a set of statements describing and explaining the relationship between human behaviour and the factors that affect or explain it. Best (1970) wrote that 'a theory establishes a cause-effect relationship between variables with the purpose of explaining and predicting phenomena' (p. 6). Kerlinger, also writing in 1970, arrived at a similar definition when he suggested that a theory was 'a set of interrelated constructs, definitions and propositions that presents a systematic view of phenomena by specifying relations among variables with the purpose of explaining and predicting phenomena'. It may be thought that these definitions would be of questionable validity in the social sciences, including education, where it is notoriously difficult to establish cause and effect relationships, let alone predict events. Cohen and Manion (1995) cite Mouly's (1978) definition which has general applicability: 'If nothing else, a theory is a convenience — a necessity, really — organising a whole slough of unassorted facts, laws, concepts, constructs, principles, into a meaningful and manageable form. It constitutes an attempt to make sense out of what we know concerning a given phenomenon.'

However, the role of theory as a framework for research is not in dispute. Silverman (1993), highlighting the importance of theory, writes that '. . . theories provide a set of explanatory concepts. These concepts offer ways of looking at the world which are essential in defining a research problem . . . without a theory, there is nothing to research'. Thus, a theoretical framework helps the investigator summarize previous information and guide the future course of action. Sometimes the formulation of a theory may indicate missing ideas or links and the kinds of additional data required. Thus, a theory is an essential tool of research in stimulating the advancement of knowledge still further. It is also true to say that not all research is designed to test existing theories or generate new ones. Theories can range from the very simple to the extremely complicated ones. In fact, some researchers prefer to avoid complex theorizing as much as possible.

In its simplest form, theory may mean a speculation, a hunch or an idea. For example, a teacher concerned with practical problems in the classroom has some idea about the best method of teaching humanities. A more complicated theory may be a synthesis of facts, an analysis of a set of variables to demonstrate their relationships with one another, or a plausible general principle to explain and predict certain phenomena. Examples of such theories may include studies which attempt to explain pupils' motivation, their learning patterns or self-concept.

Good theories are built upon facts, sound evidence and previous research evidence, and not on mere speculation. The work of most natural and social scientists can be related to the use or construction of theories of some kind. However, the distinction can be made in at least two ways. Those whose work is primarily concerned with the development of theories are often called rationalists (Travers, 1978); those who focus their attention on the collection of data or facts are often referred to empiricists. Skinner's (1959) work, for example, can be described as an empirically oriented approach to research. In practice, however, most social scientists are both rationalists and empiricists. Another broad distinction can be drawn: some researchers spend a great deal of time in the formulation of theories and may not be concerned with their practical application, while others are primarily concerned with the application of new knowledge for the solution of everyday problems. However, even in pure research, a theory, once established, may suggest many applications of practical value. Thus, the status of theory varies considerably according to the discipline or aspect of knowledge under study. Some theories are highly sophisticated and complex while others are characterized by unevenness and simplicity.

Many teachers are often suspicious of theories developed by educational researchers. They seek practical 'advice' and 'guidance' for the solution of classroom problems. They want to know *why* a child is poorly motivated rather than *what* the relations are among various elements contributing to that behaviour. Teachers, also, have their views, ideas or opinions about low motivation that are based on many years of experience or observation. Their main concern, however, is with practicalities, that is, with techniques for solving specific problems in the context of things as they are. The product of all research in the social sciences is a set of conclusions that indicate or imply a theoretical model, which may be quite different to the theory from which it began.

Teachers, on the other hand, develop their theories primarily from observations which can be unsystematic. Such 'theories' are not based upon rigorous analysis of inter-relationships between fragmented facts and observations. One of the advantages of teachers' theories, however, is that they are easily communicated to other professional colleagues in layman's terminology. It is also true to say that many educational practices and policies are based on teachers' judgments. There is the need to increase the understanding of educational researchers to further the relationship between theory and practice. The challenge for the research process in education is to relate theory and practice in such a way that meaningful answers to questions are provided on the basis of scrupulously gathered, evaluated and reported evidence.

The term 'construct' is often used in the social sciences. The concept is a construction of social scientists' imagination which helps them to understand the underlying mechanisms of an individual's thought and behaviour. For example, many theories of learning refer to a motivational factor in human behaviour. Motivation is not directly observable — it is a theoretical construct — and hence social scientists describe the term 'motivation' as a construct. Constructs are used to provide a plausible explanation of consistency in human behaviour.

Another term frequently used by both natural and social scientists is *model*. This means a close representation of certain aspects of complex phenomena used in order to gain insights into the phenomena that scientists wish to explain. Models are essentially analogies (Chapanis, 1961). For example, a teacher can help pupils to conceptualize the Earth by showing them a globe with countries, continents, mountains and oceans marked on it in different colours. Thus, the globe is a convenient model representing the important features of the earth in a way that can be easily understood by pupils. Models may also be symbolic. An example of a symbolic model is an engineer's plan for a house construction. In the field of education, Piaget's model of the intellect is a good example.

Simulation, one of the procedures used by behavioural scientists for the development of ideas within the context of discovery, is based on the idea of a 'model'. The use of models is quite common in the teaching–learning situation. Models may consist of words, mathematical symbols, pictures or physical objects, and can be very useful in thinking about complex phenomena. A model can provide a very simple representation of quite complex events and make them more intelligible. Models are simply tools that are used in the construction and testing of theories.

Both 'model' and 'theory' may be regarded as

> explanatory devices or schemes having a broadly conceptual framework, though models are often characterised by the use of analogies to give a more graphic or visual representation of a particular phenomenon. Providing they are accurate and do not misrepresent the facts, models can be of great help in achieving clarity and focusing key issues in the nature of phenomena. (Cohen and Manion, 1980)

Research in the Social Sciences and the Natural Sciences

Research in the social sciences has become an important activity in most advanced societies. Although the social sciences are not perceived as having the same 'scientific' status as the natural sciences (in terms of explanation, control and prediction) a great deal of progress has been made in the systematic study of human behaviour since the beginning of this century. Such knowledge of human behaviour has provided the basis for a variety of social technologies. The importance of research in the social sciences such as education, anthropology, economics and social psychology cannot easily be overestimated.

It is also acknowledged that the greatest obstacle to progress in the social sciences is the extreme complexity and variability of human behaviour. Many people argue that it is much more difficult to develop sound theories of human behaviour from which predictions can be made than it is to develop theories that predict events in the physical sciences. Similarly, in the field of psychology, it is far more difficult to understand and explain the development of an individual's personality or the processes involved in human thought and problem-solving than the forces operating in physics and chemistry. In the natural sciences, rigorous controls of systematic observation and analysis are often applied, whereas such control is often not possible with human subjects.

Despite the difficulties outlined above, the social sciences have made a significant contribution to our understanding of the society in which we live. It would now seem appropriate to attempt a brief examination of some of the crucial differences between the two broad groups of sciences.

- In the social sciences, many researchers deal with events or occurrences which are unique in time or in individual development. Historical and many descriptive studies, for example, are concerned with unique and non-repeatable phenomena. Also, there are many social events which cannot be observed directly. For example, an individual's past experience cannot be observed directly; the researcher has to rely upon written information or a person's recall of past events. It may be possible to assess children's reading levels and vocabulary but it will be difficult to determine the motives or the intensity of the feelings of individual children objectively. On the other hand, a pathologist can test a blood sample and the findings can easily be reproduced by other pathologists.
- In the social sciences, it is often impossible to control the factor or factors being studied. For example, in a classroom situation there are very few factors which can be identified and controlled (e.g. age, sex, and height of pupils), others can be identified but not controlled (e.g. hobbies), and many other significant factors can neither be identified nor controlled. The natural scientist is rarely confronted with the same kind of problem.
- In most cases, natural science has to deal with a limited number of variables that are amenable to manipulation and precise measurements. The social scientist, on the other hand, may have to deal with a large number of variables simultaneously in order to explain phenomena satisfactorily. Another difficulty for the social scientist is the complex nature of variables such as temperament, attitude, motivational and personality characteristics which are not only difficult to assess but they interact in subtle ways.
- In the social sciences it is difficult to make wide generalizations, because no two individuals are exactly alike in feelings, drives or emotions. What may be a reasonable explanation for one may be irrelevant for another. Furthermore, no one person is normally consistent from one situation to another because of intervening experiences. For example, if a student took psychological tests for the second time his or her behaviour would not be quite the same as that of the one who had not taken the tests previously. The response is likely to be influenced by the interaction with various elements in his or her environment. In the natural sciences it is often, though not always, possible to repeat the situation, without prejudicing the outcome.
- The behaviour of an individual is influenced by the research process itself. The knowledge of being involved in an investigation makes individuals

conscious that their behaviour is being observed or studied, and this can affect their response to the situation. However, natural scientists face similar problems. Heisenberg in the 1920s formulated the uncertainty principle which demonstrated that it was impossible to determine the velocity and position of a sub-atomic particle because the process of measurement changed its velocity in ways that could not be predicted. This led to the development of quantum mechanics theory which does not predict a single definite result for an observation but provides for a number of possible outcomes and says how likely each one of these is. Quantum mechanics theory therefore creates an unavoidable element of unpredictability in science. It is important to stress that it is an extremely successful theory and underlies nearly all of modern science and technology (Hawking, 1988).

• In the social sciences the researcher's interests, background, ability, prejudices, attitudes and values are likely to affect the research process and consequently its outcome. In the natural sciences, however, this situation is less likely to occur.

• In the natural sciences, complex constructs are defined in operational terms whereas the social sciences have been limited by a lack of adequate definitions. Many human characteristics (e.g. anxiety, hostility, motivation) are not directly observable. As constructs they can only be postulated, and inferred on the basis of test scores. Furthermore, there is a poverty of tools or instruments for 'accurate' measurement in the social sciences which makes it more difficult to describe many of the constructs.

It must be stressed, however, that the researcher working in the field of social sciences must exercise great caution in making generalizations from the findings. There is a need to adopt a research strategy incorporating qualitative judgments and quantitative measurements. By using a variety of techniques or tools, it may be possible to generate sound theories to explain human behaviour.

Types of Research

Research has been classified in various ways, e.g. by method, by area of academic discipline (sociological, psychological, anthropological, etc.), by type of data collection procedure (e.g. psychological tests, observation, questionnaire, and so on) or by purpose (whether contributing to knowledge or having policy implications). There has been considerable controversy among decision makers as to which type of research is of most value. However, if we define science in a broad sense it is possible to produce a taxonomy of types of research. Hitchcock and Hughes (1989) point out that the term 'research' is often prefixed by concepts like 'pure', 'basic', 'applied', or 'action'. They also attempt to explore the connections between these types of research. From the various combinations available in the literature the following classifications would seem appropriate, although these do not represent discrete categories:

- pure or basic research;
- applied or field research;
- action research;
- evaluation research.

This typology has the advantage of highlighting some critical differences between research that is oriented to the development of theory and that designed to deal with practical problems.

Pure or Basic Research

This type of research is typically oriented towards the development of theories by discovering broad generalizations or principles. It has drawn its pattern and initiative from the physical sciences emphasizing a rigorous, structured type of analysis. The main purpose of 'pure' or 'basic' research is to discover facts which are fundamental and important in the sense that their discovery will extend the boundaries of our knowledge in a particular area or discipline. Pure research is not primarily concerned with understanding practical problems. It is usually carried out in a laboratory or other carefully controlled situation which implies that control and precision are maintained at the cost of reality. In recent years, most learning theories have been questioned on the grounds that studies were conducted in a controlled situation with animals as subjects and therefore the findings cannot be directly applied to human problems. However, the findings of many basic psychological research studies have been applied to educational problems — the work of Skinner, for example. It is true to say that the findings from such work may take some time before they are brought into prominence or become part of the general stock of knowledge.

Applied or Field Research

This type of research is concerned primarily with the application of new knowledge for the solution of day-to-day problems. This does not mean that it is less rigorous in its approach than other forms of research. Although applied or field research has some of the characteristics of pure research (e.g. the use of sampling techniques, inferences about the target population) its purpose is to improve a process by testing theoretical constructs in actual situations. Most educational research is applied research, for it aims at establishing generalizations about teaching–learning situations. As one would expect, control is often sacrificed in field research in order to conduct the enquiry in a setting similar to that in which the findings are applied.

It should be mentioned that sometimes applied research also utilizes experimental techniques, and hence in such research designs it is difficult to make a clear distinction between basic and applied research. However, applied research needs to be conducted in order to determine how various theories operate in the actual situation.

Action Research

The term 'action research' was first introduced in the fields of social psychology, social work and education. It is a type of applied social research differing from other types in the immediacy of the researcher's involvement in the action process.

Action research is more concerned with the immediate application rather than the development of theory. It focuses on a specific problem in a particular setting. In other words, its findings are usually judged in terms of their applicability in a specific situation. Action research is similar to applied research in many ways but the fundamental difference is that applied research allows generalizations of its results. Furthermore, applied research usually involves a large number of cases for studies whereas action research can be conducted in a modest way by using a very small sample (e.g. a single classroom or a group of children within it).

In recent years, action research has generated a great deal of interest in the field of education. It has been employed in curriculum development, professional development, institutional improvement and policy development. It is now widely acknowledged that limiting educational research to professional researchers alone is to take a narrow view of the educator's role. Classroom teachers can be better decision-makers and more effective practitioners if they are encouraged to conduct action research. For example, if it is proposed to alter the organization of a school and its curriculum, it is most useful to have one or more researchers on the staff who can monitor the effects of the changes. Thus, action research is usually conducted with the aim of implementing a change in a given situation (for further discussion, see Chapter 5).

Evaluation Research

The term 'evaluation research' is often used to refer to the systematic procedures which are adopted over a period of time to collect and process data concerning the effectiveness of a particular programme or set of events. For example, a teaching programme can be evaluated at several stages. If evaluation is carried out at intermediate stages to implement changes in the programme, it is called 'process' or 'formative' evaluation. Evaluation at the completion of the planning programme is known as 'summative' evaluation.

Evaluation research has been widely employed in the last four decades. Many social action programmes and curriculum innovations have adopted this type of research in order to monitor the effectiveness of such programmes. Evaluation research highlights the symbols of measurement and scientific neutrality but attempts to minimize the influence of the behavioural science perspective. Evaluation research of the summative type is often used to assess programmes designed to engineer change (see Chapter 5 for more details).

In concluding this discussion, it is important to mention that there are several ways in which the term 'research' is used which can be conducted at various levels of complexity. It is a process which consists of a series of linked activities which has a beginning and an end. Meaningful and acceptable research may even be of the simple descriptive fact finding type. But under whatever condition research is undertaken, it is essentially an intellectual and creative activity.

References

BEST, J.W. (1970) *Research in Education*, 2nd edition, Englewood Cliffs, New Jersey: Prentice Hall.

CHAPANIS, A. (1961) 'Men, machine and models', *American Psychologist*, **16**, pp. 113–31.

COHEN, L. and MANION, L. (1980) *Research Methods in Education*, 2nd edition, London: Croom Helm.

COHEN, L. and MANION, L. (1995) *Research Methods in Education*, 4th edition, London: Routledge.

COLLINS COBUILD ENGLISH LANGUAGE DICTIONARY (1987) Editor in Chief, John Sinclair, London: Collins.

CRONBACH, L.J. and SUPPES, P. (1969) *Research for Tomorrow's Schools: Disciplined Inquiry for Education*, New York: Macmillan.

DEWEY, J. (1993) *How We Think*, Boston: Raytheon Education Co.

ENCYCLOPEDIA OF THE SOCIAL SCIENCES (1934) Volume 13, New York: Macmillan.

HAWKING, S.W. (1988) *A Brief History of Time*, London: Bantam Press.

HITCHCOCK, G. and HUGHES, D. (1989) *Research and the Teacher*, London: Routledge.

KERLINGER, F.N. (1983) *Foundations of Behavioral Research*, 3rd edition, New York: Holt, Rinehart and Winston.

KUHN, T.S. (1970) *The Structure of Scientific Revolutions*, 2nd edition, International Encyclopedia of Unified Science, enlarged, first published 1962, Chicago: The University of Chicago Press.

KUHN, T.S. (1972) 'Scientific paradigms', in BARNES, B. (ed.) *Sociology of Science*, Harmondsworth: Penguin.

LAWRENCE, D. (1973) *Improved Reading Through Counselling*, London: Ward Lock Educational.

MOULY, G.J. (1978) *Educational Research: The Art and Science of Investigation*, Boston: Allyn and Bacon, Boston.

PENGUIN ENGLISH DICTIONARY (1965) Harmondsworth, Middlesex.

PIAGET, J. (1926) *The Language and Thought of the Child*, London: Routledge and Kegan Paul.

PIAGET, J. (1932) *The Moral Judgement of the Child*, Glencoe: Free Press.

SILVERMAN, D. (1993) *Interpreting Qualitative Data*, London: Sage Publications.

SKINNER, B.F. (1959) 'A case history in scientific method', in KOCH, S. (ed.) *Psychology: A Study of a Science*, Volume 2, New York: McGraw Hill.

SNOW, R.E. (1973) 'Theory construction for research on teaching', in TRAVERS, R.M.W. (ed.) *Second Handbook of Research on Teaching*, Chicago: Rand McNally and Co.

SPINDLER, G. (1970) *Being an Anthropologist*, New York: Holt.

TRAVERS, R.M.W. (1978) *An Introduction to Educational Research*, 4th edition, New York: Macmillan Co.Inc.

VAN DALEN, D.B. (1966) *Understanding Educational Research*, New York: McGraw Hill.

WISE, J.E., NORDBERG, R.B. and REITZ, D.J. (1967) *Methods of Research in Education*, Boston, DC: Heath and Co.

Chapter 2

Educational Research: Mapping the Domain

In the previous chapter, very little was said specifically about educational research, although in the discussion of research in general, examples from the field of education were cited wherever it was appropriate. We also considered some of the differences between the natural and social sciences. The present chapter attempts to map out the domain of educational research to enable the reader to have a better understanding of the nature and process of educational research which follows in the next chapter.

The nature of educational research is more difficult to describe than many educators would seem to appreciate. One of the problems is the diversity of techniques, tools and approaches that are employed in the study of educational phenomena. Another problem in characterizing educational research lies in the methodological issues surrounding it. Seeking to provide a map of educational research in the 1990s, Bassey (1992) wrote:

> What a curious gathering of people come under the banner of research, with different interests, different methodologies, even different vocabularies. My concern is that there is a tendency for each group to reject the others, saying 'we are the true researchers, we have seen the light; they are but parasites on our back'. I believe this is unhelpful; we need to accept diversity of practice and march together in order to be effective in the world of education.

Inevitably, as this book proceeds, a wide range of techniques, approaches and methodologies used in educational research will be explored. A full understanding of its nature and process is not possible without doing so. However, there is some commonality of concern among educational researchers, which is as Bassey (1992) asserted

> the carrying out of systematic and critical enquiry on educational topics, within a twin ethic of respect for truth and respect for persons. These are the cardinal principles to which I believe all educational researchers subscribe.

Before proceeding to consider subject matter which is at the core of research, not least educational research, it is proposed to consider briefly some of the opinions held about the nature of research in education, as compared with that in other disciplines. Some writers have seen no essential differences between educational research and psychology and sociology, others do. For example, Cronbach (1962) maintained that 'most educational research, though not all, is psychological'. Taylor (1966), on the other hand, pointed to 'the centrality of practical judgments which distinguish educational research from other kinds of research which use similar methods'. Writers, like Travers (1978), consider educational research to be similar to research in the natural sciences in that both seek to make generalizations from their findings. Others, are critical of making generalizations about human behaviour. Gowin (1972), for example, argued that the search for generalization in educational research was bound to prove fruitless because human behaviour is 'context-dependent'.

However, many of the problems facing educational researchers are of the same nature as those confronting researchers in other fields of the social sciences. There are, of course, specific issues which present challenges to educational researchers, as will become evident in the course of this book. The nature, purpose and process of educational research has been the subject of much debate over the years, as educational research has sought to forge its own identity and justify itself as a separate and useful discipline, yet conducted with the same rigour as that in other fields of inquiry.

Turning attention now to the subject matter will enable the reader to begin to appreciate why educational research generates much debate about its nature, process and outcomes. In any field of research, theoretical and methodological considerations are heavily influenced by the nature of the subject matter under investigation and by the perspective being brought to bear on it.

Education in its various forms and contexts is a very broad field. Hence a variety of approaches and tools have been and are employed in order to obtain a better understanding of it. Such is its breadth that researching education can involve many disciplines and, increasingly nowadays, the use of techniques borrowed from a variety of disciplines and approaches developed in other fields of inquiry. However, in pursuing this discussion we run the risk of putting the cart before the horse, so we shall turn now to subject matter.

The Subject Matter

Subject matter in educational research can be broken down into seven major dimensions. To some extent the choice of these dimensions is arbitrary but they will provide the reader with an indication of the range of topics commonly investigated.

Individual Performance

Everybody is different, or so the saying goes. Everybody has a set of attributes or qualities that have a bearing on how he or she behaves or performs. Research into individual performance can cover investigation into any number of those attributes or qualities. Research might seek to determine how much progress an individual is making in school, or whether he or she has particular aptitudes that could be developed by specialist training. Sometimes the purpose of such research might be to determine the potential of a particular individual to become, say, a doctor or an architect.

Other probes into individual performance serve what can be called diagnostic purposes. A particular child might be experiencing difficulties in school. An investigation into his or her performance and/or behaviour could well help to identify areas of particular weakness. The causes might relate to cognitive processes (problems with his or her thought processes), or affective (problems in the way he or she relates to other people, e.g. teacher, other pupils, peers, family). Having identified the nature of the problems faced by the individual, it may then be possible to provide appropriate remedial action.

Group Performance

In some respects, the investigation of group performance is very similar to that of individual performance. This is particularly the case where attainment is being examined. Obviously, the focus tends to be broader than that employed when investigating individual performance.

Group performance has always been a very important aspect of the investigation of educational processes, never more so than now. Governments in the Western world invest a lot of money in education systems to develop people to become productive members of the nation's workforce. They look for answers to questions such as 'Do certain groups of children do better or worse than others in school?' and 'What factors are involved in this?'

The group 'units' vary in size considerably and in terms of their 'naturalness'. For example, group performance might be investigated on the basis of different classes of the same age group in one school or a group of schools, the 'natural' group units being the class groupings in which the children received their instruction.

Other groups might be 'constructed' for the purposes of the investigation. This often occurs when the basis of investigation involves an experimental approach. Sometimes, and perhaps more frequently, the groupings are only made for the purposes of analyses of performance, with the groupings being determined by a particular characteristic, for example, boys and girls. In Britain the issue of social class is often seen as an important variable in educational performance. Children who come from families where parents are well-educated and/or are well-off are considered to have advantages when it comes to schooling that are not enjoyed by other children. (There is a series of assumptions in this which cannot be considered in full here, like choice of school attended, quality of teaching received, facilities available in school, degree of parental support for the child and even for the school, and so on). Other variables often include regional variations (e.g. the performance of children in the north of England as compared to that of children from the south of England, that of children in cities and towns as compared to that of children in rural areas).

Another variable which has dominated a lot of recent research in the field of education in Britain is ethnicity. Do children from ethnic minority families get a fair chance to succeed within the existing educational system? What factors militate against success for such children? Smith and Tomlinson (1989) would be an example of this kind of inquiry.

Another type of group performance investigation is what are referred to as international comparability studies. Initially, such studies were motivated by academic curiosity. Latterly, however, economic considerations seem to have acquired an important influence. Much of the impetus has come from the field of economics and the constant battery of statistics published on the economic performance of the industrialized nations, and the strength of their technology. This statistical information has focused attention on education not only nationally but also internationally. Why is Japan or the USA achieving greater economic growth — is it because it has a better trained workforce? Is its education system being more productive than Britain's? This line of inquiry has given rise to larger scale international comparability studies of performance in mathematics and science of young people in Britain, the USA and Japan.

School Performance

This dimension overlaps the previous one, group performance. In recent developments, research into school performance has focused on what is called school effectiveness. A concept borrowed from the world of business, effectiveness looks to evaluate schools on a series of criteria including pupil performance, in order to determine the extent to which a particular school or group of schools could be considered effective, often expressed in terms of 'providing value for money' — a term of approval employed by inspectors from OFSTED (The Office for Standards in Education) in summarizing the performance of British schools.

In an age in which there are increasing demands for a highly skilled and adaptable workforce and in which audit-like mechanisms are applied to public services especially education, it is important for schools to demonstrate their effectiveness (or for their delivery to be accredited with being effective).

School Management/Management of Schools

To some extent consideration of school management and the management of schools *after* school performance is misleading, for in terms of the chronology of their development, school organization comes before school performance. Indeed, a lot of any applied benefits to be derived from the examination of school performance could not have occurred without a better understanding of how schools could/ should be organized.

It also seems likely that many of the school performance research criteria could not have been as clearly delineated without prior investigation of how schools work, how schools are managed, the study of which owed much to the study of business methods used in industry. The fundamental educational research question: 'what makes a good school?' still remains a question today, and one which some would argue still remains largely unanswered. What change there has been in the attempts to answer the question is the way in which it is addressed. Today, in Britain and elsewhere in the western world, the question is driven by economic and audit-driven factors.

Interpersonal Relationships

Interpersonal relationships are an area of study which is typically socio-psychological in character. Such studies investigate how people get on with one another. For example, a study was undertaken by Verma, Zec and Skinner (1994) into the way that pupils from differing ethnic and cultural backgrounds get on. Interpersonal relationships in schools are very important since schools are composed of adults and youngsters and various types of relationships are to be found there. In a school setting there are four main types of interpersonal relationships. These are headteacher–staff, teacher–teacher, teacher–pupil and pupil–pupil. Such relationships can involve one-to-one situations and group situations and occur both in formal settings, when lessons or other organized activities are in progress, and informal ones, such as at recreation time or in the lunch hour.

Schools, now more than ever before, are expected to respond to the challenge of educating children from different social, cultural, and religious backgrounds. Teachers, at all levels, have to confront racism, sexism and classism, which they ignored in the past. Quality research is essential to help educators not only to understand the problems but resolve them so as to help schools to provide equality of opportunity to all. In an attempt to examine questions relating to unequal opportunity, anthropologists have looked at schools as agents of cultural transmission, arenas of cultural conflicts, and sites of potential micro and macro level change. The multicultural dimension should be an integral part of educational research, particularly as it relates to the teacher as researcher. Educational researchers must examine the hidden implications of their own research questions/hypotheses and their own theoretical frameworks.

Headteacher–staff relationships are obviously important in terms of how schools are organized and the ways in which they respond to the needs of their pupils. Inter-staff relationships are also important in that respect. Teacher–pupil and pupil–pupil relationships are of importance in terms of the teaching/learning process.

Pupils and students need to have confidence in their teachers in order to learn well. They also need to be able to get on with one another. Some find it more difficult than others to make friends; some may be easily frightened or bullied by other students and this stops them from learning as well as they might. Some children and young people are disruptive and attention-seeking. This can spoil the learning chances for other students and themselves. It may also mean that the teacher is unable to devote as much time to helping them to learn, because of the distractions caused by such pupils.

The study of interpersonal relationships can provide interesting insights into how classrooms operate, how different groups of youngsters interact with one another and with their teacher. Moving a youngster into a different class so that he or she is not with others who make him or her silly or disruptive may change the whole character of the classroom. In another class, the offending youngster may quickly settle and start to work and behave properly again. The study of inter-relationships may help to identify children with particular relationship problems that might then require counselling or special help from an educational psychologist to help them to adjust appropriately in the classroom and to get on with other pupils and teachers.

Curriculum

The curriculum is at the heart of the teaching/learning process and maps out what is to be taught and learnt. The study of curriculum can be approached in many ways. The two most common are curriculum development and curriculum evaluation. The former is concerned with building a curriculum or parts of it, the latter is concerned with how effective the curriculum is proving to be in terms of its objectives and student learning.

The study can be broad-based looking perhaps at the total programme to be put before the youngsters in a country, a region, or one school. It might involve work on a curriculum programme (or 'blueprint') perhaps to determine how consistent it is with its objectives, that is to say what it is that the students are expected to learn or what skills they are expected to develop. It might involve work on a specific area or subject within the curriculum. It might be narrow in focus, concentrating on a particular unit of instruction. For example, a group of teachers may have built up a detailed working curriculum plan to meet part of the requirements of the overall curriculum of the school or of a subject or topic in it. That work might involve the production of learning materials and learning stimuli. Study of the work will help to see how it has developed, and the effects it has had on the pupils and teachers, the changes considered necessary to make it more effective, and so on.

If such work was being evaluated, one would expect not only the materials and documents developed to be studied by the researcher but also the lessons in which the programme was being taught, the materials used and the way those materials were delivered by the teacher to be observed in order to assess their impact. Interviews would be conducted with and/or questionnaires administered to the users, teachers and pupils, to gauge their reactions to the materials. Also involved would be some form of test to assess the learning (cognitive) gains made by the pupils, possibly as compared with other ways of teaching to those objectives.

Curriculum development can also involve the study of learning theory and pedagogy (or teaching style). If a curriculum is to be effective, it is not just a matter of writing down what youngsters are expected to learn and how this might be done. An understanding of learning theory will help to sequence objectives and learning experiences in a manner appropriate to the age and ability of the pupils.

Teachers

Teaching is central to what goes on in the classroom. The demands placed on the teachers are considerable. Quite apart from the need for a high level of knowledge and skills related to the subject(s) that they teach, there is also the need for a good understanding of group dynamics, classroom management, classroom equipment e.g. audio-visual equipment, information technology, communication skills and the presentation and preparation of learning materials, and so forth. Understanding of appropriate curricular objectives and what these mean in terms of pupil perform-ance and how this can be assessed accurately is also needed.

The acquisition and development of this knowledge and those skills have implications for the training of teachers, both prior to starting their careers (initial teacher training or ITT) and, increasingly nowadays, as their teaching careers un-fold (inservice training or INSET). Part of the increasing need for INSET results from the ever-growing body of knowledge, especially in the field of science but in other subject areas as well and the need to restructure and uprate what the teacher knows. Part of the need for INSET is because of changes being introduced into the education system, often the result of major curriculum reforms. The latter may have implications for the sequence in which knowledge and skills are taught and for the way(s) in which these are to be assessed.

In Britain — in England and Wales to be precise since separate arrangements exist for Scotland — a national curriculum has been in place since 1988. One of the changes in curriculum terms has been the change in 'control' over the curriculum itself. Prior to the Education Reform Act 1988 and the introduction of the national curriculum, much of the authority on matters to do with the curriculum rested in the school with the headteacher whose power was only limited by the examination requirements of the examination boards at 16 and 18 and by some degree of influ-ence held by the local education authority (LEA) in which the school was located. The LEA had a powerful influence in the appointment of headteachers and provided some inspection and guidance links with each school.

The new system involves a close specification of what is to be taught during each of the four phases (key stages) that cover the ages of compulsory schooling (5–16). It is further supported by externally controlled testing at the end of each key stage (7, 11, 14, and 16). Teachers are required to make regular assessments of individual pupils' progress against carefully defined levels of performance in a series of attainment targets for each subject, as set out in the national curriculum documentation. These assessments have to be reported to parents at least once a year and those reported at the end of each key stage have to stand alongside the levels obtained by the pupil on national tests. The reforms have thus required the development of new skills in teachers, especially in the area of assessment skills.

Part of the need for these reforms has come from dissatisfaction expressed by the government and industry with the levels of knowledge and skills acquired by students in the course of their compulsory period of schooling. Part of it is also due to the fact that the demands for an educated population to work in a technically increasingly more complex society have required not only reform of the system but also ever greater sums of money from governments to finance the system.

Britain is not alone in embarking on major curricular reform and with it major implications for ITT and INSET. For example, Malaysia introduced major curricular reforms in the 1980s. Unlike Britain, changes in content requirements were not particularly different from what was taught previously. The major difference arising from the reforms in Malaysia was in the change expected in teaching style. Previously curriculum delivery had been teacher-centred, i.e. where all learning was expected to come through the teachers and at the pace that they thought was appropriate to the needs of the class. The Malaysian reforms in the primary and secondary school curricula sought to shift the teaching style to one that was child-centred, i.e. one in which the children were not passive recipients of learning but were actively involved in the advance of their own learning. Such a major shift had considerable implications for teacher training both in ITT and INSET.

Discussion of teaching thus so far has concentrated on the transmission of knowledge and skills that are central to the main curriculum. Other aspects of teaching also exist, certainly as far as the role of the teacher is concerned. Some relate indirectly to the main subjects as defined in the curriculum and reflect important issues of the day. These aspects are covered by cross-curricular skills and themes within subject curricula (Verma and Pumfrey, 1993; Verma and Pumfrey, 1994). In History, for example, themes include the consideration of such issues as citizenship, environmental education, health education and careers education and guidance (DES, 1991). In Britain, some attention is given to sex education, to the dangers of drugs, to the need of exercise and a balanced diet as a means of avoiding heart disease in later life. The provision of such information is a new departure as far as many teachers are concerned. Overlapping those curricular areas are the issues of child abuse, welfare rights and so on, which require teachers in their pastoral role to keep an eye on their pupils to ensure that no child in their class is a victim. Another area in which teachers are expected to exert a powerful influence is in the matter of social and moral values, areas traditionally more the responsibility of the churches and parents.

These topics can be and are approached from a variety of angles. Such angles are properly referred to as perspectives and we now consider what is meant by this.

Perspectives

In simple terms, perspectives reflect the way in which particular research topics are addressed. The perspectives are part of the tradition of educational and social science research from which much of it is descended and indeed from the wider traditions of scientific research.

Those traditions have two elements underpinning them. Firstly there are philosophical and theoretical considerations arising out of the discipline in which the researcher trained. Those philosophical and theoretical considerations have implications for the approach made to the investigation of the particular topic and for the quality and nature of the evidence required. This in turn influences the methods employed to gather that evidence. Reference to the literature on educational research will turn up several key terms. These include empiricism, experimentalism, quantitative, qualitative, psychometric, sociometric and interpretative. It will be useful to consider each of these approaches in turn and to explain their significance in the field of educational research.

If the fact that educational research uses a lot of perspectives is surprising then one needs to reflect on the wide range of topics that are of vital concern to understanding what goes on in the name of education. Primarily this is because education is very much concerned with people: pupils, students, teachers, parents and others both as individuals and as members of a group in classrooms, in schools, colleges, universities and communities. Not only that, but the participants in education do not only exist in one environment, e.g. classroom or lecture room. They also have lives beyond those rooms, at home, at play, with their families and with their friends and other people in society at large.

It is equally true that children, adolescents and adults learn not just from teachers and other people but from their contact with things like books, television, newspapers, computers and other information sources. In addition, there are also the individual differences which cause people to make greater or lesser progress than others or at quicker or slower rates. Some people can be very good at some subjects in school but poor in other subjects.

Some pupils learn better with some teachers than with others. Equally, some schools do better than others because of the way in which they are organized and because of the way in which the teachers, teachers and pupils get on with one another. Some schools do better for their pupils than others because more money is spent in those schools than other ones. Some schools do better than others because of the area in which they are situated or the type of pupils that attend them.

Because of the variety of factors which have a bearing on schools, pupils, students and their educational achievements, a variety of perspectives is needed if we are to understand better how things work and to make improvements for the future which will be of benefit to schools, to individuals and to the society in which they live.

Empiricism

The distinction is often made in the literature between empiricist and rationalist. B.F. Skinner has been regarded as the prime example of the empiricist's approach to research. Researchers whose work is primarily focused on the development of theories are often called rationalists. However, most social scientists are both rationalists and empiricists.

In essence, in the empiricist approach to a research problem the starting point is observation or experiment with a view to explaining afterwards what happened or what were the important factors influencing the observed behaviour. What this implies is that a research problem should be addressed with an open mind and that any interpretation of what happened will not be attempted until after the data have been collected. Such an approach, philosophically at least, is looked upon as the purest form of research.

In contrast to this is the situation in which the starting point for the researcher was a theory or series of theories that had not yet been proven. The purpose of such an investigation would be to test that theory in a 'real' situation. The difference, again philosophically at least, would be that an investigation set up on the basis of an unproven theory or series of theories would or could produce data that were 'corrupted'. By this is meant that, if the researcher tackles a research problem in order to prove a theory, the investigation will tend to gather data that might support the theory, rather than collecting data in a neutral way, before attempting to theorize.

Some readers may already be wondering how a research problem can be approached 'neutrally' or 'with an open mind'. They may argue that it is all very well to talk of only attempting to interpret something after data have been collected, i.e. after the observation or experiment has already been done, but how can one undertake an investigation without preconceived ideas as to why a problem occurs? It may even appear to be a contradiction, especially as far as educational research is concerned. However, if there is a contradiction, it is not one made by the authors of this book. Rather, it is argued, it illustrates one of the dilemmas that educational research has faced in seeking to establish itself as a legitimate research form.

This philosophical dilemma is also apparent in other forms of research, especially in the social sciences and others which seek to investigate problems relating to human behaviour. The empiricist tradition goes back to the early days of scientific research when the types of problem being investigated did not include human behaviour, as will be apparent from the previous chapter and from what has been said so far in this one. Educational research being closely associated with human behaviour focuses on a complex series of interactions; dynamic interpersonal ones, social and cultural ones as well. It is therefore often impossible to narrow down the focus of an educational research problem, since all variables affecting it are never fully exposed.

What the readers should seek to understand from this discussion on empiricism is that it represents, again philosophically at least, an approach to research problems that is as open-minded and as broadly focused as possible. Furthermore, the notions implicit in the empiricist approach represent an important goal for educational researchers, whatever perspective they bring to bear on a research problem. Among those are discipline, clear thinking, scrupulous preparation, meticulous accuracy and care in the collection of data and of their analysis; and balanced interpretations of and conclusions drawn from the data collected.

Experimentalism

Experimentalism is perhaps best understood as the attempt to investigate a research problem by the use of an experiment or series of experiments. It is nonetheless worth pointing out that not all educational research problems lend themselves to the experimental approach. What an experiment seeks to do is to test a theory or an hypothesis under closely controlled conditions. In its purest form an experiment is something that would be conducted in a laboratory, i.e. in very controlled conditions, which another researcher could 'replicate' (set up in similar fashion) in order to confirm the results obtained. In those conditions, everything which might influence what happened can be isolated — and therefore be measured — in order to identify significant factors and possibly to calculate their relative contribution to what happened.

Once again this type of situation is somewhat alien to educational research, again because of its human interaction elements, which make it difficult to isolate all potentially significant factors. In the main, although there is an experimental tradition in educational research, this has tended to be experimental not in the fullest sense as exemplified by experimental research in the natural sciences, but in a more limited sense.

Educational experimental research, where this has been conducted under laboratory conditions, has tended to focus more on individuals rather than on groups, because of the greater interactional complexity of group situations. Moreover, the investigation of human behaviour in a group situation, if conducted under laboratory conditions, can only indicate with any degree of confidence what happened (or happens) in a laboratory setting, not what will or may happen in a 'natural' educational setting, i.e. a classroom. However, because we are able to determine what happened in one classroom at the time of the investigation, it does not mean that it would happen in identical or even similar fashion in another classroom.

Before considering what features of experimentalism are influential in educational experimental research, attention should be drawn to a form of experimental research which is widely used in educational (and other social science) research: the quasi-experiment. Since this is dealt with at greater length in Chapter 5 we will merely note here that this was a term first used by Campbell and Stanley (1963). In essence, a quasi-experiment retains the main features of a pure experiment but is one that is carried out not in a laboratory setting but in a natural one, most typically a classroom.

The principle behind an experimental design is one of control. This is to enable several purposes to be achieved. Firstly, an experiment is so designed as to enable the effect of one variable upon another to be measured in some shape or form. Secondly, it enables (or should enable) the experiment to be repeated in similar circumstances with similar results being obtained. This links up with an important concept in educational research (as in other areas): reliability. More precisely, reliability attaches to the instruments used to measure the effect of a variable. Does the instrument measure the effect accurately and does it go on measuring that effect consistently? If one is trying to grasp the idea, think of the speedometer in a car. The purpose of a speedometer is to provide an accurate indication of how fast a car is travelling at any given moment. Does it always provide a true reading of the car's speed and in whatever the condition of the road? There is a similar requirement and expectation with a research instrument.

Apart from having to meet reliability requirements, an instrument also has to have validity. In simple terms this means that not only does the instrument always measure accurately, it has to measure in an appropriate way. Validity refers to the appropriateness of that measurement. Think about the car speedometer again. It could be considered reliable because it measures the car's speed accurately. However, its validity might be questioned if the read-out was only calibrated in 10s whether of miles per hour or kilometres per hour, e.g. 10, 20, 30, 40. That would probably be acceptable if it was just a matter of making sure that the driver did not break any speed limits. However, suppose that for a particular and important purpose, the driver needed to know that the car was travelling at 28 or 34.5 mph/kph. The speedometer, although accurate (and therefore reliable) would not be valid because the readings in 10s were inappropriate for the purpose(s) required of it.

Of course, in educational research, nothing works as mechanically as a speedometer. An intelligence test may have 100 as its baseline for children of a particular age group. On the face of it, IQ scores may seem as secure as a speedometer reading: 100 is greater than 95 whether in terms of intelligence or speed. However, the processes by which an IQ score is computed are far more complex than those governing the calculation of the speed of a car. An IQ score is based on a child's test performance and this may be conditioned by a number of factors relating to the level of education already received, including any preparation for that type of test that the child has already had, quite apart from any innate qualities in the child and how tired or alert or confident he or she felt at the time of the test. Moreover, there still remain the issues of cultural, gender or class bias in such tests.

A car of a particular make and engine size will be capable of attaining the same speed as that of other cars of the same make and engine size. This makes the calibration of a speedometer for a particular type of car relatively easy to set up. The factors governing or influencing the IQ score of a child are many and there will be considerable differences in what a group of similar aged children can achieve. As a result, there are a number of factors that need to be taken into consideration before using an instrument like an IQ test, or any other measures devised to measure children's (or other human beings') performance.

Quite apart from using instruments that are reliable and valid, there is another concept from the scientific research tradition which is very important in education research. This is termed 'probability'. In essence, when results of a research study are presented, the attempt is made, where appropriate, to calculate the likelihood of the results being the product of unique conditions. If the probability that the results of an investigation would occur by chance only once in 1000 times, then one would feel very confident that the results would hold for other similar settings. Probability is considered in more detail in Chapter 8 but it is worth pointing out here that it is a statistical calculation generated from the relationships between the numbers obtained. It is still critical that the assumptions behind the instruments used to gather the data are reliable and valid.

Another key concept associated with probability is that of sampling. In essence, sampling refers to the processes by which subjects are selected for the research study. Sampling is considered in more detail in Chapter 8. At this stage we can just note that if researchers are to be confident that the results obtained in their study are generalizable to other settings then they need ideally to be able to demonstrate that the sample used in their study was a random one, i.e. that the subjects eligible to be in the sample had equal chances of being included in the actual sample. There are other forms of sampling some of which are quite complex in character and the ideal sampling frame is conditional on the type of investigation being conducted.

Quantitative/Qualitative

Strictly speaking neither 'quantitative' nor 'qualitative' is a discrete perspective on research. However, both make an important contribution to educational research and, as we said earlier, the choice of a particular perspective has implications for the type of evidence to be collected and the mode of analysis used in the investigation of a research question or issue.

Quantitative as its name suggests refers to any approach to data collection where the aim is to gather information that can be quantified; that is to say it can be counted or measured in some form or another. Thus, quantitative research is concerned with the acquisition and interpretation of data which can be presented in the form of discrete units that can be compared with other units by using statistical techniques (Maykut and Morehouse, 1994). A quantitative approach is therefore central to an experiment-based investigation and to many others. The units of measurement may take a variety of forms. In the course of quantitative investigations, it is often necessary to create particular units or scales. The design of quantitative research can be more difficult, relative to qualitative research, because it requires more explicit prior specification of the kind of data to be collected. However, once this is determined and the data collection complete, the analysis of quantitative data can be more straightforward.

Perhaps one of the best known — but contentious — scales in educational research is the IQ (intelligence quotient) score. Although the IQ score will be considered in more detail in the psychometric section of this chapter, it is worth noting at this point that an IQ score is derived from an individual's performance in an 'intelligence' test. There are many intelligence tests and derivatives, for example the VRQ test (verbal reasoning quotient). All work on the same principle. The score for any individual is based on his or her actual test score (sometimes referred to as the raw score). That score is then usually converted on to a scale, where the baseline is expected to be 100: very often the conversion is conditioned in part by the age of the individual.

As a result, the raw score of two individuals who had done the same test might be the same, before the age factor was taken into consideration; one individual might end with an adjusted score of 105 and the other with one of 95. The difference in adjusted scores would be entirely attributable to difference in age, the higher score being awarded to the younger of the two individuals. The reason why the adjustment is made is in part because older pupils might be expected to know more than a younger one. In matters of intelligence measurement, age is an important factor, especially for younger pupils, whose rates of development vary quite considerably. The baseline is usually aimed at the mid-point age of someone in a particular school year. In that year the age range of pupils may show a difference of up to 11–12 months, from oldest to youngest. The adjustment of scores is to take account of such differences.

Qualitative, on the other hand, is an approach to evidence gathering which although disciplined relies less on scales and scores. Typically, it involves the gathering of evidence that reflects the experiences, feelings or judgments of individuals taking part in the investigation of a research problem or issue whether as subjects or as observers of the scene. There may be some element of quantification even in a qualitative approach, as for example, the researcher reporting the numbers of individuals with similar judgments or experiencing similar feelings. Qualitative research is often concerned with social processes. The main feature of qualitative research methods is that meaningful explanations of social activities require a substantial appreciation of the perspectives, culture and world-view of the actors involved.

Ideally, qualitative-based evidence should come from a clearly definable base, so that the readers are able to form their own judgment on the plausibility of the evidence presented. That base might be established by a careful description of how the sample of subjects was selected to be interviewed and how the interview data were analysed. Very often too, when collecting qualitative data that relates directly to the topic being investigated from the subjects, some relevant biographical data on each are also collected; those biographical data, dependent on the topic of the research and the nature of the subjects, might include age, length of teaching experience, level of education received, size of family and so on. Those background data can be critical in enabling the reader to be convinced by the research evidence produced and the conclusions drawn from them.

Finally, it should also be pointed out that quantitative and qualitative are not mutually exclusive. That means to say, if a researcher decides to use a quantitative approach to the investigation of a problem, there is no obligation to ignore any qualitative data that are collected in the process. Similarly, if in another study it was decided that a qualitative approach was best suited to the topic being investigated, it could still include quantitative data. It should be recognised that often researchers may not appear to have to make a decision about whether to adopt a qualitative or quantitative approach. The way research questions are formulated and the research agenda specified make it clear what approach is most appropriate and trustworthy.

Psychometric/Sociometric

The nature of these approaches has already been touched on in this chapter. As the suffix 'metric' indicates, both psychometric and sociometric involve measurement. Each emphasizes the measurement of particular factors central to, or contributory to, the topic under study.

Psychometric refers typically to the measurement of mental capacities and processes. The most common examples are intelligence and related tests, e.g. reading ability, verbal/non-verbal reasoning ones. Other examples include measures of mental states, for example, personality and some attitude tests.

Sociometric, on the other hand refers to the measurement of social relationships with groups of people and/or attitudes arising out of membership of a particular social group. Social groups can be defined in a variety of ways depending on the focus of the research study. One notion of a social group might be what is loosely termed 'social class'. In Britain, reference is still popularly made to people being of 'working class' or 'middle class'. In research terms, not just in educational research but also generally in the social sciences, social groups are more precisely defined using socio-economic groupings as classified by the Registrar General of the Census Office. Such classifications are considered better indicators of distinct groupings. The advantage of socio-economic group classifications is that they are legitimated by the Census Office, one of the most important sources of objective information about the population of Britain. Middle and working class may have once been relatively distinct groupings in Britain but with a steadily evolving country, socially and economically, that distinction has become increasingly blurred. Today, while it may still be possible to draw some cultural distinction between the two groups, the relative rewards gained from being in either manual or non-manual employment are no longer as clear cut as they used to be and people in the more highly skilled manual sector may enjoy higher earnings, if not necessarily the same security of employment, as those in the non-manual or white collar sector.

In Britain it has long been held that middle class parents placed greater value on education than their working class counterparts and that the education system, through the values it sought to transmit and the rewards that it offered seemed to be loaded in favour of middle class children. Equally, it was held that children from working class families suffered a double disadvantage in that, not only did the education system work against them, but also that the deprived nature of their home circumstances meant that they were less able to benefit from the education provided by schools. Poor housing, poor health and ignorance of the value of education meant that working class children generally were doomed to fail in school. It is difficult enough when researching education to unpick the realities from the popular and often erroneous myths surrounding the impact of home background on educational performance, without using misguided conceptions of social groupings.

Ethnicity forms the basis of another form of social grouping. In the British context, the Office of Populations Censuses and Surveys used the following ethnic groupings in the 1991 census: Black Caribbean; Black African; Black Other; Pakistani; Indian; Bangladeshi; Chinese; Any other ethnic group (OPCS, 1991). Another way of grouping people might be by their religion: Islam, Sikhism, Buddhism, Hinduism for example.

Sometimes the social grouping might be conditioned by school type or location. Thus a group might be defined as single sex schools (that is, schools for boys or girls only) or mixed schools; or it could be urban or suburban as against rural or inner-city. The last grouping is typically used to refer to schools serving inner-city neighbourhoods with the implication of old and poor housing, high levels of unemployment, poor diet, poor health and so forth.

The issue of schools and their social settings and the relative impact of external influences on school outcomes as opposed to the effectiveness or otherwise of individual schools' management or curriculum delivery are currently topics of particular concern in countries like the UK where governments are concerned to raise standards in education while at the same time trying to control rising expenditure on education.

One of the objectives of education legislation in the UK since the late 1980s has been to raise standards, hence the need, so the government has argued, for a national curriculum together with an associated form of testing and assessment at age 7, 11, 14 and 16. This has been accompanied by budgetary reforms giving schools greater control over, and responsibilities for, their individual financial arrangements and greater parental choice over the schools attended by their children and a more frequent inspection of schools to ensure that they are well run and meet their curricular obligations.

Other forms of social group can extend to quite distinct sub-groups, even within a school. In one classic study of its kind, Willis (1977) explored the attitudes of disaffected youngsters in relation to school and teacher and peer group expectations. Our understanding of such groups has clear implications for the way in which we teach and plan our curricula, especially in societies in which, increasingly, higher skill levels are required in order to strengthen the country's economic performance. What is important and should be stressed is that social groups, just like any other variable seen to be important in our understanding of educational — or any other social process — needs to be clearly defined.

Interpretative

The interpretative approach is part of the qualitative. The particular focus is seeking to explain why things have happened from the insider's point of view. The interpretative approach does not necessarily require an 'insider' to be part of the research team. Very often, the researchers rely on their experience of particular settings to be able to 'read' the information provided by the subjects involved in the study.

While, arguably, interpretation involves deduction from the data obtained, it relies more on what it feels like to be a participant in the action under study. For example; if one was investigating the impact of a curriculum package, one way of assessing it would be to rely on the achievement test scores of pupils who had followed the package and compare their scores with those of similar pupils who had covered the same topic using the traditional teaching/study methods. If the pupils using the new package performed better than the others, the usefulness of the package could be said to have been demonstrated.

Alternatively, or additionally, data could be obtained from pupils and teachers using the new package to determine the degree of interest it generated among them. Motivational benefits could provide an additional argument for the wider use of the package. If the package was a prototype, the data from the teachers and pupils on how it worked and the areas or aspects in which it might be improved would be of considerable value to the designers of the package. Even in areas of test development, information from the candidates on what the paper 'felt like', or on questions or instructions which were difficult to understand, could all help to improve the test's construction. Objective evidence taken from the analysis of answers from different candidates may attest to the relative suitability of different items. However, the mathematical logic cannot take into account cases where the right answers have been given for the 'wrong' reasons. In areas like national curriculum testing and assessment, where pupils are awarded levels on the basis of their test performance and which consist of a series of short answers, two answers, right or wrong, could make the difference of a whole level in terms of the outcome.

References

BASSEY, M. (1992) 'Creating education through research', *British Educational Research Journal*, **18**, 1.

CAMPBELL, D.T. and STANLEY, J.C. (1963) 'Experimental and quasi-experimental designs for research on teaching', in GAGE, N.L. (ed.) *Handbook of Research on Teaching*, Chicago: Rand McNally and Co.

CRONBACH, L.J. (1962) *Educational Psychology*, 2nd edition, New York: Harcourt Brace.

DEPARTMENT OF EDUCATION AND SCIENCE (1991) *History in the National Curriculum*, England: HMSO.

GOWIN, D.B. (1972) 'Is educational research distinctive?' in THOMAS, L.G. (ed.) *Philosophical Redirection of Education Research*, Chicago: University of Chicago Press.

MAYKUT, P. and MOREHOUSE, R. (1994) *Beginning Qualitative Research: A Philosophical and Practical Guide*, London: Falmer Press.

OPCS (1991) *Total Period Fertility Rate Tables*, Office of Population Censuses and Surveys, London: HMSO.

SIMON, B.S. (1978) 'Educational research: Which way?' *Research Intelligence*, **4**, 1.

SMITH, D.J. and TOMLINSON, S. (1989) *The School Effect: A Study of Multi-racial Comprehensives*, London: Policy Studies Institute.

TAYLOR, P.H. (1966) 'The role and function of educational research' — 3, *Educational Research*, **9**, pp. 11–15.

TRAVERS, R.M.W. (1978) *An Introduction to Educational Research*, 4th edition, New York: Macmillan.

VERMA, G.K. and PUMFREY, P. (1993) (eds) *Cultural Diversity and the National Curriculum: Vol 2 — Cross-Curricular Themes in Secondary Schools*, London: Falmer Press.

VERMA, G.K. and PUMFREY, P. (1994) (eds) *Cultural Diversity and the National Curriculum: Vol 4 — Cross-Curricular Themes in Primary Schools*, London: Falmer Press.

VERMA, G.K., ZEC, P. and SKINNER, G.D. (1994) *The Ethnic Crucible: Harmony and Discord in Secondary Schools*, London: Falmer Press.

WILLIS, P. (1977) *Learning to Labour*, Farnborough, England: Saxon House.

Chapter 3

Educational Research: Nature and Process

This chapter introduces a range of issues, some of which will be taken up and dealt with at greater length later in the book. We begin by offering some definitions of educational research, describe some trends and continue with a discussion of some of the issues inherent in the process. These are followed by operational strategies, a classification by purpose, some observations on the nature of the audiences the researcher seeks to address and the chapter concludes with suggestions on how the evaluation of a piece of research might be undertaken.

Definitions

It is extremely difficult to give a definition of the term 'educational research' which would be acceptable to all those concerned with educational decisions and practices. Lovell and Lawson (1970) neatly summarize the situation by saying that 'it is virtually impossible to give a definition of the term ... which would command universal acceptance, as there are innumerable meanings that can be given to the word education.' Traxler (1954) holding a similar view, stated that the overlapping of educational research with research in the other social sciences is inevitable because of the nature of the process of education itself. (Anyone wishing to pursue the notion of education as a discipline could refer to Walton and Kuetha, 1963, and/or to Bruner, 1962.) However, definitions are a valuable aid in understanding a concept or an idea and not a means of forming inflexible categories.

During the 1930s, educational researchers adopted the idea that all terms should be defined in operational terms (Travers, 1978). This strategy has not proved useful in eliminating the vagueness of educational language. For example, many psychologists have defined the concept of intelligence through intelligence tests, but the tests have proved far less valuable than test designers had hoped for.

Watson (1953) asserted that 'In education we would do well to stop mimicking the physical sciences. Educational research is ultimately concerned with people. It is best shared as lay and professional educators are involved.' Such a perspective would obviously appeal to many classroom teachers who have come to see research as the private concern of a particular group of people — as something accomplished for its own professional interests. Corey (1953), one of the pioneers in action research, agreed with the previous author that limiting educational research to professional researchers alone is to take too limited a view of the education function.

Education research literature indicates that many writers have conceptualized educational research in a broad sense. Travers (1978), for example, defined it as 'an activity directed toward the development of an organised body of scientific knowledge about the events with which educators are concerned.' According to him, the goal of educational research is to discover laws or generalizations about behaviour that can be utilized to make predictions and control events within the educational context. Not all of those engaged in educational research would feel sympathetic to this idea of using research as a means of achieving this end. Ary, Jacobs and Razavieh (1985) state that 'When the scientific method is applied to the study of educational problems, educational research is the result.' In this simple description of research it is implied that educational research has the same general goals as other research.

Peters and White (1969), expanding the boundaries and questioning the assumption in much of the literature that most educational research is psychological or social scientific (e.g. emphasized by Cronbach, 1962), defined research as 'systematic and sustained enquiry carried out by people well-versed in some form of thinking in order to answer some specific type of question'. The authors have attempted to enlarge the dimension of research in order to include all those disciplines which are engaged in 'the more reflective side of scientific work'.

Earlier, British contributors to the discussion of the nature and scope of educational research seem to have adopted a narrower perspective. Thouless (1969) in the preface to his book, *Map of Educational Research*, offered the following definition: '... educational research was to be understood as embracing empirical and experimental researches, but not historical and comparative studies in education'. A similar definition was suggested by Nisbet and Entwistle (1970), restricting it to 'areas which involve quantitative or scientific methods of investigation', and pointing out that 'there are other important forms of research in education, such as historical or philosophical enquiry'.

Anderson (1990) exploring the nature of educational research wrote:

> Research in education is a disciplined attempt to address questions or solve problems through the collection and analysis of primary data for the purpose of description, explanation, generalization and prediction.

Such a view of educational research implies that it is basically a problem-solving activity and addresses a question or tests an hypothesis. Anderson further argues that the problem-solving nature of educational research is preferable because it seeks to address specific questions generated by data for the purpose.

However, it should be stressed that most people conduct research in areas in which they feel a certain value commitment, but this must not interfere with the researchers' objectivity. They should not have too strong a vested interest in the outcome (Anderson, 1990).

Stenhouse (1984) regarded educational research as

> systematic activity that is directed towards providing knowledge, or adding to the understanding of existing knowledge which is of relevance for improving the effectiveness of education.

He then went on to say, more succinctly, that it was 'systematic activity that is made public'. Notice here that Stenhouse introduces the idea of an audience and implies that research can, and should, have some practical value — ideas to which we will return later.

Finally, there is the Economic and Social Research Council definition which is of interest to many researchers and would-be researchers, not least because of its powers to influence the direction of research effort in Britain. For the ESRC:

> Educational research within the social sciences may include any disciplined enquiry which promotes theoretical understanding of educational processes and settings or which serves educational judgements and decisions about policy and practice. Such research may be conducted in formal educational settings, in industrial, commercial and professional situations or in informal contexts (such as parent–child interaction, self-help groups and local communities). This disciplined enquiry necessarily draws on the theoretical and methodological resources of philosophy and of social science disciplines, such as anthropology, linguistics, social history, sociology, psychology, or economics. However, it may also involve methods and techniques originating from the distinctive nature of educational knowledge. In addition, the generation of new methods may itself be a focus of educational research. (ESRC, 1996)

It should further be pointed out that the ESRC's influence is exerted in part through its role as a sponsor of projects. Researchers seeking funding from it are invited to submit proposals to the Council. Each proposal is subjected to judgment by independent and experienced experts working in the field in question and rated on its relevance, the appropriateness of its methods, design quality and feasibility. Proposals with the highest ratings on those criteria are then assessed by a panel which decides which ones are to be accepted for funding. The winning of such funding confers status on the researchers and the host institution. Quite apart from its role in acting as a watchdog for public funds, allocated for research, the ESRC exerts a controlling/monitoring role on what constitutes research and its conduct. (Other agencies, typically charitable trusts, like the Nuffield Foundation, the Leverhulme Trust and the Rowntree Trust, invite research proposals, and operate similar scrutiny processes, but the prestige of such awards varies, according to the status and reputation of the agency.)

Despite the differing conceptions of the goal of educational research, the common element passing through most of the ideas is the application of systematic methods to the study of educational problems. Given this dimension to the definition, the search for meaningful and trustworthy knowledge becomes central to the whole process. It should also be remembered that research in education has been greatly influenced by research in other disciplines such as psychology, anthropology and sociology. Nevertheless, it has made progress since the beginning of this century, and many educational decisions have been implemented as a result of the processes of research. It should be emphasized that there is no universal recipe for conducting educational research. All research studies are characterized by some general format which is consistent with the basic procedure of the method of research outlined in Chapter 1.

Trends in Educational Research

While reading studies related to education, one becomes aware of the division of opinion regarding the nature of educational research. Some researchers seem to be convinced that the experimental technique is the most powerful research method to deal with educational issues. The opponents of this method assert that only the non-experimental approach can discover the 'reality' which is inaccessible to this quasi-scientific educational research. Thus, the distinction is often drawn between experimental and non-experimental approaches to the study of educational phenomena. In spite of this diversity of opinion, there is a fairly clear description in the literature of what educational researchers have in recent years achieved. Yet, many practitioners (teachers, educational psychologists) conceive of research within a narrow framework.

During the early part of this century, research was primarily concerned with the collection of descriptive data concerning educational phenomena, and with the development of test instruments. By the middle of the 1930s, leaders in the field began to question the quality of research data since much of the work was repetitive, biased and fragmented in design and methodology (Van Dalen, 1966). Such studies made little contribution, if any, to the knowledge and understanding of education.

From about 1940, research workers began to make detailed examinations of the shortcomings that existed in educational research, in the tools used and in the gaps that existed in the overall production of research findings. Furthermore, in an attempt to expand the frontiers of educational knowledge, educational researchers raised questions about the nature of learning and the processes by which children learn. Upon becoming familiar with the various theoretical explanations of learning, educators began to appreciate that learning was a more complex process than they had thought (Van Dalen, 1966).

The work of Tyler (1949) represents another research related trend that challenged some existing school practices. He introduced into the learning–teaching situation the idea that educational objectives should be specified in precise terms, a doctrine that has continued to have an impact on school systems, particularly in the United States. Although Tyler made some contribution to curriculum construction, his main thesis of defining educational objectives with precision did not lead to any significant advances either in education or in the thinking behind it. His attempt to reduce the complexity of educational phenomena to simple behavioural components did not prove to be a useful way of describing human intellectual performance, and did not seem to generate any provocative educational research.

The emphasis of much educational research in recent times has been on the solution of educational problems through various research methods. As a result of this emphasis, many methodological advances have been made in the domain of educational research. Page (1975) pointed out that the period between 1965 and 1975 had been one of great achievement 'for concept after concept has been sharpened and tested, and myth after myth has been exposed'. Tremendous impetus has been given to educational researchers over the last three decades by providing them with generous financial support. In Britain, attempts were made to promote the development of educational research from the earliest part of this century. However, substantial financial support for educational research is a product of the last 40 years. For example, Douglas's (1964; Douglas et al., 1968) longitudinal study, Pidgeon and Yates's (1957) work on secondary school selection made some impact on the educational climate of the country. Because of the time, effort and money which have been expended, both the quality and quantity of research in education have increased (see Ward, Hall and Schramm, 1975).

Another significant change which has taken place in the character of educational research is the involvement of many disciplines. Since the beginning of this century, researchers from many disciplines have, from time to time, turned their attention to the school as the locus of historical, psychological, philosophical and sociological problems. As a result of this, much of modern educational technology seems to represent an attempt to bring a multi-discipline approach to the solution of educational problems. Modern social science research is increasingly dissolving the boundaries between disciplines, and successful researchers are likely to require an understanding and appreciation of research techniques beyond the domain of their own immediate discipline. A great deal of innovative research in the last two decades has been conducted across disciplinary boundaries. The current trend clearly shows that interdisciplinary studies are likely to play an important role in research in the future. It is necessary therefore that researchers acquire skills and competencies across a range of research perspectives and techniques. Stouthamer-Loeber and Kammen (1995) suggested two crucial skills: firstly, the ability of the researcher to pose research questions of societal or theoretical importance; and secondly, once the problem to be studied has been formulated, practical skills are required to carry out the research.

The expanding boundary of educational research reflects, in part, the fact that society has put its faith in, and therefore placed enormous responsibilities on, the educational enterprise. This may, in turn, imply that the central problems of education are concerned with issues that are related to the values society holds. As Bloom (1966) rightly remarked, 'Education is looked to for solutions to problems of poverty, racial discord, crime and delinquency, urban living, peace, and even for problems arising from affluence.' It seems, however, that for many social problems, decision makers turn to education for their solution. In the last few decades, research workers have become more aware of the need for evaluating critically the varied and conflicting explanations of educational phenomena, and to test them in a wide variety of settings.

In the early 1960s, the OECD (Organization for Economic Cooperation and Development) paid some attention to research in the field of education, but nothing tangible appeared. In the late 1980s, there was a revival of interest which is apparent from the following declaration of the OECD Ministers of Education at the end of their meeting in November 1990 (OECD, 1994).

> The potential of educational research as an integral element of improvement remains
> largely underdeveloped, whether at the national, regional or local level. Traditional
> academic research has its own special part to play. More important still, much

research and development needs to be grounded on practice, involving staff and institutions, whether individually or collectively, in a constant process of diagnosis, comparison and analysis.

In recent years, some researchers have introduced the notion of 'paradigm', a term originally developed by Kuhn, into the language of educational research (see Parlett and Hamilton, 1977; Esland et al., 1972). This is a theory about relationships in the natural world. Kuhn (1970, 1972) argued that paradigms pre-structure what is seen and understood in science. Thus, instead of dealing in all possible laboratory manipulations, science selects those which allow for the fruitful elaboration of the dominant paradigm. Kuhn thus raised the serious question for a view of science that sees it as value-free and as developing through the challenging of theories following their systematic testing against empirical movements. In a brilliant article, McNamara (1979) argued that 'the introduction of the term paradigm into educational research is based upon a misunderstanding or inaccurate representation of Kuhn's work and that it can lead to muddled and unclear thinking among educationists, especially those involved with curriculum evaluation'. This shows the way in which research workers in the field of education operate. Researchers from different 'discipline' backgrounds adopt individual techniques and approaches in a somewhat eclectic way (McNamara, 1979), a point mentioned earlier in this section. A glance through the literature suggests that there is a body of opinion that is doubtful about the use of the 'positivist' paradigm in educational research. An alternative approach, claimed to be more flexible and more holistic, has been advocated in the field of education (Elliot and Adelman, 1978), curriculum development (Wheeler, 1967; Stenhouse, 1975), and organizational change (Clarke, 1972).

A review of the literature points to a dichotomy between positivism or objectivity and anti-positivism or subjectivity. Researchers tend to align themselves with one or other of the two research paradigms, and elect to use either quantitative or qualitative research methods accordingly. However, there is now an increasing recognition that combining the two main research traditions within an educational framework has considerable benefits, rather than making exclusive use of one or the other.

Many educational research programmes seem to adopt a 'combination of methods' from so-called differing research traditions known as 'triangulation of methods' or the 'multi-method approach'. It is widely accepted that all research methods have both strengths and weaknesses. Bryman (1988) has shown that '. . . the tendency to view the two research traditions as reflecting different epistemological positions, and hence divergent paradigms, has led to an exaggeration of the differences between them . . .'. Similarly, Silverman (1985) wrote, '. . . that there are distinctive advantages to be gained from the juxtaposition and integration of these two styles of research . . .'.

In spite of the complex nature of educational research, most producers and consumers of research data hold the view that its main function is to provide meaningful and trustworthy information (knowledge). It is also emphasized that research knowledge must lend itself to practical application in the solution of educational problems. In other words, the results of research should be obtained and then used by educators who convert the findings of the research worker into practical applications. As pointed out by Eggleston (1979), 'philosophers and educational researchers who have reflected on the nature of the educational research enterprise have frequently emphasised the centrality of practical concerns'. Thouless (1969) agreed with this rationale of educational research. According to him, education is an applied science, which implies that educational research should be conducted in response to questions arising from an educational context, and that success can only be achieved when the findings are applied to current educational practices. Some educationists view this perspective as restricting the domain of educational research, as we will see presently.

However, the application of research findings is a difficult task. Therefore, practising teachers ought to have an understanding of research terminology and methodology in order to make intelligent educational judgments. The critical evaluation of research reports by teachers will keep them informed of educational developments, and might reduce the gap between research findings and their applications. The current resurgence and reorientation of research efforts show a growing awareness amongst educators that research is a slow but effective tool for educational progress. As a result, schools have come under the focus of interest of professional researchers in recent years. This increasing interest is reflected in the number of educational research projects accomplished over the last three decades.

We conclude this section on trends in educational research with a few lines on post-modernism and post-structuralism. Those researchers practising within this movement adopt a wholly different stance from that traditionally taken by educational researchers. Much of what has been written so far in this book (and, indeed, informs what follows) takes, as its starting point, a set of assumptions including the belief that a research programme, properly constructed and conducted, will result in an identifiable addition to knowledge upon which further research leading to greater knowledge and understanding can be safely undertaken.

Post-modernists and post-structuralists, however, influenced by the work of Lyotard, Foucault and Derrida, take the view that truth-making in the research process is seductive but essentially naive; that there is a multiplicity of truths, all of which have a legitimacy and are dependent on the positioning of each actor in the research context (see for example, Griffiths, 1995). An examination of the theoretical bases for this movement are well outside the scope of this book but we return to the subject in a little more detail in Chapter 4.

At this point in the discussion, we turn to examine some issues in educational research as more conventionally understood.

Issues in Educational Research

The field of education is at least as complex as, and some would argue, more complex to research than the biological and physical sciences. In spite of the many useful contributions research has made to education (e.g. in the areas of learning, transfer of training, motivation, classroom dynamics, teaching methods and assessment techniques) it has not provided all the answers educators seek to make educational judgments. There seem to be many reasons for its falling short of their expectations.

Educational researchers have to deal with many variables simultaneously, and some of them cannot be controlled or quantified. Furthermore, educational research is complicated by factors such as the interaction between the investigators and their human subjects of study, and this can influence the way the conclusions are drawn. Such an interaction may even produce changes in human behaviour (in the subjects of the study) which might not have occurred otherwise. Such an interaction can also influence the way the conclusions are drawn. However, in practical terms, it is extremely difficult for researchers to dissociate themselves from the phenomena under study.

In the classic division in the general sciences between researchers and their fields of study, a number of principles seem to have wide acceptance. These include three propositions. Two of these relate to objectivity: the maintenance of an objective stance towards the subject under study, and the centrality of the quest for objectivity in investigations. Thirdly, there is recognition of the need for accuracy and precision in measurement, to be achieved through the employment of statistical principles. Researchers recognize the importance of the need to maintain an 'objective' stance towards what they are studying, avoiding to the best of their ability any intervention that might result in distortion of the data collected. The quest for objectivity is central to all investigation work. Despite its widespread acceptance as an essential element, the achievement of objectivity in the social sciences is more difficult than in the natural sciences. The use of the scientific method in the social sciences attempts to deal with events whose occurrence, in principle, can be agreed upon by everyone. However, researchers' personalities and values can all too easily intrude upon and influence their observations of phenomena and assessment of the findings, possibly affecting consequently the validity of any attempted generalizations from the results.

In educational research, the above mentioned principles and methods have often been applied in large-scale social surveys. In these, the major research effort has been to produce effective instruments of enquiry, and once data have been collected, to analyse them. This analysis is usually undertaken by statistical methods, and advancements in computerization have greatly facilitated this process.

In recent years, a substantial body of social scientists (including educational researchers) have rejected this positivistic approach and the physical sciences' model from which it is drawn. They have argued that these principles have little to offer in terms of relevance in the study of complex social situations and human behaviour. Some of them have highlighted the need for qualitative research and analysis of interpersonal structures, and their approaches have been based on a quite different set of assumptions. This view stresses a more involved role by the researcher in seeking to understand the reality from the point of view of the individuals being studied. It should be mentioned that the qualitative approach itself is not free from weaknesses.

Ethical considerations also need to be taken into account by all researchers. Until recently, researchers did not have to confront these issues. For example, Dennis (1941) investigated the role of social stimulation on child development by raising a pair of twins in virtual seclusion for a year. Today, the situation has changed, and ever-increasing attention is being given to the ethical considerations of research with human subjects. The research procedures may produce undesirable psychological side effects. Additionally, human beings have the right to refuse to participate in research, the right to remain anonymous, and the right to ask the researcher to treat data about them confidentially. When conducting classroom research, the investigator often obtains personal information about the pupil, sometimes by means of deceptive methods. These practices raise both ethical and legal questions concerning the rights of research subjects. The human subject should not be viewed as an ingredient in the research laboratory. These ethical issues obviously make educational researchers re-think their research strategies.

Another type of problem concerns the way society perceives social science research, in contrast with the natural sciences. As early as 1949, Remmers had remarked that our thinking about research was quite different in the fields of natural and social sciences. Such attitudes still seem to prevail. For example, it is hard to change public attitudes, beliefs, values and traditions in the light of new ideas and findings based on social research. However, there has been some positive shift in society's expectations from educational enterprise in recent years as mentioned earlier (Bloom, 1966, Travers, 1978), and this has resulted in the increased funding of educational research.

Yet, while many people are reluctant to accept change recommended in light of social research findings, even if this would improve their way of life, some people are seemingly ready to accept findings unquestioningly. An example of this is the reaction to the notorious study by Jensen (1973). His findings, published in the book *Educability and Group Differences*, argued that black children had inherently lower intelligence than white children. Many researchers have pointed out methodological weaknesses in Jensen's work (see, for example, Bagley, 1975; Flynn, 1980). However, many educators accepted Jensen's results without examining the research critically. This can seriously affect the performance and achievement of a black pupil in two ways: first, by teachers being openly prejudiced in their interaction with the black child, and secondly by having low expectations of the child's abilities and achievement. Both these attitudes can be found among white teachers in British schools (Giles, 1977; Troyna, 1992). It must be stressed that both researchers and consumers should evaluate critically any research findings, and should avoid acceptance or rejection on emotional grounds.

A recent trend in educational research has been a greater emphasis on applied rather than basic research. Many researchers believe that this has created a vacuum in the theoretical aspects of education. Whether or not there has been less emphasis on basic research, most consumers (particularly classroom teachers) agree that there is a wide gap between research findings and practical applications. This gap can be narrowed if more and more teachers are involved in practical research, and solutions to many of the classroom problems are sought in the natural settings. That is to say, teaching and research should become co-activities. Both professional researchers and teachers can make significant contributions in bridging the gap. Researchers should conduct their studies from sound theoretical positions, should make their hypotheses or research questions explicit and should disseminate their research findings and implications in a form that makes them readily understandable to teachers. Teachers should also develop research sophistication in order to appreciate research findings and their implications.

In summary, it can be said that educational research has not improved educational practice to the extent that had been hoped for. In the current international economic situation, it is doubtful whether sufficient funds for educational research will be made available. However, it would seem that one of the essential strategies is to spend some of the resources and time available at the disposal of educational researchers to improve the training of both producers and consumers of research. Educational practitioners have a vital role to play in implementing educational change in any society. It is to be hoped that one day many classroom problems can be effectively studied by the teacher when research becomes a natural consequence of teaching. In a chapter on 'The Teacher as Researcher', Stenhouse (1975) rightly observed that '. . . it is difficult to see how teaching can be improved or how curricular proposals can be evaluated without self-monitoring on the part of teachers. A research tradition which is accessible to teachers and which feeds teaching must be created if education is to be significantly improved'.

Operational Strategies in Educational Research

In Chapter 1, a number of investigative methods were described as a broad framework in the execution of systematic research. These are:

- the selection of the problem: development of the hypothesis;
- collection and analysis of data; and
- drawing appropriate conclusions.

Generally speaking, educational research follows a similar pattern except that it is limited in scope defined as educational. Sometimes it becomes difficult to make a clear cut distinction between educational and non-educational issues. However, the tendency in educational research is to try and focus upon the unique characteristics of educational phenomena. Writers have suggested various strategies to conduct research which is regarded as a process having a series of linked activities. Dixon, Bouma and Atkinson (1987) have outlined the research process simplistically into three phases:

- Phase 1 — the researcher clarifies the issue to be researched and selects a research method;
- Phase 2 — collection of evidence about the research question;

- Phase 3 — the researcher relates the evidence to the research question, draws conclusions about the question, and points out the limitations of the research.

All research activities, regardless of type or discipline, are characterized by some general format. Although the methods developed in the natural sciences gave impetus to the development of research in education, the differences between the two sciences are recognized (see Chapter 1).

1 The first and foremost task of educational research is to establish the purpose of the study in a clear concise way. The problem must be recognized as worthy and capable of investigation. A clearly stated problem provides the most essential element in constructing a frame of reference that can give direction to the study. Too wide and too general a purpose, such as 'to investigate teaching styles', may prove too complex and diffused.

2 When a problem has been identified, the next phase requires a systematic and critical analysis of the research problem. This analysis involves the search of available information specific to the area of study, and definition of the problem in a logical way. For example, an educational researcher might begin with a thorough study of the previous literature that has a direct or indirect bearing on the research problem. This helps in defining the research topic satisfactorily. Many educational terms have several meanings e.g. 'sociability', 'maladjustment', 'intelligence'. A study of text books and journals would help to do further analysis of these terms and concepts. Sometimes, a review of the literature raises more questions rather than providing clues as to how to resolve things. It might even suggest that the original research problem needs to be modified, and if so, what would be the form and nature of the revised hypothesis/es or research question/s? This activity provides insight into the work of other investigators who have explored a similar area. At this stage of the research, the investigators are likely to crystallize the meanings of various concepts and ideas related to their investigation.

3 Although the formulation of hypotheses is not always essential in educational research, their use provides a direction in deciding upon the research methodology to be adopted. However, the research worker might decide to formulate research questions rather than hypotheses. The key to hypothesizing is careful preparation and analysis of available information (see Chapter 1).

4 Depending upon the nature of the problem and the resources available, the researcher decides whether to use an experimental design (e.g. psychometric approach) or a non-experimental one (e.g. case study, interviews, observations). The choice of research design often dictates the kinds of tools and procedures which are to be utilized in order to study the variables/factors. Sometimes, appropriate tools may not be available or may be inappropriate in a particular cultural setting. Some insight into the problems of measurement

is necessary to be able to select the correct instruments or tools (Verma, 1979). A number of standard designs and types of research exist (see Chapters 5 and 6), but many modifications to them are possible.

In educational research, the discussion should not be centred around the best methodology, but rather consideration should be given to the most appropriate methods or techniques which can be employed in a given situation. Most research projects require the use of more than one method or technique. Researchers, therefore, need to keep abreast of a wide range of research designs and methods, and be confident of making an appropriate selection from them.

5   The next step involves actual data collection and analysis. This also includes administration of instruments (if used), interviews, observations, or other research tool or combination of tools. The need to understand the procedures of analysis cannot be overestimated. In educational research, the investigator often deals with a large number of variables which require the help of a mathematical process, i.e. statistical analysis. Dependent upon the research design, statistics can play an important role from the planning stage right through to the evaluation of the results. Most professional researchers would agree that some knowledge of statistical techniques is essential for both producers and consumers of educational research studies.

6   The final stage of research is perhaps the most delicate and complex one. This is concerned with discussion and the presentation of research findings. The investigators need to draw the conclusions in an intelligent form in order to communicate the findings to their target audience. It is also essential that the conclusions of the study are kept within the boundaries set out initially by the definition of the problem. This part of the research report should also contain a consideration of the implications of the study's findings, with particular attention given to the extent to which the findings can be generalized. In essence, this involves an objective assessment of the grounds for believing that the findings might hold true in settings similar to those in which the study was conducted. The major drawback in many research reports is the tendency to make incorrect/invalid generalizations. This stems from a failure to appreciate the complexity of factors. For example, in a classroom situation there are a very few variables which can be identified and controlled. The research worker is often forced to use common sense or intuition in identifying and interpreting the controlled or floating variables. The researcher's personality or bias is another factor which is likely to influence the way conclusions are drawn. In view of the above-mentioned factors, the researcher must exercise extreme caution in making generalizations from the findings.

A word about the reporting of research findings ought to be included here. People have different abilities and experiences which can influence the way they receive and use research reports. Technical or statistical information may not be meaningful or comprehensible to some people. One of the reasons often cited for the slow advancement of educational research is that there is a wide gap between professional researchers and classroom teachers (consumers). In recent years, the present authors in the course of their research projects, were able to confirm this proposition from a large number of teachers in British schools. Very few seemed to have any knowledge of the research evidence which appears at the end of the projects. Ideally, the researcher ought to make the findings available in a simple and intelligent manner, using a minimum of jargon, so that they may be followed by the widest possible audience. In practice, however, researchers tend to write for a more immediate audience, either the body or agency which has sponsored the study, or for fellow professionals. Sadly, there often never seems to be the time or the resources to re-present the findings in a form available to that wider audience. (The issue of audience is an important one in terms of research, especially in a field as complex and significant as education, and is considered later on in this chapter.)

It must be emphasized that the operational strategies described in the preceding paragraphs should not be taken as a rigid framework. These strategies overlap considerably, and depending upon the nature and design of the research one may need to move back and forth from one step to another. For example, systematic reading of the literature may suggest a redefinition of the problem and a consequent amendment of the enquiry.

Classification of Educational Research

Any attempt to classify educational research into categories poses a difficult problem. A glance through the literature indicates that research in education has been classified from many points of view: according to discipline (e.g. psychological, philosophical, sociological, and so on); according to the type of data collection procedures (e.g. interviews, observations, testing, and so on); according to the methods employed (e.g. historical, descriptive and experimental, see Chapter 5).

A simple dichotomy frequently used in the classification of social science and educational research is that between quantitative and qualitative or psychometric and reflective/illuminative. The advancement of computer technology and the improvements in statistical methods have resulted in a rapid increase in quantitative studies during the last two decades. However, these labels do not represent discrete categories or clusters, but are merely endpoints of a continuum. Sometimes a piece of research may fall into more than one of these categories. Some writers have classified research methodology in a general way such as library, life and physical science, social and technological research (Rummel, 1964). This categorization seems less clear, and does not appear to make a significant contribution to our understanding of research methods. In view of methodological advances, it would be difficult to devise a single categorization scheme to include all the possible combinations of methods used in educational research. Lincoln and Guba (1985) and Lofland and Lofland (1984) are among many writers who present a variety of terms for research conducted within this post-positivistic, naturalistic paradigm:

> Social science is a terminological jungle where many labels compete, and no single label has been able to command the particular domain before us. Often ... researchers simply 'do it' without worrying about giving it a name. (Lofland and Lofland, 1984).

Another useful way to classify or categorize educational research is by purpose. Purpose could be seen as lying along a continuum from the most basic to the most applied. That is to say, a piece of research might be designed to add knowledge to the field of study which may or may not be of any immediate value (basic), or might be designed to be of immediate practical application (applied). In the educational context, problems studied in basic research can range from learning, and the transfer of training (materials to be learned) to the development of systematic knowledge (e.g. how children think, or studies of interaction in various types of classroom groupings). The findings of basic research tend to push forward the boundaries of some new or established knowledge, and may not have any immediate practical relevance. It is argued, however, that findings of basic research may provide vital knowledge as a link in a practical situation at a later time.

Applied research is often designed to solve specific problems or to provide information that is of immediate use. A great deal of contemporary educational research would seem primarily to be of the applied type. It covers a wide range of possibilities, but often takes the form of a survey of some kind. This type of research tends to be carried out by experienced researchers and may include participant observation or unobtrusive measures. In this, the researcher observes the situation but does not interfere. Examples of applied research include the transfer of new teaching methods, teaching approaches or strategies from experimental schools to a representative group of schools, where teachers may be trained to use them. It should be remembered that the distinction between pure and applied research (i.e. between theory development and implementation) is based primarily upon the purpose of the research in question.

The above description of these research categories clearly shows that basic and applied research are difficult to distinguish in many studies. In many ways, pure and applied research have a great deal in common. According to Van Dalen (1966), the purpose of investigation may be different in 'pure' and 'applied' research, but the techniques used in each may be almost indistinguishable. Hilgard (1945) pointed out that the distinction is really a continuum rather than a dichotomy. Travers (1978), differentiating between the two terms, wrote that:

> Basic research is designed to add to an organised body of scientific knowledge and does not necessarily produce results of immediate practical value. Applied research is undertaken to solve an immediate practical problem and the goal of adding to scientific knowledge is secondary.

The recent trend in the educational field shows that much of the research accomplished has been concerned with the immediate application of its findings. This would obviously be favoured by most classroom teachers who would argue for more applied research that can produce simply practical and immediately useful information. For example, practising teachers might well prefer to contribute to applied research for the development of a machine to teach maladjusted or ESN pupils rather than a fundamental contribution to the knowledge of learning–teaching situations.

Many of the earlier psychological studies were conducted with the intention of expanding the frontiers of knowledge. However, a large proportion of modern research in the field of testing and measurement is applied research. There has been considerable debate among educators with regard to which type of research is of more value. Cronbach (1966), like many social scientists, argued for more basic research:

> Educational improvements that really make an impact on the ignorance rate will not grow out of minor variations of teaching content and process. Effective educational designs, worth careful development and field trial, can emerge only from a deep understanding of learning and motivation.

Similarly, other social scientists believe that basic research is of more importance than applied research with regard to its impact on education (Kerlinger, 1977; Travers, 1978). Such views imply that the findings of basic research seek to make fundamental contributions to the knowledge of education whether this new knowledge has any immediate or practical application at the time.

In basic research, knowledge of more than one discipline is often involved in the search for new facts, elaboration of new theories, or the re-appraisal of old ones. The investigators deal with any problem which they regard as important, and this decision does not need to be hampered by considerations of practical use to which their results will be put. Basic research is not very popular among many educationalists because it demands skilled researchers and is time-consuming and expensive. However, its potential value at some later stage cannot be denied; it requires creativity and imagination, and often leads to further research of a more obviously utilitarian nature.

In addition to the basic and applied research dimensions, other terms have also been used in the characterization of educational research. Rowan (1976) offered an outline of eleven kinds of research which, according to him, broadly cover the range used in social research and educational research: pure basic; basic objective; evaluation; applied; action; intervention; existential; experiential; phenomenological; ethnomethodological and dialectical. Rowan believed that the first four of these approaches tend to be alienated types of research, which treat people as objects to be described externally. He was also critical of these types of research on the grounds that the true purpose of the study is often concealed from those who provide research data. According to Rowan, the last seven types of research tend to be much more 'genuine' because people are not deceived.

Anderson (1990) presented four levels of educational research: descriptive; explanatory (internal validity); generalization (external validity) and basic (theoretical). According to him a researcher needs to have some understanding and perhaps working knowledge of each of the four levels. The levels are by no means discrete; they often build on one another in an interactive way (Anderson, 1990).

The belief that for most problems one particular research approach is superior to all others rarely seems to be based on rational grounds. Such a conviction may lead to the use of methods inappropriate to a given problem. The appropriateness of any type of research strategy should be determined by the nature of the problem, the goal of the research, the kind of data required, and the time and resources available. For example, the broad objective of research may be oriented towards the clarification of a theoretical concept or to the solution of a practical and immediate problem. However, the eleven kinds of research outlined by Rowan (1976) do seem to overlap, and do not form a logically consistent pattern: they are not mutually exclusive.

The aspects of educational research which have received a great deal of attention from educationalists in recent years are evaluative research, action research and consumer-oriented research. The term 'evaluative research' is often used to refer to the systematic methods used in the collection and analysis of data regarding the effectiveness of an educational experience. This type of research has become an essential ingredient in the field of curriculum studies (see Hamilton et al., 1977). Much of the thinking attempts to view evaluation studies as a part of a decision-making process. Cronbach (1963) defined the concept of evaluation as 'the collection and use of information to make decisions about an educational programme'. He pointed out that evaluation is almost inevitably concerned with decision-making, and discussed three types of decision where evaluation may be involved: course improvement, decisions about individuals and administrative regulation. The evaluation studies movement has attracted a new generation of research workers, and has developed its own vocabulary and also a large amount of theoretical literature (see Hamilton et al., 1977).

Important terms often used in connection with evaluation research are developmental, formative and summative. One can evaluate in some way the process that goes into the design of a curriculum or a programme (developmental); when the programme is put into use, one can evaluate the learning of pupils at various levels of proficiency and also determine the effects of changing various components of the programme (formative or process evaluation); then comes the evaluation of the final and total effect of the programme (summative evaluation). Summative evaluation is supposed to provide a final judgment on the value or worth of the programme.

Evaluation research is the dominant type of research in the relationships of exchange between researchers and professional practitioners. However, there are many who express doubts about the utility of evaluation research, and may not even want to label evaluation as research (Guga, 1969). Notwithstanding, most social action programmes and curriculum innovations should be systematically evaluated both during the programme, to facilitate improvements, and at the end, to assess the outcome, i.e. summative evaluation. The product of such research activity almost always comes out as some kind of evaluative judgment in the course of action. Thus, evaluation research is often a decision-oriented activity. For many policymakers, 'research' is seen as a process conveying some kind of approval of or respectability to their policy initiatives. Unfortunately, when this view is adopted, the findings of the research tend to be ignored unless they support what they believe on ideological grounds. For others, research is perceived as an academic exercise, undertaken by academics and divorced from the reality of the classroom. (For further discussion of evaluation research, see Chapter 5.)

Action research, according to Corey (1953), is undertaken by practitioners in order to improve their practices. It is a type of applied research, but in this process the researcher is the same person as the practitioner. In other words, the researcher is the person who will be affected by the results. The thesis behind this dual role is that the strategy to change the behaviour of practitioners is to get them involved in conducting research on problems which concern them (Helmstadter, 1970). Corey (1953), the originator of the term, argued that teachers can become better decision-makers and more effective practitioners if they conduct action research. It is suggested that this type of research can guide, correct and evaluate decisions and actions, and can provide solutions to immediate problems in schools. Action research is a form of self-evaluation usually employed by teachers, though increasingly it is used by teachers in collaboration with students or other members of school communities (Kemmis and Stake, 1988). Its focus is 'on the improvement of educational practices, understandings of practices and the situations in which teachers practise' (Kemmis and Stake, 1988).

Consumer-oriented research seems to be preferred by many educators today. It is concerned with the kind of data which are of value to the consumer. Teachers, other researchers, employers, and parents would seem to be the main consumers of the results of this type of educational research. Cronbach and Suppes (1969) used the terms 'conclusion-oriented' and 'decision-oriented' enquiry as synonymous with 'consumer-oriented' or 'audience-oriented' research. The 'audience-oriented' terminology, however, has come into frequent use in the discussion of educational research in the last 20–30 years. Wrigley (1976), drawing a distinction between various kinds of research, listed five possible audiences: 'Other researchers in the field; teachers in the classroom; policy-makers at local and national level; the general public interested in educational matters; the press.' Barnes (1979) argued that there were four groups of audience whose interests need to be taken into account: 'scientist', 'citizens', 'sponsors' and 'gate-keepers'. Sometimes, there is also a conflict between producers and consumers of research. Unfortunately, there are no guidelines to offer advice to the beginner researcher on how to act, from a moral point of view.

However, there seems to be little doubt expressed in the literature that teachers need to be consumers of the results of educational research (see Chapter 9). In this connexion, it is frequently said that educational researchers do not choose as the subjects of their study those matters which are of interest and concern to teachers, parents and students. They are often accused of working and writing for an audience composed of other researchers rather than practitioners. This is true in many cases, and, it has to be stressed, a perfectly proper thing for them to do, particularly if they are engaged in what we have defined as 'basic' research. It must also be added that many professional researchers are not always free to follow their inclinations. Their subject matter is often dependent on grants from funding agencies who have their own views about what is valuable and important.

We approach the end of this section with the following thought. The revolution in information technology and a growing demand in most democratic societies for significant improvements in their education systems suggest that a new set of relationships needs to be created. This will require the different partners — whether researchers, decision-makers, practitioners or those responsible for education reform — to work together if common goals are to be attained. New technologies have the potential to forge closer links between the producers and users of research and to facilitate the speed and ease with which research-generated information is disseminated.

Educational researchers, policy-makers and various audiences are all important partners in the education process. The ability of all to generate and/or manage knowledge and information significantly determines the degree of success in the implementation of change.

In summary, it is apparent that educational research can take many forms; a variety of dimensions, perspectives and rationales have been presented in this chapter. The most important point to be remembered is that the focus of educational research must be *education*, and that the foremost function is to assist teachers, parents, decision-makers and all concerned in the field, with the aim of improving the quality of the educational process, and thus enhancing the quality of life.

Audiences

When engaged in the business of educational research, one important aspect to bear in mind is the audience. This affects the work in two ways. Firstly, the type of audience at whom the findings of the research are to be directed will have an influence on the way in which the study is conceived (its subject matter, the methods used, the issues addressed) and on the way those findings are presented. Secondly, the way in which the research is conceived and the findings presented have implications for how 'understandable' the research is. It is of course possible, and indeed, often is the case, that a piece of research may be reported in more than one manner. The research may be reported in a technical specialist manner (typically to meet the requirements of those sponsoring the study) and then in a way that makes it more generally understandable so as to make the information (or some of it) available to a wider audience. This has bearing not only on the content but also on the style in which the research is presented. A research study prepared for a group of specialists might well be written in a style that uses a lot of technical terms and specialist concepts readily understood by the specialist audience and for whom very little explanatory context is required. A reader, unfamiliar with those terms, might find the report inaccessible or, at best, difficult to access.

Some of the detail in such a report might well be only of significance to its immediate audience. Yet, if the study was targeted at a wider audience it would be necessary to set out more fully the context in which the study had been conducted and to explain the concepts on which the study was built, including a full spelling-out of their implications. This is often the case when educational research is set in a particular and, possibly, unfamiliar context.

A report on the delivery of aspects of the curriculum in secondary schools in Scotland might well pose problems of comprehension to someone not familiar with the Scottish secondary education system. Another person working in the Scottish education system or with a child at a secondary school in Scotland might find the report largely understandable.

Other Researchers

As a researcher writing for other researchers, it is reasonable for the author to assume that his or her readers are familiar with the field in which he or she is operating. Such research reports tend to be difficult to read and of little interest to the general reader since they often deal with highly theoretical aspects of the research process: of value to other professional researchers but with little relevance to the work of teachers or policy-makers or the lives of parents or children. It is in this kind of report that the nature of the subject matter and the audience for whom it was written most clearly dictates the way in which it is presented.

Educationists

When writing for educationists, the researcher can assume that the readers will have a general background knowledge of the area in which the study was placed. In all probability, they will also have undertaken some research themselves as part of their training. Thus, they are unlikely to welcome lengthy descriptions of routine research processes or techniques with which they are perfectly familiar. On the other hand, they will be interested to know — and will expect to be clearly told — significant aspects of the research design. What these aspects are will vary from one study to another but, to take an example, if the study depends heavily on the results of a survey of a sample of a population from which the researcher draws conclusions about the whole population, an audience of educationists will be very interested in the way the sample was constructed. They will expect to be reassured about such matters as its size: was it large enough to produce reliable results for the whole population? They will also need to be confident that its membership was not biased: that, for example, the age profile and gender balance reflected the population norm. These and many other considerations relating to sampling (a subject covered more fully in Chapter 8) will be of vital interest to them.

Teachers

In writing for teachers, many of the considerations that apply to educationists apply equally well. Increasing numbers of teachers have some knowledge of research and those numbers are likely to grow in the future. The major difference is likely to be in the subject matter of the study. Whereas educationists might be — indeed, ought to be — interested in such matters as the latest study of the impact of deprivation on attitudes towards learning in 7-year-old children, many teachers may well feel they have a perfectly adequate working knowledge of this from their day-to-day activities in the classroom. Teachers are much more likely to be interested in research into effective ways of teaching number to 5-year-olds, or reading skills to children whose first language is not English. They will, in addition, need to be persuaded that the conclusions reached by the researcher are valid for them in their working situations. For this reason, this chapter ends with a check list of questions for use in evaluating a research report.

Decision-makers and Policy-makers

Of all the audiences a researcher might write a report for people who can make decisions and create policies are at once one of the most important and the most difficult to address successfully. Their importance is obvious. It is not often that a researcher's work may have an immediate and practical impact and form the basis for decisions that will affect large numbers of people. The presentational problems arise from the fact that the audience will probably be unversed in the business of research and may well know little about much of the subject matter contained in the report. It must also be assumed that they have neither the time nor the inclination to study all 273 pages of prose, tables, graphs and appendices that constitute a major report, nor to make nice assessments about whether the evidence collected and the elegant rigour of the argument lead to the conclusions and recommendations arrived at. One way they avoid having to do this is to ask for an Executive Report of perhaps 5–10 pages which sets out the essentials of the full report. They also employ experts who *will* read the full report and make judgments as to its merit.

The General Public

In this context, the general public are likely to be parents and perhaps grandparents of children and young people in school. Clearly, researchers can make no assumptions about their audience's knowledge about research. In writing for this audience, it is likely that the researchers have already published their findings elsewhere as a book or in a journal addressed to one of the more specialized audiences considered above. For successful access to the public interest, the researchers will need to have addressed an issue that is, of itself, of interest to the public.

Evaluation of Educational Research

In order to evaluate research findings critically, educators ought to ask themselves a few questions when they read a particular research report. Since there is no universally accepted yardstick (as mentioned earlier) for judging research reports, the following format might provide a useful guide to those who wish to embark on research activities of their own or to teachers who are anxious to improve their educational practices in the light of research findings. Briefly, the questions should be concerned with the theoretical aspects of the study, the significance of the problem, the appropriateness of the hypotheses or the goals, the research methodology, meaningfulness and trustworthiness of the techniques (if these are used, then their reliability and validity), the representativeness and adequacy of the sample, the conclusions and implications of the study. So, to arrive at a critical appraisal of a study, the following questions should be at the back of the reader's mind:

1 Does the title of the study explicitly indicate the problem area?

2 Does the problem/issue have a precise theoretical position or a theoretical assumption? Has it been stated clearly and accurately? Is the problem/issue significant and worthy of investigation?

3 Has the previous literature been thoroughly reviewed covering the relevant variables under study?

4 Has the evaluation of previous studies helped the investigator to generate hypotheses or to formulate research questions?

5 Has the researcher stated the hypotheses, null hypotheses or research questions in a clear, concise way? If the hypotheses are developed to test facts and to examine the relationships between variables, has this been made clear? Are the stated hypotheses testable? If so, are the assumptions or inferences on which they are predicated made clear?

6 Has the investigator provided any operational definitions? Have the relevant terms and concepts concerning the research been defined and analysed clearly?

7 Are the techniques, procedures and materials used to attain the goal of the research trustworthy and reliable? Have they been adequately described?

8 Has the sample been adequately described including the criteria for selection?

9 Has the investigator pointed out any probable source of error in the data that might have influenced the results of the study?

10 Have any statistical techniques been used for the analysis of data? If so, were they appropriate and adequate in view of the research objectives?

11 Have the data been analysed objectively, clearly and accurately?

12 Are the results presented intelligibly and free of all ambiguity? Has the researcher mentioned the limitations of the study? Can the findings and their implications be understood by many educators and other audiences?

13 Have the conclusions been clearly stated showing their support from the data obtained? Have the findings been over-generalized?

14 Has the researcher suggested further investigation in the area highlighting the gaps in existing knowledge?

These questions are suggested in order to make the reader of research reports critical. It should be mentioned that research reports do not always use specific headings e.g. the problem, hypotheses. This is not crucial. What is important, however, is that these aspects are dealt with in the research report. It should also be emphasized that one of the essential characteristics of research is the degree of flexibility when seeking the solution of problems or the answer to research questions.

It must also be recognized that the techniques required in educational research, particularly in quantitative research, include some knowledge of statistics. This is necessary even in comparing the difference between test scores of an experimental and a control group. The investigator needs to ascertain whether the difference between the two groups on any characteristics under study is 'significant'. For many research purposes, it is also essential to be able to calculate a correlation coefficient (see Chapter 8 for a discussion of statistical concepts). However, those who read the research findings of others need perhaps less knowledge of statistical techniques than those who contribute to research. Nevertheless, it is desirable for readers of research reports to have some grasp of the general principles of research methodology and of the determination of significance.

References

ANDERSON, G. (1990) *Fundamentals of Educational Research*, London: Falmer Press.

ARY, D., JACOBS, L.C. and RAZAVIEH, A. (1985) *Introduction to Research in Education*, 3rd edition, New York: Holt, Rinehart and Winston Inc.

BAGLEY, C. (1975) 'On the intellectual equality of races', in VERMA, G.K. and BAGLEY, C. (eds) *Race and Education across Cultures*, London: Heinemann.

BARNES, J.A. (1979) 'Who should know what?', *Social Science, Privacy and Ethics*, Harmondsworth: Penguin.

BLOOM, B.S. (1966) 'Twenty-five years of educational research', *American Educational Research Journal*, **3**, 212.

BRUNER, J.S. (1962) *The Process of Education*, Harvard University Press: Cambridge, MA.

BRYMAN, A. (1988) *Quantity and Quality in Social Research*, London: The Academic Division of Unwin Hyman Ltd.

CLARKE, P.A. (1972) *Action Research and Organisational Change*, London: Harper and Row.

COREY, S.M. (1953) *Action Research to Improve School Practices*, New York: Bureau of Publications, Teachers' College, Columbia University.

CRONBACH, L.J. (1962) *Educational Psychology*, 2nd edition, New York: Harcourt Brace.

CRONBACH, L.J. (1963) 'Evaluation for course improvement', in HEATH, R. (ed.) *New Curricula*, New York: Harper and Row.

CRONBACH, L.J. (1966) 'The role of the University in improving education', Bloomington, Indiana, *Phi Delta Kappan*, **47**.

CRONBACH, L.J. and SUPPES, P. (1969) *Research for Tomorrow's Schools: Disciplined Inquiry for Education*, New York: Macmillan.

DENNIS, W. (1941) 'Infant development under conditions of restricted practice and of minimum social stimulation', *Genetic Psychology Monographs*, **23**, pp. 143–89.

DIXON, R., BOUMA, G.D. and ATKINSON, G.B.J. (1987) *A Handbook of Social Science Research*: Oxford University Press.

DOUGLAS, J.W.B. (1964) *The Home and the School*, London: MacGibbon and Kee.

DOUGLAS, J.W.B., ROSS, J.M. and SIMPSON, H.R. (1968) *All Our Future*, London: Peter Davies.

EGGLESTON, J. (1979) 'The characteristics of educational research: Mapping the domain', *British Educational Research Journal*, **5**, 1, pp. 1–12.

ELLIOTT, J. and ADELMAN, C. (1978) *Classroom Action Research*, Ford Teaching Project, Unit 2, Centre for Applied Research in Education, England: University of East Anglia.

ESLAND, G. et al. (1972) *The Social Organisation of Teaching and Learning*, Units 5–8 in Course E282, Bletchley, England: Open University Press.

ESRC (1996) *ESRC Postgraduate Training Guidelines*, London: Economic and Social Science Research Council.

FLYNN, J.R. (1980) *Race, IQ and Jensen*, London: Routledge and Kegan Paul.

GILES, R. (1977) *The West Indian Experience in British Schools*, London: Heinemann.

GRIFFITHS, M. (1995) 'Making a difference: Feminism, post-modernism and the methodology of educational research', *British Educational Research Journal*, **21**, 2.

GUGA, E.G. (1969) 'Significant differences', *Educational Researcher*, **20**, 3.

HAMILTON, D., JENKINS, D., KING, C., MacDONALD, B. and PARLETT, M. (1977) *Beyond the Numbers Game*, London: Macmillan.

HELMSTADTER, G.C. (1970) *Research Concepts in Human Behavior*, New York: Appleton-Century-Crofts.

HILGARD, E.R. (1954) 'A perspective on the relationship between learning theory and educational practices', in HILGARD, E.R. (ed.) *Theories of Learning and Instruction*, Part I of the 63rd Yearbook of the National Society of the Study of Education, Chicago: University of Chicago Press.

JENSEN, A.R. (1973) *Educability and Group Differences*, London: Methuen.

KEMMIS, S. and STAKE, R. (1988) *Evaluating the Curriculum*, Geelong, Australia: Deakin University.

KERLINGER, F.N. (1977) 'The influence of research on education practice', *Educational Researcher*, **6**, 8, pp. 5–11.

KUHN, T.S. (1970) *The Structure of Scientific Revolutions*, 2nd edition, International Encyclopedia of Unified Science, enlarged, first published 1962, Chicago: The University of Chicago Press.

KUHN, T.S. (1972) 'Scientific paradigms', in BARNES, B. (ed.) *Sociology of Science*, Harmondsworth: Penguin.

LINCOLN, Y. and GUBA, E. (1985) *Naturalistic Inquiry*, Beverley Hills, CA: Sage.

LOFLAND, J. and LOFLAND, L.H. (1984) *Analysing Social Settings: A Guide to Qualitative Observation and Analysis*, Belmont, CA: Wadsworth.

LOVELL, K. and LAWSON, R.S. (1970) *Understanding Research in Education*, London: University of London Press.

McNAMARA, D.R. (1979) 'Paradigm lost: Thomas Kuhn and educational research', *British Educational Research Journal*, **5**, 2.

NISBET, J.D. and ENTWISTLE, N.J. (1970) *Educational Research Methods*, London: University of London Press.

OECD (1994) 'Innovation in Education', News from the OECD, Paris.

PAGE, E.B. (1975) 'Accentuate the negative', *Educational Researcher*, **5**.

PARLETT, M. and HAMILTON, D. (1977) 'Evaluation as illumination: A new approach to the study of innovatory programmes', in HAMILTON et al. (eds) *Beyond the Numbers Game: A Reader in Educational Evaluation*, London: Macmillan.

PETERS, R.S. and WHITE, J.P. (1969) 'The philosopher's contribution to educational research', *Educational Philosophy and Theory*, **1**, pp. 1–15.

PIDGEON, D. and YATES, A. (1957) *Admission to Grammar Schools*, the third interim report on the allocation of primary school leavers to courses of secondary education, London: Newness.

REMMERS, H.H. (1949) 'The expanding role of research', *North Central Association Quarterly*, **23**, pp. 369–76.

ROWAN, J. (1976) *Ordinary Ecstasy*, London: Routledge and Kegan Paul.

RUMMEL, J.F. (1964) *An Introduction to Research Procedures in Education*, 3rd edition, New York: Harper and Row.

SILVERMAN, D. (1985) *Qualitative Methodology and Sociology*, England, Aldershot: Gower Publishing.

STENHOUSE, L. (1975) *An Introduction to Curriculum Research and Development*, London: Heinemann.

STENHOUSE, L. (1984) 'Evaluating curriculum evaluation', in ADELMAN, C. (ed.) *The Problems and Ethics of Educational Evaluation*, London: Croom Helm.

STOUTHAMER-LOEBER, M. and KAMMEN, W.B.V. (1995) *Data Collection and Management*, Applied Social Research Methods Series, Vol. 39, London: Sage Publications.

THOULESS, R.H. (1969) *Map of Educational Research*, Slough, England: National Foundation for Educational Research.

TRAVERS, R.M.W. (1978) *An Introduction to Educational Research*, 4th edition, New York: Macmillan.

TRAXLER, A.E. (1954) 'Some comments on educational research at mid-century', *The Journal of Educational Research*, **47**, pp. 359–66.

TROYNA, B. (1992) 'Ethnicity and the organization of learning groups: A case study', *British Educational Research Journal*, **19**, 1.

TYLER, R.W. (1949) *Basic Principles of Curriculum and Instruction*, Chicago: University of Chicago Press.

VAN DALEN, D.B. (1966) *Understanding Educational Research*, New York: McGraw Hill.

VERMA, G.K. (1979) 'Attitude measurement in a multi-ethnic society', *Bulletin of the British Psychological Society*, **32**, pp. 460–2.

WARD, A.W., HALL, B.W. and SCHRAMM, C.F. (1975) 'Evaluation of published educational research: A national survey', *American Educational Research Journal*, **12**, 2, pp. 109–28.

WALTON, J. and KUETHA, J.L. (1963) (eds) *The Discipline of Education*, Madison: The University of Wisconsin Press.

WATSON, F. (1953) 'Research in the physical science', Bloomington, Indiana, *Phi Delta Kappan*.

WHEELER, D.K. (1967) *Curriculum Press*, London: University of London Press.

WRIGLEY, J. (1976) Social Science Research Council Newsletter, October, quoted by SIMON, B.S. (1978) 'Educational research: Which way?', *Research Intelligence*, **4**, 1.

Chapter 4

Educational Research: A Short History

The problem of defining the nature of 'educational research' has been dealt with in Chapter 3. As we have seen, the term does not mean the same thing to everyone in the field of education, and no single definition is universally acceptable. This may be due to the huge range of often disparate activities that form the education process. This chapter briefly describes the emergence of research activities in the field of education, and outlines the work of a few individuals who have exerted a significant influence on the development of educational research.

Although interest in solving educational problems through research began to stimulate educators' minds in the late nineteenth century, it was only at the turn of the century, when the social sciences established their identity, that researchers in many fields started turning their attention to the school as the locus of historical, psychological, philosophical and sociological problems which were asking for solutions. As a result of their interest, educational research, from its inception, embraced elements of many disciplines and utilized a wide range of strategies and tactics in its quest to acquire information across the whole field of educational endeavour.

The current practice of research methodologies vastly differs from that of the early part of the century. Contemporary social scientists do not follow any simple routine in research programmes that can be written and communicated to others. They attempt to synthesize a complex set of techniques and approaches to acquire knowledge about educational problems. Because of the sophisticated research designs and techniques of statistical analysis now available, researchers are able to tackle many of the complex and fundamental educational problems that once had to be ignored. During the last 40 or 50 years, research has greatly expanded the scope of its activities, and has gradually exerted influence on the practices in most areas of education (e.g. psychology, the curriculum, administration, teaching methods and evaluation). Today, educational research is accepted as a necessary element in the diverse activities of any advanced society.

The Historical Development of Educational Research

Although educational research is a fairly recent development, it is difficult to pinpoint its formal beginning. One might say that seeds of the research movement sprang up in Leipzig in 1879 when W. Wundt established the first laboratory. In England, at about the same time, Galton and Pearson were working on developing their statistical methods which were to be used in educational research. However, most writers in this field seem to agree that it was at the turn of the century that the science of education made a positive approach to the solution of educational problems. Realizing that simple improvements in the efficiency of education could be produced through systematic studies of pupils and teachers, some educators tried to establish more efficient and objective methods to achieve this. Another significant feature of this era was an emphasis on measurement and testing. In fact, psychometric measurement formed the cornerstone of the research movement, as reflected in the following statement:

> For there cannot be a science without fairly precise quantification: not that science is measurement, but those traits which are devoid of any reasonably definite quality simply do not have the required specificity for entering into the careful thinking essential to science. When quantities are disregarded almost any generalisation is true. (Scates, 1947, pp. 253–4)

It seems that this kind of perspective was inculcated in the mind of many research workers of the pioneer period who were influenced by Thorndike's (1918) famous slogan: 'Whatever exists at all exists in some amount' (p. 16). Thorndike inspired many educators who began to employ quantitative methods to obtain 'scientific' and precise information about various aspects of human behaviour.

Other influential people whose work on measurement and testing made a significant contribution to the development of educational research were Darwin, Huxley, Spencer and Galton. Some people believe that Joseph M. Rice was the forerunner in the educational research movement. His two articles, published in the same year (Rice, 1897), were concerned with the spelling achievement of school children in the United States. This work is regarded as the turning point in the contemporary movement for an objective study of educational problems. The findings of Rice's investigation pointed out the weaknesses in the existing methods of teaching spelling, and suggested that teaching methods in terms of how well children could spell should be evaluated. This point of view clearly implied that teachers should assess the strengths and weaknesses of their work in the classroom.

Galton, often called the 'father of mental testing', was extremely interested in the study of individual differences. His famous book *Hereditary Genius* was published in 1869 and had a tremendous bearing upon educational philosophy. By 1886, Galton had established his famous anthropometric laboratory devoted to the measurement of physical and sensori-motor characteristics of human beings. He was the first person who worked out the concept of statistical correlations, and applied the technique in the analysis and understanding of individual differences (although Karl Pearson worked out the actual product–moment correlation formula). However, Galton's statistical methods were employed by Pearson, Spearman, Burt and Thompson in England, and by Kelly, Thurstone and Guilford in the United States. The use of statistical inference and other quantitative concepts has become an essential element of today's development and application of measurement and evaluation in educational research.

Turning to the first quarter of the century, we find that Thorndike's work through research made a strong impact on the educational scene. His interest and many years of studies questioned the existing beliefs concerning the concept of human learning within an educational context. His early work, *Elimination of Pupils from School* published in 1907, seems to have inspired many educational leaders of his time. Thorndike's other major work, *Introduction to the Theory of Mental and Social Measurements* published in 1904, introduced statistical methods into educational research. Thereafter, Thorndike and his students constructed a number of tests and scales for measuring the academic achievement of children. The Stone Arithmetic Test appeared in 1908, and the Thorndike Handwriting Scale in 1910. An evaluation of his work seems to suggest that he was one of the earliest scientists whose influence on the research movement created a whole new line of research strategy which is still being practised today by many psychologists. Thorndike, like some of his contemporaries, endeavoured to change educational philosophy and practices through research.

One of the major criticisms levelled at Thorndike's research is that he pursued the traditional role of a laboratory scientist, having had no contact with schools and teachers. His critics say that he was divorced from reality. Thorndike himself believed that a scientist should spend most of his time in the laboratory, doing research that would have implications for educational practice. This kind of approach is not uncommon in the present educational world. Many theorists, particularly in the United States, ask their graduate students to collect data from schools, while working themselves on theoretical aspects of research. These researchers are likely to be unaware of the practical problems faced at the data collection stage. In the social sciences, it is misleading to suggest that researchers work in the order set out earlier or finish with facts that are unquestionable. Research in education — or indeed in any other field, including the natural sciences — is not just a mechanical but a creative activity, often making progress through intuitive leaps and the actual process of research may not always follow a logical pattern (as discussed in Chapter 3).

One of the contributions of Thorndike's laboratory research to education which has survived so far is the emphasis it placed on providing the learner with knowledge of how he or she was doing. Thorndike called this 'rewards' and later psychologists described this process as 'reinforcement'. A related concept, which Thorndike referred to as the 'law of effect', was subsequently given the name of the 'law of reinforcement' by Skinner. Thorndike's emphasis on the law of effect had impact because, previously, children in schools were given very little information about their performance and whether what they were doing was right or wrong (Travers, 1978). The relevance of the 'law of effect' in the learning–teaching situation is, or certainly should be, recognised by every practising teacher today.

Thorndike's research has been attacked quite often because of his superficial contact with the classroom situation. However, some of his ideas, derived from laboratory research and embodied in school experience, have had widespread impact. For example, one of his findings was that what pupils learned in one situation was difficult for them to generalize to other situations. Thorndike's well known research on 'transfer of training', as it was called, was interpreted by educators to mean that one could not generally expect much transfer, and that it would be more sound educationally if the material was learned directly. Thus according to this theory, learning Latin would not help the child to learn English vocabulary.

This conclusion produced radical changes in the school curriculum, because his research showed that no school subject had any special powers for training the mind. This might be a convenient moment to comment again on the slowness with which educational research has worked through to affect educational belief and practice. For example, it was not until the 1960s that the University of Cambridge dropped the absolute requirement of a qualification in Latin at GCE level for entry on to any undergraduate course it offered. Similarly, a degree in Latin or Greek was still thought of as the best sort of mental training for anyone aspiring to become a leading figure in public service and allied fields — the diplomatic corps for example — until World War II. One could argue that the multiplicity of specialist courses which now exist at undergraduate level can be attributed to Thorndike's work in the early years of the century. The work of Thorndike on army testing during World War I contributed to the development of measures of intelligence, although this did not have as marked an impact as his research in other areas of education.

In addition to the emphasis on measurement and testing in the pioneer period of educational research, another theme emerged which generated some enthusiasm amongst educational leaders. The school survey idea, which came into being in the early 1900s, is still one of the popular types of educational research in America. This kind of research design involves a description and evaluation of one or more aspects of a school environment. The school survey became almost an institutional feature of the educational research movement with the result that standardized tests began to be employed on a large scale. Since there was already some scepticism about the use of psychological tests, and with the increased emphasis on achievement and intelligence testing in school surveys, a great controversy about the validity and accuracy of obtaining such data started. Opponents of objective measurement enquired into the 'propriety' of test data, and leaders of the research movement of the day defended the psychometric measurement (Barnes, 1960). Thorndike put the axe to the debate when he stated: 'If a thing exists, it exists in some amount; and if it exists in some amount, it can be measured' (Thorndike, 1914).

Despite the arguments for and against educational measurement, the National Association of Directors of Educational Research was created at a meeting in 1915, which became the American Educational Research Association (AERA) in 1930. One of the objectives of this Association was 'the promotion of the practical use of educational measures in all educational research' which acted as a motivating force for the growth of the educational research movement. Consequently, researchers felt encouraged to utilize psychometric measures in their study of various aspects of education.

During the Thorndike era, Terman's (1931) longitudinal study of gifted children was another classic work which made an impact on education. Contrary to the general belief held by teachers, his findings indicated that there was nothing 'abnormal' in gifted children, and that they could adjust well in any social situation. Of course, not all of his contributions were on the same solid ground. His work on the English version of Binet's intelligence tests was a controversial issue. Karier (1973), examining the development of the testing movement in America, summarized the work of Terman (one of the movement's leaders):

> Designing the Stanford-Binet intelligence test, Terman developed questions that were based on presumed progressive difficulty in performing tasks he believed necessary for achievement in ascending the hierarchical occupational structure. He then proceeded to find that, according to the results of his test, the intelligence of different occupational classes fit his ascending hierarchy. Little wonder the intelligence quotient reflected social-class bias. It was based on the social-class order.

Nevertheless, the age of Thorndike did produce some useful ideas for educational research, although the emphasis was placed on the use of tests. For example, the publications of J.M. Cattell's 'Mental Tests and Measurements' in 1890, the development of an intelligence scale by Binet and Simon in 1905, and the development of the handwriting scale by Thorndike in 1910 were some of the contributions made in the development of techniques for educational research. In recent years, these techniques and tools have been questioned by many social scientists on psychological, social and ethical grounds. Still, these early studies should be treated as precursors of new methods.

The next period in the development of educational research, between 1920 and 1945, was regarded as the 'publications' era. During this period, well known leaders of the research movement started educational organizations and publications with a view to disseminating their findings and advancing their work. The number of psychological tests increased tremendously, and most of these became commercially available. Buros began publication of the *Mental Measurements Year Book* containing critical reviews of the available standardized psychological tests. A number of educational journals and periodicals appeared during this period of expansion. *The Review of Educational Research* published by AERA (American Education Research Association) started in 1931. A number of original books were also written during this time (Buckingham, 1926), some of which are still regarded as useful literature for the purposes of educational research.

Britain did not lag behind in the educational research movement. Many scholars made significant contributions to the development of educational research from the early part of this century. Cyril Burt, who started as a school psychologist in 1913, was long recognized as one of the leading educational researchers of this century, although he has come under increased attack in recent years because of fraudulent misrepresentation of data (Flynn, 1980). The studies of Susan Isaac on child development, of Lindsey on educational opportunity, of Cyril Burt on the assessment of abilities, of Hartog and Rhodes on the way examiners awarded marks, influenced the educational research climate of the 1930s and 1940s in Britain (Taylor, 1973). Another proponent in British educational research was Rusk (1912) who strongly argued for more experimental work in education. Further impetus to the organization and development of educational research came from the creation of the Scottish Council for Research in Education in 1928, and the Education section of the British Psychological Society in 1919. In a review of 'British Research in Education' Brehaut (1973) showed that research in education has a longer and more complex history than some people suggest. However, the fact that Britain has been one of the pioneers of educational research is not in question.

Modern Educational Research

Since about 1945, social scientists have been engaged in the re-evaluation of educational research in the light of improvements that research has brought about in the education process. Research methodologies in education have undergone extensive refinement in order to obtain more reliable and valid information. With the advancement of computer science, more sophisticated statistical techniques have been developed for analysis of data. New terms and meanings have been introduced in the literature to communicate the knowledge to a large audience. Memory, capacity, power, speed of operations and steadily reduced costs have made the computer readily available to researchers, resulting in widespread use of statistical analyses of data. This reappraisal of educational research can be attributed to a new generation of educational leaders, who followed Thorndike, Terman and others, and include names such as Sidney Pressey, B.F. Skinner, R. Tyler and Jean Piaget, to mention but a few. This generation provided ideas through research which have had an impact on education.

Pressey first introduced the idea of mechanical devices for teaching. These devices were designed to have a dual function — to test as well as to teach and to provide immediate feedback about the correctness of students' responses. Pressey promoted this machine as a good way of self-teaching, particularly when students were required to learn some routine types of material. He was one of the first to publish a textbook on educational psychology which showed the relevance of psychological research in solving educational problems.

The work of Skinner has been of great significance for classroom teachers. He, unlike Thorndike, visited classrooms, observed the learning–teaching situation, and, on the basis of this experience, concluded that positive and frequent reinforcement was essential for effective learning. He avoided the problems that Thorndike's law of effect had by defining reinforcement as anything that increases the probability of a response. Skinner and his followers still hold the same view with regard to this issue of learning. These ideas not only revolutionized thinking about learning and reinforcement, but eliminated the possibility of measuring habit strength indirectly by keeping track of the number of reinforced responses. The work of Skinner, though based on behaviourist assumptions, is pragmatic rather than theoretical. He did not attempt to predict what should be reinforced and why, but concentrated on showing the effects of reinforcement on learning. Most of his initial work was carried out on hungry animals, but according to him the underlying principles seemed to work for well fed humans too. Many teachers are critical of his approach on moral grounds, but seeking to change behaviour by reinforcement need not necessarily be immoral. Teachers are well aware that, in a wide sense, any curriculum is an attempt to change the behaviour of pupils whether this objective is explicitly stated or not.

Skinner's contribution to education through research is often associated with programmed learning and teaching machines. He first developed the teaching materials to be used with the teaching machine, but later on the development of the programmed text made it possible to use materials of the same format, without the use of the machine. The use of programmed text and teaching machines did not gain popularity in schools partly, perhaps, because of expense and technological limitations, but also because they seemed to threaten the professionalism of teachers in that they were inflexible in their use and removed the power to handle student learning problems in their own way. Now that the national curriculum has come into the equation together with, relatively, cheap computers, it is noteworthy that much of the instructional material is constructed on what are essentially Skinnerian principles.

In the 1930s, Ralph Tyler started a movement to change the educational process through curriculum research. His work played a part in encouraging schools to depart from some of their traditional practices. He introduced into education the idea that educational objectives should be defined in terms of specific behaviours or learning outcomes, a theme that has continued to have an impact ever since it was first advocated. Tyler's model for curriculum construction was first articulated in 1934, and received favourable support from many educators (Tyler, 1949). Undoubtedly, the Tylerian doctrine has exerted a powerful influence in curriculum research on both sides of the Atlantic during the last three decades.

As a result of Tyler's behavioural specification of objectives, sometimes called the 'Engineering Model', investigators both in Britain and the United States made efforts to define the desired course outcomes with great precision. Sometimes, educational objectives were defined in enormous detail. However, this approach has for some the substantial merit of simplicity, rationality, utility and practicality. Although this kind of educational thought did not make much advance in understanding the complexity of learning–teaching situations, it encouraged psychologists to make greater use of psychometric measurement. Another weakness of this model is that it has not proved to be a useful way of describing human intellectual performance. Consequently, Tyler's idea of pre-specifying the behavioural outcomes of any educational programme has come under severe attack in more recent years. Nevertheless, his contribution to curriculum construction has had a significant impact on education.

The impact of Piaget's research on education has been rather slow, partly because of the style of his writing which draws heavily from logic and biology, and partly because his theory of the nature of the human intellect is complex. (For an overview of Piaget's work, a specialist study, such as Beard (1969), should be consulted.) The main thesis of both Skinner's and Tyler's work was to reduce complex educational objectives to simple behavioural components, whereas Piaget's basic premise is that the complex forms of human behaviour cannot be reduced to simple components. According to Piaget, complex phenomena should be studied in all their complexity, since laws governing complex forms of behaviour operate differently from those governing simple forms of behaviour.

Piaget's studies of the intellectual development of the child have had an enormous impact on subsequent research activities in the area. His model of intellectual development, and description of the conditions that would improve this development have been recognized by many educators. The Piagetian model has been widely used as a basis for designing school teaching materials, particularly in the area of mathematics and science. For example, the Nuffield Science and Nuffield Mathematics Projects designed the teaching materials on Piagetian lines. These programmes were widely used in British and North American schools. In Britain, in the Science 5–13 Curriculum Project (Schools Council, 1973), a rigorous objective type of approach was adopted which was claimed to be essentially 'child-centred'. The project was set out with a clear statement of broad aims followed by a precise classification of nine sets of objectives, illustrated with possible examples at each of three Piagetian stages. Although criticisms of the Piaget model are often made on the grounds of vagueness (Ennis, 1975), his programmes of research have undoubtedly made a significant contribution to the classroom practice. The greatest strength of Piaget's work is in the mapping out of children's mental operations which has obvious implications for educational practices.

The contribution of Bruner's work has had some bearing on learning situations, and consequently on education. In fact, Piaget's work provided a framework for Bruner's research (1966). His research which led to the idea of translating the key concepts of knowledge into materials that can be understood by children has interesting implications for the curriculum. He first worked out this hypothesis with mathematics and then applied it to the social sciences in his *Man: A Course of Study* (MACOS) Curriculum Project. Bruner's well known statement that any subject can be taught in some intellectually honest form to any child shows the need to understand how children structure their knowledge if their learning is to be maximized. The question arises as to whether any teacher can teach anything, given it is possible to teach anything to any child. Although Bruner has been criticized on several grounds (Jones, 1972), his active interest in the effects of teaching and experiences as a teacher has made his research more relevant for classroom teachers.

In addition to the above-mentioned individuals whose contributions to education through research work have been widespread, there are others who have also made an impact on many aspects of education. J.P. Guilford (1967), for example, has provided educators and researchers with an idea of the intellect which makes a distinction between divergent and convergent thinking. His model has made some contribution to the development of aptitude tests, and has put forward ideas about components of the human intellect which can be considered for training. Kohlberg's (1964, 1975) work on moral development has been verified in many different cultures in the world. His model, a topological scheme describing general structures of moral thought, has been criticized on philosophical and psychological grounds. Nevertheless, his theory has proved valuable in the field of education and has relevance for the classroom teacher. It should be mentioned that although most theories in the social sciences have, at one time or another, been contradicted or modified by subsequent pieces of evidence, many still seem to hold their position, partly because no alternative models offering a greater degree of research credibility are available. The work of Kurt Lewin, Carl Rogers and others should not be omitted when considering the impact of research on the educational world.

The reader should not get the impression that educational change has been brought about by psychological research alone. Philosophical, historical and sociological considerations have also played a part in educational research. The term research incorporates a wide range of activities within the field of education (see Chapter 3). For example, the historian has studied the progress of education as one of the many factors in the general development of civilization. The sociologist has attempted to find out in the school community paradigms of social behaviour. Similarly, the philosopher has from time to time been interested in applying principles of epistemology and ethics to an understanding of education. The psychologist has provided conceptual models and information assisting teachers in educational planning. The impact of psychological research on education has also been in terms of methodologies which are adapted for educational enquiry. For example, theories of learning, theories of cognitive and emotional development, group dynamics, individual differences in ability and personality, models of attitude formation and change, theories of motivation, all seem to have an obvious relevance to the planning of learning–teaching situations.

Educational Research Today

As mentioned in Chapters 2 and 3, research workers from various disciplines have come together in recent years through an interest in studying education, and this has resulted in a broad, inter-disciplinary approach to educational research. One of the implications of a new network concerned with educational research has been the recognition of a wide variety of approaches and techniques as opposed to the narrower dimensions of the past. Other developments such as the rise of educational technology and the development of sophisticated statistical techniques have also contributed to the refinement and classification of methodological issues in educational research. Thus, research activity has been greatly expanded in its scope in the last two or three decades. Schools throughout the world have made striking changes in all aspects of the curriculum.

The European Educational Research Association was founded in Strasbourg in June 1994. It was felt that such a Europe-wide association could serve a valuable role in heightening discussion of research quality, improving communication amongst researchers and potential users of research, disseminating research findings and in raising public awareness of the value and contribution of research in educational debate and decision-making (Calderhead, 1995). There is still much to be achieved in organizing and developing an educational research community within Europe.

In spite of this critical appraisal and the broadening of methodological issues, educational research is still underdeveloped. Much of the work in defining educational phenomena may still be described as 'hunting expeditions'. There seem to be so many difficulties at both the conceptual and technical level concerning the methodology of research in education. For example, human behaviour — the concern of most educational researchers — is at least as complex to understand and interpret as the forces operating to make up the content of the physical sciences.

There are not many people outside the realm of education who understand the complexity of the problem faced by educational researchers. Some people may even be inclined to suggest that much research has had little impact in promoting effective learning. Such a view lacks knowledge of the educational field as a whole. There is sufficient information in the literature to suggest that the analysis by various scholars since the turn of the twentieth century of the complex dynamic processes involved in the learning–teaching situation is a continuing guide to the conduct of research and its evaluation. As discussed earlier in this chapter, the work of Thorndike, Terman, Skinner, Bruner, Piaget and many others has had a substantial and significant influence on educational practices. Research has obviously influenced education in terms of teaching materials and methods, conceptions of the nature of the learner, and of the various means of solving educational problems.

The concepts of action research, applied research and evaluation research have played an important part in bringing educational researchers closer to practitioners (see Chapter 3 for a brief discussion of these concepts). Most people would agree that the two partners have at least started a dialogue, although the gap between them is still wide. There is some evidence today of a greater acceptance by teachers of research findings than was the case, say, 30 years ago. Moreover, many educational researchers have now accepted, in principle, that research data must be made accessible to a wider audience including teachers (potential consumers) for both the improvement of educational practice and for the general benefit of society. Today, educational researchers seem to be less dogmatic, and are willing to consider both the achievements and limitations of research design and methodology.

Most recently, post-modernism and post-structuralism have influenced the work of a small but growing number of researchers in education. It can be argued that these movements are more usefully seen as providing new tools for researchers rather than as research methods. Many of the approaches engendered by these movements are particularly useful when they are applied to the perception, recording and analysis of everyday situations. Many situations are the products of such well-established power structures that, like the air we breathe, we can easily be unconscious of their existence. It is, perhaps, for that reason that post-modernism and post-structuralism have been found attractive by many feminist researchers and writers.

The situation is very complex since these theoretical stances have no unified body. At this stage in their development, writers and researchers feel free to use the ideas of different writers with differing theoretical stances. Their practical value to educational research in the quest for knowledge and understanding which will result in better teaching or more effective learning, remains unproven. Readers whose interests have been aroused might find that a copy of the *British Educational Research Journal* for 1996 (Volume 22, No. 6) provides an insight into the kind of studies resulting from them.

There is, however, no denying that the progress of research in education has been slower than in other fields. Of the many factors contributing to this lack of progress, the attitudes of teachers, administrators and decision-makers on the one hand, and researchers on the other, have not been favourable. Indeed, it would be fair to say that, in the UK, the last 15 years have been a period of growing tension, particularly between researchers and politicians concerned with education.

A notable factor in this was the decision by the Thatcher government to carry out major reforms in the education service. This involved a massive legislative programme climaxing (though not ending) with the Education Reform Act 1988. An analysis of the motives underlying this legislation and the details of its application is not our concern here, suffice it to say here that it had some fundamental objectives. Among these were:

i.   the reduction in the powers acquired over the years by the *providers* of education (the Local Education Authorities),

ii.   an increase in the power of the *consumers* of education, defined as the parents of children in schools,

iii.   a determination to move away from the comprehensive system to one which would provide diversity, and therefore choice for parents — effectively a market-oriented system, and

iv.   a determination to enhance the educational achievement of pupils in schools by introducing a new system of inspection for schools and testing pupils at regular intervals — what might be called the managerial approach to education.

This was seen by many in education as a blatant exercise in the politicization of education. Few, if any, of the government's legislative decisions were based on research evidence. Researchers felt that they and their work had been marginalized and many responded in the only way, perhaps, that they felt was open to them: and it was not surprising that they investigated the processes and outcomes of the reforms with particular interest, nor that their findings were generally unsympathetic.

Relations between researchers and the then Department of Education and Science became increasingly strained — a situation that was probably not helped by, on the one hand, a lack of understanding on the part of ministers about what researchers were able to do and the environment in which they operated and, on the other, considerable mistrust on the part of researchers of the motives of their political masters.

The exasperation felt by both sides is, to some extent, understandable. Let us take as an example the issue of class size and the impact this has on the achievements of pupils. This, it might be thought, is a fundamental question that should have been addressed and answered long ago. On the face of it, the question is a simple one: What is the optimum class size for effective learning and teaching? The obvious assumption might be that children can be taught more effectively in smaller classes yet a Minister of State for Education was able to say 'I do not believe there is any proven connexion between class size and quality of education' (Eric Forth,

The Independent 3/3/93). It should be noted that the same claim has been made by other Ministers and Secretaries of Education in the U.K., before and since. What have researchers actually contributed to the subject? (The following quotations are taken from Blatchford and Mortimore, 1994.)

> Reducing class size to the point where student achievement would likely benefit . . . is prohibitively expensive. (Tomlinson, 1990)

> The evidence . . . suggests that . . . reducing class size will not itself make a substantial difference in student achievement. (Slavin, 1989)

> The outcomes of this research effort (into the connexion between class size and educational attainments) have been conflicting, inconclusive and disappointingly meagre. (Burstall, 1992)

> . . . drastic class size reductions in the early grades seem to offer the best hope yet advanced . . . How much more evidence do leaders need before they apply these strong findings to help improve schooling? (Achilles et al., 1993)

> Large reductions in school class size promise learning benefits of a magnitude commonly believed not within the power of education to achieve. (Glass et al., 1982)

> . . . the smaller the class the greater the effect on the instructional process, on pupil effect and on achievement. (Glass et al., 1982)

What Blatchford and Mortimore's (1994) paper powerfully suggests is that plenty of research evidence exists, notably from a major experiment in Tennessee involving 7,000 pupils in 79 schools, to show that small classes (perhaps between 13–17 children) *in the first two or three years of schooling* result in higher levels of attainment — especially for disadvantaged children — *and* that this benefit is retained when class sizes return to normal as they move up the school. They also make the point that it is true that small class sizes later in school life appear to have no measurable beneficial effects. Finally, they provide statistics giving average class sizes for 1992 in England, Wales and Scotland. They show that for the three countries, primary school classes had between four and six *more* children in them than did secondary classes. They also make the point that having two adults — a teacher and a teacher's assistant — in a large class seems to be an ineffective strategy. What matters is the size of the class. Their paper concludes with a plea for a serious study to be conducted in Britain into the effects of reducing class sizes in the first three years of schooling on teaching processes and children's achievement.

It is easy to see how the exasperation developed between the two sides. On the one hand, there were the researchers who believed that evidence existed which showed that small classes in the early years have a lasting beneficial effect on children and yet who heard Ministers state that they were unaware of the existence of any such research evidence. On the other hand, there were the ministers who had to make decisions and who seemed to believe that researchers had failed to address the issue adequately with the result that the advice they received was contradictory.

Unfortunately, mutual exasperation became too mild a term to describe the relationship between government and researchers. By 1992, the President of the British Educational Research Association made the following observations in his inaugural lecture:

> The present government and their advisers have treated educational researchers, among other educational professionals, to what Stephen Ball (1990) calls a discourse of derision . . .
>
> It has been constantly reiterated that standards are falling, that many teachers are either weak or subversive, that important subjects in schools are neglected, that teacher education is failing, and that LEAs are conniving in this deterioration. . . .
> As Ball says, 'The role of expert knowledge and research is regarded as less dependable than political intuition and commonsense accounts of what people want.' . . . This discourse of derision has served to prepare the ground for ideological change. Ball stresses that the ideological change which our education system and schools are experiencing is not simple. He refers to: 'the messy realities of influence, pressure, dogma, expediency, conflict, compromise, intransigence, resistance, error, opposition and pragmatism in the policy process.' (Bassey, 1992)

This clear expression of reasoned resentment demonstrates only too well the breakdown of any kind of effective working relationship between many researchers and the political decision-makers at that time. Thus, the notion that educational research stands outside the political agenda or has a neutral stance is naive. Having said that, it should also be stressed that education policy research in particular adopts a variety of styles and strategies which are positioned differently in relation to the processes of reform and also in relation to the traditions of the social sciences.

Some writers make a clear distinction between 'policy-oriented' and 'practice-oriented' research. Ball (1997) points out that 'a great deal of research about education or schooling is not "about" policy at all'.

Arnot (1997), reflecting on the current trends in educational research, writes that:

> By the mid-1990s, new educational research in the UK began to develop around the concept of citizenship and the political processes, languages and meanings attached to such concepts historically and in the post-war period. Such research, although not a coherent body of work, raises important new themes and questions about education.

However, there is a growing realization amongst all concerned, that no matter how elusive the term 'educational research' may be, or the activity it is meant to describe, they share a common view with regard to the objective of educational research. Research is identified as being a systematic enquiry or investigation conducted to gain an overall understanding of the education field, and directed towards a closer understanding of the learning–teaching process, with a view to improving it. Many people even believe that for all kinds of social problems, the solution lies with education (e.g. eradication of illiteracy, reduction in inter-group hostility and conflict, racial discord, crime and delinquency). In these respects, the value of research to education cannot be overestimated.

The fact remains, unfortunately, that one of the distinguishing features of the past two decades has been a growing sense of impatience with the academic research community felt by governments and other agencies with decision-making responsibilities about education. The main thrust of the criticism has been that too little of what has been undertaken under the aegis of educational research has been concerned with improving practice in schools. This theme is taken up from a different perspective in Chapter 9. Suffice it to say here that the criticism was long resisted but has recently begun to have effect. Perhaps one of the most evident responses has been from BERA (The British Educational Research Association) which, in its 1997 Newsletter, proposed a new Journal, focusing on the usefulness of educational research. The proposal gave the aims of the new journal as:

1 to demonstrate and highlight the usefulness of educational research;
2 to encourage educational researchers to devote energies to scholarly consideration of the implications of research for policy and practice and to reward them for so doing through the prestige of publication in the journal;
3 to provide a channel for communicating with scholarly practitioners, such as curriculum developers and teacher educators, about the implications of research for policy and practice;
4 to provide a forum for debate about different ways in which research can be of value in informing policy or practice; and
5 to provide a scholarly foundation for a parallel popular series of pamphlets for practitioners and policy-makers reporting the conclusions of papers in the journal.

How these aims might be interpreted in practice would be in the hands of the editorial board. However, as stated, the aims make it possible for the editor to give powerful support to researchers whose concern is with applied rather than basic research *and* with those aspects of research which are most likely to be of immediate value to teachers in schools.

However, what is significant in this short history of educational research is not what one new journal may turn out to be but the fact that such a journal, sponsored by the research community and emphasizing the *usefulness* of educational research, is seen to be necessary as well as desirable. The theme of the usefulness of research was taken up by McIntyre (1997). Citing Elliott (1989) he writes:

> . . . educational research is a form of practical inquiry which fuses inquiry with practice. There can be no educational research if teachers play no important role in the process of articulating, analysing and hypothesising solutions to complex educational problems.

On the same theme in discussing a paper by Stenhouse in Ruddock and Hopkins (1985), Elliott observes:

> For Lawrence Stenhouse educational research . . . was 'systematic inquiry . . . to provide a theory of educational practice . . . made public'. For me, these are the key concepts in relation to *professional* educational research: the conduct and claims of the research must be open to public scrutiny and criticism; the inquiry must be systematic, with all the complex requirements that entails; the purpose must be to improve our theoretical understanding; and it should usefully inform the development of educational practice.

In this context, we draw particular attention to the last phrase.

However, McIntyre does not restrict himself to considering the extent to which research should be an activity that is of value to teachers and policy makers. He also touches on the importance of managing a *rapprochement* between researchers and teachers and policy makers. He cites with approval Brown (1991) who argued for the need to engage in civilized dialogue with policy makers, 'even where we found their values and assumptions quite alien'. Indeed, he goes so far as to quote Hargreaves (1996), with approval 'in principle':

> Practitioners and policy makers must take an active role in shaping educational research as a whole, not just in influencing a local project in which they happen to be involved; and researchers need to know that users are powerful partners with whom many aspects of research need to be negotiated and to whom in a real sense the research community is in part accountable.

These may, of course, be no more than straws in the wind. However, it is possible to discern strong pressures developing in favour of the directions McIntyre is indicating. A coming together of researchers as providers and policy-makers as users of their products in a more harmonious relationship might well be seen as a more productive, and desirable, relationship than has been the case for the past 20 years.

There are potential problems on the horizon, however, that will have to be negotiated. Historically, researchers enjoyed enormous freedom to pursue their interests and to gratify their intellectual curiosity. Many, most perhaps, have done so as individuals. Research was what they were employed to do and for which they were paid, usually by their universities or by sponsoring organizations. Their work was circumscribed only by ethical requirements and the disciplines of the research process itself. This freedom has been jealously guarded, understandably so. Unfortunately it was this freedom which led, in part, to the virtual breakdown of working relations between educational researchers and policy-makers. If that breakdown is to be repaired, it will require changes in the practices of both parties. So far as researchers are concerned, the idea that research is an individually defined project conducted by the individual may have to become, largely, a thing of the past. The price of support for research by policy-makers may well be that individually defined projects will become a thing of the past. Instead, research priorities will be defined and large scale research projects involving substantial teams of researchers will be commissioned, either directly by the DfEE (Department for Education and Employment) or by way of its agencies such as the ESRC (Economic Social Research Council). This will not entirely prevent individuals from pursuing their own interests — charitable trusts will continue to fund research that can be supported by their trustees. The main body of work, however, will be defined, effectively, by the government, since that is the source of most of the funding and most researchers will be engaged in it.

The clear danger with this sort of development is that governments may misuse their power. Careful safeguards will have to be built into the system to ensure that they cannot do so. Most important of these, perhaps, is the preservation of the researcher's right to publish, so as to prevent the suppression of unwelcome research findings or their misrepresentation.

This chapter has sought to provide a brief history of educational research from the work of the pioneers up to the present day. It has only been possible to scratch the surface of this particular topic in a book like this. The reader interested in this aspect would be well advised to pursue the topic elsewhere. However, a number of points might usefully be made in conclusion to this chapter.

What constitutes educational research has evolved considerably over the last century or so. This is in part because of the development in research techniques in general, but in the social sciences and education especially. Much of the early work was basic in character and was in part an attempt to map the domain, At the same time, there has been a considerable expansion in the numbers of people engaged in all research, let alone merely in the field of education. If the theatre of educational research was once the armchair or the laboratory of a few seeking to gain 'knowledge', this theatre has now extended to include the classroom, the education office and all places involved directly or indirectly in the process of schooling, and is an activity engaged in by many.

Furthermore, and just as importantly, education as process and system has seen considerable expansion, not just in the countries in the so-called developed world, but also worldwide. The content of education has grown beyond the basics of the 3 Rs and the system has grown, from what were once local individual units of classroom or small school, to elaborate local and nationally networked systems, paid for out of public funds, aimed at educating *all* children to enable them to fulfil ever more complex roles in adult life to contribute to the generation of national wealth and social well-being and integration. The growth has placed new demands and challenges on the system to meet the needs of producing an ever more skilled workforce, while demonstrating that the investment of public money is being wisely spent.

At the same time, the increased availability of educational opportunity has resulted in higher expectations from the consumers (parents, children, young people, *and* tax-payers). To support that growth, more elaborate structures have had to be set in place, to meet the needs of accountability. Teaching itself has changed considerably, not least because of the growth in knowledge and what is considered desirable or essential to be transmitted to those being educated. Moreover, societies have become more complex and the direction of education systems is moving increasingly to the classification of those passing through the system. This has given rise to what is referred to as the examinations industry, which seeks to provide authoritative assessments of the standards reached. The accountability movement has sought to use that sort of data as a means of monitoring the performance of the system down to the level of individual schools and teachers. The development of a full public education system has also had important implications for the curriculum to be taught. Hence the growing development of vocational education in parallel with the latter day versions of the academic education, traditionally reserved for the élite, whether having reached that status on merit or through some form of privilege, usually associated with wealth and social status.

Finally, the role of the teacher has changed substantially over the period, this arising out of the growth in the levels of public education. Whereas once, teachers enjoyed a certain distance from those they taught and their parents, the growth in alternative sources of knowledge and information has challenged their role in relation to those taught. Those sources include books, television and radio, and now, increasingly, the computer. These cannot replace the teacher entirely, but they have had and will continue to have a marked effect on the way teachers teach *and* on the relationships between teacher and taught.

As for the future, Ranson (1996) observes:

An agenda for educational research in and for the future needs to be shaped by a distinctive theoretical frame which theorises the values, purposes, conditions and practice of active learning, which can be brought to bear upon and refined as a result of analysing the issues of learning embedded in the layers of historical change affecting individuals, institutions and communities.

The cumulative effects of developments in research techniques and in the numbers of researchers and the issues that they explore, the contexts in which they work, plus the continuing changes in society and in education systems and the contexts in which they operate mean that there will be plenty of work that researchers might usefully do. The directions taken by that research and its usefulness to the system on which it focuses will, it would seem, be likely to depend in part on a greater integration between researchers, the experts within the main education system, and the bodies that fund research. While all parties will need to maintain their integrity and relative independence, a greater harmonization of purpose will need to be achieved, so that the inputs of all parties are recognized and *communicated* in a mutually meaningful manner.

References

ACHILLES, C., NYE, B., ZAHARIAS, J. and FULTON, B. (1993) *The Lasting Benefits Study in Grades 4 and 5: A Legacy from Tennessee's Four Year (Kindergarten — Grade 3) Class Size Study (1985–1989)*, Project STAR, Paper presented at North Carolina Association for Research in Education, Greensboro, North Carolina.

ARNOT, M. (1997) 'Gendered citizenry: New feminist perspectives on education and citizenship', *British Educational Research Journal*, **23**, 3.

BALL, S.J. (1990) *Politics and Policy Making in Education*, London: Routledge.

BALL, S.J. (1997) 'Policy, sociology and critical social research: A personal review of recent education policy and policy research', *British Educational Research Journal*, **23**, 3.

BARNES, J.B. (1960) *Educational Research for Classroom Teachers*, New York: G.P. Putnam's Sons.

BASSEY, M. (1992) 'Creating education through research', *British Educational Research Journal*, **18**, 1.

BEARD, R.M. (1969) *An Outline of Piaget's Developmental Psychology*, London: Routledge and Kegan Paul.

BLATCHFORD, P. and MORTIMORE, P. (1994) 'The issue of class size for young children in schools: What can we learn from research?', *Oxford Review of Education*, **20**, 4.

BREHAUT, W. (1973) 'British research in education: Some aspects of its development', in BUTCHER, H.J. and PONT, H.B. (eds) *Educational Research in Britain*, Part 3, London: University of London Press.

BROWN, S. (1991) 'Effective contributions from research to educational conversations: Style and strategy', *British Educational Research Journal*, **17**.

BRUNER, J.S. (1966) *Toward a Theory of Instruction*, Cambridge, Mass: Harvard University Press.

BUCKINGHAM, B.R. (1926) *Research for Teachers*, New York: Silver, Burdette and Co.

BURSTALL, C. (1992) 'Playing the numbers game in class', *Education Guardian*, 7 April.

CALDERHEAD, J. (1995) 'A new association for Education Research', *EERA Bulletin*, **1**, 1.

ELLIOTT, J. (1989) 'Educational theory and the professional learning of teachers: An overview', *Cambridge Journal of Education*, **19**.

ENNIS, R.H. (1975) 'Children's ability to handle Piaget's propositional logic: A conceptual critique', *Review of Educational Research*, **45**, pp. 1–14.

FLYNN, J.R. (1980) *Race, IQ and Jensen*, London: Routledge and Kegan Paul.

GLASS, G., CAHEN, L., SMITH, M. and FILBY, N. (1982) *School Class Size*, Beverly Hills Sage.

GUILFORD, J.P. (1967) *The Nature of Human Intelligence*, New York: McGraw Hill.

HARGREAVES, D. (1996) *Teaching as a Research Based Profession*, London: Teacher Training Agency.

JONES, R.M. (1972) *Fantasy and Feeling in Education*, Harmondsworth: Penguin.

KARIER, C. (1973) 'Ideology and evaluation: In quest of meritocracy', Paper presented to the Wisconsin conference on education and evaluation, School of Education, University of Wisconsin, Madison, Wisconsin, April 26–27.

KOHLBERG, L. (1964) 'Development of moral character and moral ideology', in STEVENSON, H. (ed.) *Child Psychology*, 62nd Yearbook, National Society for the Study of Education: University of Chicago Press.

KOHLBERG, L. (1975) 'The cognitive developmental approach to moral education,' Bloomington, Indiana, *Phi Delta Kappan*.

MCINTYRE, D. (1997) 'The profession of educational research', *British Educational Research Journal*, **23**, 2.

RANSON, S. (1996) 'The future of education research: Learning at the Centre', *British Educational Research Journal*, **22**, 5.

RICE, J.M. (1897) 'The futility of the spelling grind', *Forum 23*, April and June pp. 163–72, 409–19.

RUDDOCK, J. and HOPKINS, D. (1985) *Research as a Basis for Teaching: Readings from the Work of Lawrence Stenhouse*, London: Heinemann.

RUSK, R.R. (1912) *Introduction to Experimental Education*, London: Longman.

SCATES, D.E. (1947) 'Fifty years of objective measurement and research in education', *Journal of Education Research*, **41**.

SCHOOLS COUNCIL (1973) *Science 5–13 Curriculum Project: With Objectives in Mind*, London: Macmillan. (This project has been published as: HARLEN, W. (1977) *Match and Mismatch*, Edinburgh: Oliver and Boyd.)

SLAVIN, R. (1989) 'Class size and student achievement: Small effects of small classes', *Educational Psychologist*, **24**, 1.

TAYLOR, W. (1973) 'Support for educational research and development', in BUTCHER, H.J. and PONT, H.B. (eds) *Educational Research in Britain*, Part 3, London: University of London Press.

TERMAN, L.M. (1931) 'The gifted child', in MURCHISON, C. (ed.) *A Handbook of Child Psychology*, Worcester, MA: Clark University Press.

THORNDIKE, E.L. (1914) An address at the First Annual Conference on 'Educational Measurement', Indiana University *Bulletin of Extension Division*, 12, Indiana University.

THORNDIKE, E.L. (1918) 'The nature, purpose and general methods of measurement of educational products', *Seventeenth Yearbook of the National Society for the Study of Education*, Part II. *The Measurement of Educational Products*, Bloomington, Illinois: Public School Publishing Company.

TOMLINSON, T. (1990) 'Class size and public policy: The plot thickens', *Contemporary Education*, **62**, 1.

TRAVERS, R.M.W. (1978) *An Introduction to Educational Research*, 4th edition, New York: Macmillan.

TYLER, R.W. (1949) *Basic Principles of Curriculum and Instruction*, Chicago: University of Chicago Press.

Chapter 5

Approaches to Researching Education

A glance through the literature suggests that there is no generally accepted scheme for classifying educational research studies. However, the reason for generating and using some forms of classification stems from the fact that the criteria for evaluating educational research become clearer when they are related to the specific methodological characteristics of each category. Another advantage of using some sort of classification is that it makes the analysis of research processes more intelligible and comprehensible, because modern educational research, as we have seen earlier, embraces elements of several related disciplines and makes use of a number of techniques. The three broad categories of research methodologies are:

- The historical method of research;
- The descriptive method of research; and
- The experimental method of research.

None of these categories is intrinsically superior to the others. Each makes its own particular contribution to educational knowledge. A piece of research may fall into more than one of these categories, and often does. For example, after identifying the problem to be investigated, the research worker may usefully begin with an historical study to determine what has been done in the past, and then go on to collect information about the present state of affairs regarding the problem, and which would constitute a descriptive or experimental study. Many research programmes in education make use of all three methods. It should be remembered, however, that the methods and strategies employed in a research programme should always be dictated by the nature of the problem and the kind of data sought.

The Historical Method of Research

The researcher uses the historical method to understand the present in the light of past events and trends. Historical research may be described as 'the systematic collection and objective evaluation of data related to past occurrences in order to . . . test hypotheses concerning causes, effects or trends of those events that may help explain present events and anticipate future events' (Anderson, 1994). It can be summarized as viewing today retrospectively. On the basis of information about the past, the researcher is better able to predict the direction of future developments with some degree of confidence. The historical study of an educational institution, for example, can provide a perspective which helps in the understanding of the present educational system, and this understanding may help to establish a basis for further progress and improvement. During the 1920s and 1930s, historical educational research received a great deal of attention and a number of books were published. In more recent times, the historical method in educational research has regained the reputation which it lost during the 1930s because of the misuse of the method by several research projects in the USA (Barnes, 1960). Today, the focus and strategy of historical research have changed, attempting to achieve rigorous critical standards in dealing with educational problems. Thus, modern historical research may be described as the application of systematic and rigorous methods of inquiry for understanding the past; it is an interpretative synthesis of past events and records. According to Travers (1978), historical research 'involves a procedure supplementary to observation, a process by which the historian seeks to test the truthfulness of the reports of observations made by others'.

The research methodology consists of the collection, organization, verification, validation and analysis of information in accordance with a set of specific standards. All these steps in historical research provide the kind of evidence which may lead to a new understanding of the past and of its relevance to the present and the future.

Studies of an historical nature in educational research consist of a large and broad collection of data. They may include histories of the lives and work of leaders in educational thought and practice, and past information about educational movements and trends. The historical with the British context approach has been used in research into educational issues, such as school discipline, the 11+ examination system, mixed ability teaching and methods of teaching. The problems involved in the process of historical research make it a somewhat difficult task. Barzun and Graff's (1970) work is interesting, because it suggests how to deal with the basic problems in treating historical information.

As with other approaches, the essential steps in the use of the historical method in educational research are: defining the problem, gathering the data, evaluating and synthesizing the data and finally, presenting the findings. However, the data gathering process is largely a mechanical exercise. The second process, evaluating the data, draws heavily upon logic, and reporting the findings is based on facts and opinions.

In data collection, the researcher can turn to two sorts of sources: primary and secondary. As the term implies, primary sources are first hand, original data related to events in the past. The sources for this sort of data are documents, such as diaries of eye-witnesses, court records and statistics; artifacts, such as tools and art objects from the past; and on-the-spot records, such as files and photographs. The major part of the data is derived from primary sources which constitute the basic materials of historical research. Thus, for example, if a researcher is studying the historical development of the tripartite system of education in the UK, he or she must address the primary sources.

Secondary sources of information include the accounts of persons who relate the testimony of an actual witness of an event. Common examples of secondary sources are history textbooks, newspaper reports of an actual event not written by an eye-witness, biographies and other secondhand descriptions. This kind of evidence obviously has limited value because of the distortion of facts which is likely to take place in transmitting the information from one person to another. Because of this limitation, historical researchers tend to use primary sources as much as possible.

It is not always useful to make a rigid classification of source materials because the same source may be either primary or secondary depending on how it is used. For example, if a piece of research is designed to study the policies of a local education authority concerning multi-cultural education at a particular time, the local newspaper's editorials on the subject during the time would be secondary sources. On the other hand, if the aim of the research was to explore editorial policy towards the local education authority on multi-cultural education, the editorials would be treated as primary sources. A main concern in the collection of data in historical research in education should be to locate primary sources, that is, to obtain data that are as close to the facts as possible.

Historians have developed various procedures for the evaluation of historical materials. They have given educational researchers two levels of criticism to consider: external criticism and internal criticism. External criticism attempts to distinguish between a misrepresentation and a genuine document or authentic relic, monument, or any other source of data; however, the genuineness of data does not always establish the accuracy of its contents. Internal criticism, on the other hand, aims at determining the validity and accuracy of actual historical data. In other words, the main concern of internal criticism is to reveal a true picture of what actually happened at a particular place and time. Thus, truthfulness becomes the guideline for internal criticism.

Having subjected historical data to external criticism for genuineness or authenticity and to internal criticism for trustworthiness or relevance of material, the question of synthesis and reporting becomes an important one. This is a philosophical process in which the researcher draws the threads together in a meaningful pattern and then applies the result to test the hypothesis or answer the question formulated at the outset. Although hypotheses are not always explicitly stated in historical investigations, they are usually implied. This stage of research requires a great deal of imagination and resourcefulness on the part of the researcher who must take great care to report the facts as accurately as possible.

Historical research is an interesting exercise which can make a significant contribution to the field of education by tracing a particular aspect of it through a particular period of time in order to identify factors that have influenced the development of the concept or idea being investigated. In fact, the activities of the historian, when education is the subject of inquiry, are no different from those working in any other field. However, at this point, a brief examination of its strengths and weaknesses seems appropriate.

Since the historical researchers draw data from the experiences and observations of others, they have to depend upon inference and logical analysis for filling in the picture of the particular historical event being studied. This introduces researcher bias. The researchers have no control over which documents, relics, records and artifacts happen to be available, hence having little control over the sample materials to be studied. They can only choose to reject some of what is available. Another limitation is that it is impossible to replicate the study. Historical knowledge is invariably incomplete, since it is derived from the surviving data of a limited number of events that took place in the past. Many historical studies in education not dealing with recent events make (excessive) use of secondary sources of information. Furthermore, the researchers often interpret the meaning of a document in order to draw conclusions. This process is a difficult one, since word meanings and usage tend to change over the years.

In spite of the many limitations in historical research, there is some relevant information which cannot be obtained by other means. For example, if the researcher wishes to assess the effect of student sit-ins on the subsequent policy of higher education in the UK since 1972, then only the historical research approach can shed some light in charting the evolution of the educational institution. That particular situation may not always be duplicated, and even if it were, many circumstances would be different.

Another obvious advantage of the historical method in education is its unobtrusiveness. Since the researcher is removed from the events and situations being investigated, there is no danger of contaminating the phenomena as a result of being present at them. In most historical studies, researchers do not need to get the permission of, say, the school authority, to carry out their research. Because of this lack of personal involvement in historical research, it may be more acceptable to study even a controversial issue for which the use of other types of research would be extremely difficult. Historical research by individuals may be limited to studies of specific educational problems in schools or colleges, but the combined picture of such research can give an indication of how and why the problem arose in a particular situation. However, in view of its limitations, great care should be taken in generalizing the findings of historical research in education.

The Descriptive Method of Research

While the historical method describes past events, the descriptive method of research is primarily concerned with portraying the present. In actual fact, the descriptive method in the educational field is not exactly a method, since it embraces many approaches to the collection of data. However, each of them has one element in common — each endeavours to depict the present position of a given situation. The main difference between the various types of descriptive research is in the process of description. For example, description by interview and description by testing are two entirely different research approaches, but both of them come under the heading of descriptive research.

Early developments in educational research were concerned with making precise and accurate assessments of the educational problem and the relationships between the phenomena that existed. Even today, the investigation of some educational problems may require an understanding of the nature of the factors which gave rise to the current condition or situation before proceeding any further. For example, in order to address the problems of children's poor self-esteem, some information has to be collected about the nature of the problem, educational practices, attitudes, home background and existing levels of self-esteem.

The process of descriptive research goes beyond the mere collection and tabulation of factual data. It is not only a structured attempt to obtain facts and opinions about the current condition of things; it also involves elements of comparison and relationships of one kind and another. Descriptive research may not answer all the fundamental questions, but it does provide useful data that will serve as a basis for further research using a more rigorous research design. Thus, the discovery of meaning is the focus of the whole process. It should be mentioned that, in the social sciences, it is notoriously difficult to establish cause and effect relationships. However, by identifying the nature of factors and interpreting the meaning and significance of 'what is', it may be possible to formulate some hypotheses or research questions for further work. Although much progress has been made in recent years in identifying the variables and the relationships between them in order to deal with educational issues, there are many areas about which very little is known. Hence, there is a need to develop an understanding of the various stages in descriptive research and to be aware of its differing techniques for the collection and interpretation of data/information.

As stated earlier, descriptive research involves some interpretation of the meaning or significance of what is described. This process is often criticized on the grounds of bias towards the investigator's subjective judgments and superficial impressions of the phenomena. Nevertheless, an examination of the many theses and dissertations submitted in the last three decades will confirm that the descriptive method has been widely used. In order to mitigate the validity of the above criticism, it is necessary for researchers to adopt carefully structured plans:

1 Recognition and definition of the social or educational problem/issue which is to be studied.
2 A decision must be made about the kind of data required, and a clear statement on this made. It helps to set out the parameters of the study.
3 The formulation of the hypotheses to be tested and/or the framing research questions to be addressed must be stated clearly, pointing out the assumptions underlying them. If the study is an exploratory one, hypotheses may be more tentative or the questions broader in character, but still need to be carefully stated, it perhaps not being possible at the outset of the study to be more specific.
4 Selection and description of appropriate subjects/samples and a detailed description of the methods to be employed.
5 Selection of research tools, techniques or instruments which are to be used in the collection of data. If new/modified techniques or tools are to be utilized, a more detailed description, including their psychometric or sociometric characteristics, should be given.
6 The hypotheses should be tested and/or the questions addressed on the basis of the data collected. Sometimes, however, it may be necessary to

collect further data to do this, or even to amend the original hypotheses or questions. (Such actions should, however, be recorded and justified in the research report.)

7   Finally, the results must be described, analysed and interpreted. It is important to remember that the results must be reported in clear, precise terms.

Before leaving this section, one or two points need to be emphasized. There are often various means of data collection for descriptive research. It is often suggested that the investigator should be flexible in his or her approach. However, the decision, on the types of techniques, tools or instruments, must be made in accordance with the nature of the problem, the hypothesis/es to be tested or the question/s to be addressed and the resources available for carrying out the research. If the researcher finds that none of the existing instruments or tools is appropriate, consideration should be given to modifying them or even constructing new ones. An example of how standardized, modified and new instruments and tools can be inter-woven can be seen in the evaluation of the Schools Council's Humanities Curriculum Project (Verma, 1980).

Types of Descriptive Studies

There is no general agreement on the classification of descriptive studies. For example, an interesting study under the title *Middletown in Transition* (Lynd and Lynd, 1937) has been classified as a survey by Jahoda, Deutsch and Cook (1951), and as a case study by Young (1966). However, for the sake of convenience, descriptive research in education can be classified into the following categories:

- Surveys;
- Case studies;
- Development studies;
- Comparative studies;
- Ethnographic studies;
- Evaluation studies; and
- Action research.

Surveys

Surveys are one of the most commonly used methods of descriptive research in education and other social sciences. Surveys involve the gathering of limited data from a relatively large number of cases at a particular time. This method is frequently employed to indicate prevailing conditions or particular trends. It is not concerned with the characteristics of individuals as individuals, but it is concerned with providing information about population characteristics. Thus, surveys are broad studies of a generalized statistical nature rather than in-depth studies. Moreover, as Fowler (1993) has noted, 'there probably is no area of public policy to which survey research methodology has not been applied'.

A survey involves the clear definition of the problem and requires systematic collection of data, careful analysis and interpretation of the data, and intelligent reporting of the findings. It may be broad or narrow in scope, involve several countries or be restricted to one nation, country, local authority or school. Survey data may be gathered from the entire population, in which case it is normally called a 'census', or from a carefully selected sample of the total population.

Surveys include topics, such as population trends and movement, pupil and/or teacher opinions/attitudes on various educational matters, pupil drop-out rates, and so on. The survey method has been widely used in educational research for many years in the British context. Data have been collected through the use of questionnaires, interviews, standardized tests and other techniques and the results of such information have often helped to make decisions which have changed many educational practices in British schools.

Today, longitudinal surveys are less common than they used to be, because of the expense involved. Such a survey is usually the product of a team of researchers which might explore and evaluate many aspects of the school system, such as teaching staff, curriculum, teaching methods, financial support, buildings, and so on. This type of survey can only be conducted under the sponsorship of government departments or charitable foundations. In Britain, there is a long tradition of educational surveys being carried out by local education authorities with the findings being published in journals. One of the advantages in localized survey research is the provision of regional information which can form the basis for administrative action. However, individuals also use the survey method of research, albeit on a smaller scale.

As mentioned earlier, many types of educational issues can be explored by means of the survey. Broadly, these include various factors in and outside the school which affect pupil learning, together with information about teachers' characteristics and the educational achievements of pupils. Many surveys have also been conducted in recent years for the purpose of comparing the educational attainment of pupils in different schools, cities, neighbourhoods and countries. Chall (1967) studied reading instruction by analysing research studies on reading and teaching materials, interviewing authors of reading methods and observing over 300 classrooms in the United States and England. This was a three-year study, funded by the Carnegie Corporation. Another study (Húsen, 1967) — *The International Study of Achievement in Mathematics* — compared achievement in mathematics in 12 countries. It was a six-year survey and tests were administered to 13-year-olds and to students in their last year of school prior to going to university. More than 132,000 students, 13,000 teachers and 5,000 schools, drawn from the 12 countries, were involved. The two volume report of this survey research compared the data obtained from across cultures.

Although the survey does not seem to aspire to develop an organized body of knowledge, it does provide information for further research, possibly of an experimental nature, which may lead to the establishment of some theory. The method seems to have the advantage of being an effective way of collecting data from a large number of sources, relatively cheaply and, perhaps, in a short time. Furthermore, the results can be analysed quickly and action can be taken, if this is the objective of the study. Surveys usually make use of sampling to produce valid and reliable data which can be generalized with some confidence.

There are limitations, however, in this type of descriptive research. The researchers' role is often a minor one since, in many cases, they do not come into contact with the people who provide the data. Another weakness is that, if the problem is politically or socially sensitive, some respondents may not wish to divulge their true feelings. In surveys, mailing is almost inevitable and recognized as a major factor in non-response. Despite these limitations, the survey method has proved useful in providing the researcher with a valid description of some of the issues involved in education.

Case Studies

Case studies are regarded by some writers as being the study of a group, while others are of the opinion that a case study is of only one case. 'Case study' is a familiar term, particularly in the fields of psychology, sociology and education. Platt (1988) wrote of a case study as 'one where more than one case may be used, but if more than one is used the individuality of each case is retained and/or the number of cases falling into a given category is not treated as of significance'. Similarly, Runyan (1982) defined the case study approach as 'the presentation and interpretation of detailed information about a single subject, whether an event, a culture, or . . . an individual life'. On the other hand, writers like Becker (1968), from the sociological tradition of participant observation regarded such study as of a group with a view to understanding the group's behaviour. The above examples clearly show that writers view the case study method according to the discipline in which they have acquired their cognitive framework.

The case study is essentially a research in depth rather than breadth. The typical case study is an intensive analysis and evolutionary description of an individual. The method is not practicable with a very large sample. However, it can be employed in studying a small group of individual units or individuals. The clinical type of case study is often carried out by social workers, psychiatrists and clinical psychologists for the purpose of diagnosing an individual's problems. In this context, emphasis is upon the study of individual characteristics. The method perhaps has its origins in the Freudian approach which attempted to diagnose and treat patients with psychological problems.

In education and other behavioural sciences, the method has been employed with individual children, with all types of groups — from a small group within a class to a school itself. Today, psychologists, sociologists, anthropologists and educational researchers frequently use the case study method with a view to supplementing the survey method. Young (1966) remarked that 'the most meaningful numerical studies in social sciences are those which are linked with exhaustive case studies describing the interrelationships of factors and processes'. Case studies may reveal certain relevant information which is not and cannot be obtained through the survey method. Thus, in many research programmes the two methods operate to complement each other.

The greatest advantage of this method is that it endeavours to understand the whole individual in relation to his or her environment. Koluchova's (1972) case study of severe deprivation in twins provides an illustration of the planned way in which case studies can and ought to be carried out. Since the interviewer has to probe deeply into the dynamics of an individual's personality, he or she must be trained in the planning and structuring of the case study, in the obtaining of the necessary information and in the interpretation of the data.

There are certain weaknesses, however, in this method. One of the problems is that the information obtained is often of a confidential nature and so can hardly be evaluated by other research workers. An obvious shortcoming of the method is that the cases or the individuals selected for the study may not be representative or typical and hence generalizations will not be valid. Although the study of a single unit by this method may be thought to have limited value in establishing immediate generalizations, a major advantage is that it can be a fertile source for the generation of hypotheses or formulation of questions which can later be tested by more rigorous research. Another problem is that research based upon the study of a single case or a few cases can be very expensive in terms of time and resources.

Teachers are often engaged in studies of individual children. In order to understand the behaviour of children, they obtain information on their home background, school attainment, attitudes and interests, relationships with the peer group, intellectual abilities or disabilities, personality and standardized test results. In this instance, when case studies stem from attempts to learn about children in order to help them, the research aspect is of limited value except to those concerned with the case (although the process may help teachers to develop their awareness of other pupils as individuals). Because case study work has become increasingly popular during the last decade, we return to the subject, looking at it from a different angle, in Chapter 6, which considers research tools.

Development Studies

Developmental studies are not only concerned with the description of the current state of affairs and the interrelationships of phenomena in a given situation, but also with the changes which take place as a result of the time factor. In this type of descriptive research, investigators describe children's development over a period of months, or even of years. This method is educationally important in the sense that educators are concerned with the physical, mental and emotional development of children and it is useful to learn more about what children are like at different ages, how they differ from one another within age levels and how they grow and develop. In designing a school curriculum, it is extremely important to take into consideration the relevant characteristics of the learner. Essentially, in this type of study, recorded data are utilized with a view to determining what has happened in the past, what the present situation reveals, and what will be likely to happen in the future. For example, if the population of an ethnic community shows consistent growth over a period of time, one might say that, by a certain year in the future, the population will have reached a particular level. The assumptions are based on the possibility that the factors (such as higher fertility rates and younger age structure of the community) producing the growth will continue to exert their influence into the future.

There are two commonly used methods to study children's characteristics and the way these characteristics change with growth: the longitudinal and cross-sectional methods. In longitudinal studies, the same sample of subjects is studied at intervals (say, at the ages of 9, 10, 11 and 12, though the intervals will always be dictated by the nature of the matter under investigation). For example, a researcher may wish to investigate how reading comprehension patterns develop in a group of children over a period of time. This would be possible by measuring their achievement at each successive year and by plotting the patterns of development for each child and for the group. The cross-sectional method, on the other hand, attempts to study samples of children taken from each age level. The results are then plotted showing the pattern of development for children from 9 to 12 years of age.

Longitudinal studies have proved to be most effective in studying children's development over a period of time since they allow for intensive studies of a large number of cases and of many variables. The idea behind longitudinal studies as they have been employed in educational and social research is to answer questions about an individual's development from evidence based on a large number of cases. However, studies of this type demand a great deal of time, resources and money. Some of the longitudinal studies in America were maintained for 35 years (Terman and Oden, 1959). Two of the major longitudinal studies in Britain are still of interest and relevance to education in the broader sense. Douglas (1967) studied just over 5000 children employing a wide range of measures. Newson and Newson (1965, 1970, 1978) engaged in a long term study of children growing up in a representative English midland city. One of the findings in both the studies underlined the significant impact that social class makes on an individual's development.

Another longitudinal study inquiring into the development of delinquency was conducted by West (1969). The investigator followed a sample of London boys from the age of 8 to 18 in an attempt to trace the emergence of delinquent behaviour and to observe the psychological and sociological characteristics that accompany it. *Fifteen Thousand Hours* is another example (Rutter et al., 1979). Also conducted in London, this study was sponsored initially by the Inner London Education Authority (ILEA) and subsequently by the Ministry of Education. It followed a cohort of pupils through their five years of secondary education in 12 schools to explore the effects of different schools on pupil outcomes.

An evaluation of longitudinal studies would suggest that the way in which studies are carried out serves two main purposes: first, because the sample of subjects is studied at certain points in their development, a cross-sectional picture of a particular age group can emerge; and secondly, if the sample has been carefully chosen and is representative of all children at a particular age, this can provide information about the number of children who have reached a certain stage in development, the number with highly developed intellectual skills, the number with particular educational problems, and so on. The relationship between these measures and some relevant variables (such as sex, parental occupation, family size) can be of considerable importance. This knowledge can be of great value, particularly where the planning of educational and social policy is concerned.

Longitudinal studies have a number of inherent practical difficulties. Contact with the same sample of subjects over a long period of time can be difficult. Loss of subjects is quite common. There is also the problem of retaining the interest of subjects over the period of the research. Perhaps the occurrence of these difficulties could be minimized as long as the subjects are attending the same educational institution, but the difficulties arise once they transfer from primary to secondary school, or employment (or unemployment) begins. If the sample chosen turns out to be unrepresentative, there is no way to redress it. Furthermore, once the study has reached its final stages, it is not possible to introduce new variables for investigation. Therefore, such projects require careful planning and farsightedness, with a degree of flexibility built into the design in order to make minor changes possible at a later stage. Although the general format of contemporary longitudinal studies is the same — regular contact with a sample of children, their homes and their schools — the types of 'measurement' included and the process of data collection vary from study to study. The word 'measurement' should be taken in the broader sense to include various sorts of classification or evaluation of individuals, or their circumstances.

Some of the practical difficulties inherent in the longitudinal method do not appear in cross-sectional studies. The cross-sectional method attempts to study children of various age levels at the same point in time. Because this approach is less expensive and less time-consuming, it is more commonly used in the field of education. An investigator can collect and analyse the data in a relatively short time. Thus, one of the main advantages of cross-sectional research is its relative cheapness and the speed with which the results can be obtained. The main limitation of this approach is that it cannot answer questions about the changes in, and the relationships between, the different aspects of the child's experience with time. A further disadvantage is that chance differences between samples may bias the results. Selection of age group samples which are representative of the total population may present difficulty, especially if the study is confined to one local education authority or one city. However, if we want to know about certain physical, intellectual and emotional characteristics of typical children at various stages, the cross-sectional approach is perhaps preferable because the chances of obtaining a large sample are higher. On the other hand, if we wish to learn about certain changes in children's characteristics, the longitudinal method is perhaps better, since the researcher follows the same sample of subjects through their developmental stages. It should also be mentioned that most research students and university teachers tend to conduct cross-sectional rather than longitudinal studies, because of the lack of sufficient financial support.

Comparative Studies

Comparative studies form a link between two types of previously discussed research (case studies and surveys), and experimental methods of research. Some investigators try to make comparisons of existing situations which provide a similar kind of information to that which experimental studies might yield. Such studies may be described as causal comparative. This method is sometimes referred to as *ex post facto* design.

In a laboratory situation, the experimenter attempts to control all the variables except the independent variable, which is deliberately manipulated to see what occurs. Because of the complexity and nature of social phenomena, an investigator cannot always manipulate or even control the factors in order to study cause and effect relationships. For example, it is impossible to control and manipulate home background, intelligence or social class. In these circumstances, a study of what actually happens in a natural environment would be more relevant than that in a controlled laboratory situation.

A research worker may decide to find out the factor or factors that are associated with certain types of pupils' behaviour. For example, studies of academically motivated children may compare the social and educational backgrounds of highly and poorly motivated children. The study may well seek to identify which factors are common to the highly motivated and the poorly motivated children. Any factors common to one group but not to the other might give us some indication as to the underlying causes of poor motivation.

Many educational researchers have utilized the comparative method of research in the analysis of educational programmes, practices and outcomes. The approach employed may range from relatively simple designs to fairly complex ones in which some elements of the experimental method are also employed (e.g. the use of control groups). Studies in this category often employ correlational analysis to determine relationship. The t-test is an appropriate statistical technique to determine the level of significance of differences between defined groups. Some writers refer to this approach as correlational studies. (See Chapter 8 for discussion of some common statistical concepts used in educational research.)

It should be kept in mind that, in addition to seeking probable causes, comparative research is often used in the educational field to ascertain differences between defined groups. Investigations comparing different racial/ethnic groups or those comparing normal with handicapped groups are not aimed primarily to explore causes but to gain an insight into the relative characteristics of the groups compared. Thus, in comparative studies, two different groups are compared using the same measure or the same variables at, or nearly at, the same time. The initial procedures of comparative design are basically the same as those employed in other methods of research. However, considerable emphasis is placed upon biographical data of the subject such as family relationships, peer group relations, school records, and other information.

One of the dangers of the comparative research method is that, because variables or factors go together, some people conclude that one is the cause and the other the effect. This error of mistaking what is merely an association for the cause could lead readers of research reports to deduce a false cause–effect relationship. Although the causal-comparative method has some merit, it has several limitations as well. Failure to isolate the real significant factor/s, failure to recognize that problems may have multiple rather than single causative factors and drawing false conclusions on the basis of a limited number of occurrences may lead the investigator to misleading conclusions. Classifying subjects into comparable control and experimental groups also poses difficulties since social events are not alike except within broad categories. In comparative studies in 'natural' settings, the investigator cannot apply stringent criteria in selecting a sample of subjects. In spite of many limitations, the comparative method of research provides a means of dealing with many educational problems which cannot be explored in a laboratory situation. This method has acquired some respectability in recent years with the advent of improved techniques, tools and methods of conducting educational research.

Ethnographic Studies

Ethnographic studies imply a methodological approach with specific procedures, techniques and methods of analysis. During the last two decades, interest in the application of ethnographic research strategies has increased among educational policy and evaluation researchers. Most ethnographic studies in educational research are designed to influence educational policy and practice. They have mainly been addressed at teachers and education advisers, school governors and people in similar positions (Hammersley, 1994; Troyna, 1994). Educational ethnography as a sub-field of anthropology and education has grown rapidly because of dissatisfaction with the limitations of traditional quantitative designs (Eisner, 1979). This has resulted in the increasingly common practice of incorporating an ethnographical component into educational research studies.

Sometimes, first-time researchers use the terms 'case study', 'qualitative research' and 'ethnography' as if they were interchangeable. It is important to realize that they are not the same. Various attempts have been made to define ethnography. Some suggest that its goal is to present a theoretical account of a community, institution or culture (Hammersley, Scarth and Webb, 1985). Another attempt at defining it suggests that it provides a cultural description of a group and its activities from the viewpoint of the actors themselves (Hitchcock and Hughes, 1989). Recognising the complexity of research methodology, Hammersley and Atkinson (1992) stated that

> we do not regard ethnography as an 'alternative paradigm' to experimental, survey or documentary research. Rather it is simply one method with characteristic advantages and disadvantages, albeit one whose virtues have been seriously underestimated by many social researchers owing to the influence of positivism.

Broadly speaking, an ethnographic study has been defined as 'an in-depth analytical description of an *intact* cultural scene' (Borg and Gall, 1983). Rist (1975) saw ethnography as being 'the research technique of direct observation of human activity in an ongoing naturalistic setting'. The technique was developed by anthropologists for their particular purposes and was subsequently adopted and amended by educational researchers to meet their own needs. Ethnography has sometimes been portrayed as primarily descriptive or perhaps as a form of story-telling (Walker, 1981).

In essence, this approach requires a trained person who becomes a non-participant, or more commonly participant observer in the classroom or other natural location in which the subjects of the study conduct their activities. The researcher conducts an in-depth study of some or all aspects of a cultural, social or ethnic group or even of an entire community. For Anderson (1994), 'Ethnographic research involves participant observation, description, a concern with process and meaning and inductive analysis'.

Anthropologists such as Margaret Mead and Ruth Benedict tried to get an insight into the life of people by spending a great deal of time with them in their natural surroundings. Thus anthropologists' efforts at understanding and describing the culture (in a broad sense) of a group of people is often called ethnography (Maykut and Morehouse, 1994). In an attempt to define the essence of ethnography, Werner and Schoepfle (1987) pointed out that '. . . the ethnography variety is almost limitless'. Wolcott (1988) found it useful '. . . to distinguish between anthropologically informed researchers who do ethnography and . . . researchers who frequently draw on ethnographic approaches in doing descriptive studies'.

It is clear from the work of anthropologists that the approach was developed with a view to understanding the behaviour of people in their natural setting. The strategy depended heavily on participant observation in order to acquire a view of the situation as an insider. Some researchers attempt to integrate with the community, culture or group being studied, so as to share their experience over a period of time. The experience, of becoming a member of the group being studied, provides the researcher with a unique opportunity to understand its values, attitudes and beliefs. An important aspect of ethnographic research is the need for long periods of observation so that realities can be unravelled (Schratz, 1993). It is essential that there is no intervention by the researcher in the social or cultural processes being observed, since this would clearly contaminate the data. The ethnographic method is used at various levels ranging from the study of a complex society as a macro-ethnography to the study of a single situation as a micro-ethnography (Spradley, 1980).

Most observational research is undertaken by researchers who have already formed some hypotheses and their observations are designed to collect specific information related to those hypotheses. Yet, the essence of an ethnographic study is that the researcher starts with no specific hypotheses. On the contrary, part of their training is to learn to put aside specific preconceptions or prejudices during their observations to avoid bias in interpreting what they see. Looking at some earlier completed research, it is easy to forget how difficult it is to conduct an ethnographic study. As early as 1970, Spindler, an experienced ethnographer, wrote:

Nothing is more shocking to neophyte fieldworkers than to find that there are no cultures, kinship systems, roles, statuses or ecological systems in the field. There are only people acting, events occurring, man-made forms and nature.

In its purest form, the researchers adopt a holistic approach to data collection. That is to say, they attempt to perceive the total situation rather than focusing on a few elements within it and to record by whatever means available as much of it as possible. It is also important that, in making the records, the researchers avoid the temptation to contaminate the data by allowing their value systems to affect the record. However careful they might be, it is very difficult over the time taken to make the observations for the researchers to avoid becoming active participants in the environment being studied and thus distorting the reality they are seeking to record. Furthermore, the process is time-consuming and difficult. In practice, educational researchers start by having some theoretical framework or perhaps some very tentative hypotheses to provide a non-specific focus for their observations.

It is also to be borne in mind that, engagement in research of this type inevitably means a degree of researcher involvement in the community being studied, and that its members may well view the investigator in terms different to those which he or she holds of the role of the investigator. This is something over which the researcher has no control. Thus, in a working class community, the researcher will fail to become part of that community unless he or she is able to absorb its values and cultural characteristics (Weis, 1992). Weis strongly believed that if a researcher who is not able to follow at least three principles should not be conducting ethnographic research. These are: 'know who you are before going into the field; respect those with whom you are working; and conduct yourself with the utmost of integrity at all times'.

The approach depends heavily on the records/notes (taken by whatever means — pencil and paper, electronic or, more likely, a combination of as many as can be brought to bear), because the ethnographer believes that the behaviour of individuals can only be understood if they are seen as part of their social system. The quantity of data collected can rapidly become daunting. As the data accumulate, the researcher may well seek to make sense of them by forming hypotheses to explain the observed phenomena. It is this process which makes ethnographic studies so valuable. The hypotheses which they generate are founded on and emerge from objective observation and subsequent analysis. This process makes them a much more serious proposition than those which are little more than hunches arrived at intuitively or speculations derived from the study of the literature. Just as with the descriptive studies considered earlier, ethnographic studies may well serve to provide insights into the area under investigation, and from which hypotheses can be derived. These could form the basis for subsequent studies, designed specifically to test them.

In educational research, the ethnographic approach presents a number of problems. As well as those already discussed, the presence of an outsider, the researcher, in the natural setting may change the behaviour of those being studied, particularly if the observational phase is of short duration. In educational studies, data are gathered over a much shorter period of time than is customary in anthropological studies where the researcher may be resident over a period measured in years and so has time to become part of the environment. It is essential therefore that, in analysing the data, this issue is kept in mind. Educational researchers are often criticized for adopting ethnographic techniques since they tend to deviate from the procedures developed by anthropologists.

However, some notably successful work has been achieved. An example of the approach in educational research is the study of a school which relied heavily on the close contact and observation by the researcher over a period of time (Burgess, 1983). Studies in education attempt to understand patterns of behaviour and attitudes in a natural setting, most commonly the classroom. For example, the educational researcher may wish to find out the process of communication between the teacher and pupils in the classroom. Such an approach does not imply any preconceived ideas. The researcher simply needs to make detailed notes of the processes in the classroom which might be useful to understand and explain the observed phenomena. Thus the explanations, the hypotheses, grow out of, and are grounded in, observations of the real world.

Despite its limitations and difficulty, the ethnographic approach has unique benefits. At its best, it provides data unobtainable by other means and, as we have seen, can generate hypotheses which can then be tested by other techniques. However, for a post-graduate student, its inherent difficulties and the demands of time and resources may well make it inappropriate.

Evaluation Studies

Evaluation studies use many of the research approaches and techniques described elsewhere in this chapter. In practice, there is a great deal of overlap between educational research and educational evaluation: research designs, instruments and methods of analysis employed are the same. The difference is often not one of methods, but of purpose. Kemmis (1982) defined evaluation broadly as part of the research process of reaching judgments:

> Evaluation is the process of marshalling information and arguments which enable interested individuals and groups to participate in the critical debate about a specific programme.

Stake and Denny (1969) characterized evaluation more succinctly:

> Considered broadly, evaluation is the discovery of the 'nature and worth' of something.

Education is both vital to the economic success and social stability of a country. This is reflected in the resources that governments make available to education systems. They would be irresponsible if they were not concerned that they, as well as the taxpayers, and the pupils in schools and students in colleges and universities, were getting value for money. This overall concern is reflected at each level of the educational hierarchy. For those concerned with curriculum evaluation, it can usually be resolved in the following terms: 'How effective are the teaching materials and/or the methods by which they are delivered in achieving the desired outcomes?'

Evaluation studies are generally reckoned to be of two kinds: 'formative' or 'summative'. Both formative and summative functions of evaluation require that evidence of performance or attainment is not only generated and analysed but acted upon in some way. These actions may then directly or indirectly generate more evidence so that the cycle is repeated (William and Black, 1996).

Formative studies gather information about programmes whilst they are in progress. The data obtained can then be used to modify the programme to make it more effective or, in some instances, to provide evidence of its fundamental weakness so that it can be ended. Summative evaluation, as the term implies, is designed to measure the effectiveness of a programme on its completion. Another term often used is 'baseline evaluation'. This is effectively a summative evaluation employed to discover how effective an existing programme has been in producing certain specified educational outcomes before the introduction of a new programme. A baseline evaluation makes it possible for subsequent evaluations to measure more accurately the changes brought about by the new programme. This desirable step in the evaluation process, it has to be said, is often omitted.

The distinction between the two forms of evaluation is significant, because it tends to define the process and personnel involved. In formative evaluation programmes, the personnel involved are frequently members of the team concerned with providing the programme and may well have had an important part in developing it. This makes sense in practical terms, because they are best placed to observe its day-to-day operation and to make changes to their original plans smoothly and rapidly. Formative data tend to be acquired from student feedback in the form of post-lesson questionnaires, interviews and observation. Summative evaluations, on the other hand, are usually conducted by externally recruited researchers whose judgments are less likely to be affected, not having been involved in the creation and delivery of the programme. Their allegiances will also be different. Whilst formative evaluators have a commitment to the success of the programme and have built up a close relationship with their fellow programme developers, teachers and participants in the programme; summative evaluators have a duty to educational policy — and decision-makers. Their decisions are arrived at as a result of their analysis of data collected using a variety of instruments, including, where appropriate, standardized tests.

Since researchers are mainly concerned with summative evaluations and much, if not most, of their work is done to establish the worth of study programmes, what follows concentrates on that aspect. The first task of an evaluator is to establish clearly what the aims of the programme are. Fortunately, these are usually expressed by the programme designer/s in terms such as 'The course aims to provide the students with a clear understanding at an appropriate level of the rise of the middle classes following World War II'. This may well be followed by two or three other aims related to the subject expressed in similar terms. In addition to the aims of the course, the designers may also have provided a series of behavioural objectives which will be in a form similar to 'At the end of the course, the students will be able to: (i) show how the fiscal policies of successive governments favoured the development of the middle classes; (ii) critically comment on the role of education policies in maintaining the boundaries between the working and middle classes', and so on.

If there are no aims or objectives supplied by the designers, the first task of the evaluator is to work out what they might be. He or she will have to infer them from the course material. This should not be too difficult. If a course was developed without having any worthwhile and appropriate aims, it is hard to see how it could have any value to the students and it is unlikely that an evaluator would be employed other than to confirm that it was useless and should be discontinued.

If, on the other hand, aims and objectives are supplied by the course designers, it is a fairly straightforward task for the evaluator to match appropriate instruments and techniques to discover if the desired objectives of the course have been met. There is, however, the danger that the evaluator will be seduced by the logic of the course's construction and thus overlook important side-effects that can be attributed to the course but were not foreseen by its designers. For example, the students on the history course concerned with the rise of the middle classes might have their political beliefs substantially changed as a result of their studies. Their response to having a greater understanding of this aspect of social history may be entirely legitimate but those responsible for designing and delivering the course need to be made aware of this unlooked for outcome.

In addition to the above considerations, the evaluators will very probably have a number of other matters to consider. One of these is likely to be the cost of a course or programme of courses in relation to the observed benefits to the students. They may discover that a course is extremely successful in terms of the measurable student outcomes but that its costs are twice or three times that of courses with similar objectives mounted by the same or other institutions. Part of their job will be to discover why this is so.

Considerations, such as that, impinge on another aspect of evaluation research. How effectively is the course or programme being administered or managed? Under this heading would be included such matters as the organization of the programme; monitoring procedures to ensure that the students are, in fact, being taught what the course designers intended; that the quality of teaching is, at least, adequate; that the demands made by the teachers on the students in terms of their expectations of student performance are appropriate; that personal tutors are meeting their responsibilities to their students, and so on. All these things, and many others, have an impact on the quality of a programme, the quality of the learning experience enjoyed by the students, its cost to the institution and the outcomes of the programme.

Action Research

Action research is an approach which has grown considerably in popularity during the past two decades. It has now largely overcome its reputation as something of a 'soft option' and is accepted as a legitimate form of research with a sound theoretical basis.

Kurt Lewin is often regarded as the originator of action research. For him, it was exemplified by the discussion of problems followed by group decisions on how to proceed. Not surprisingly, he stressed the importance of intra-group relations in the context of action research (Lewin, 1946; 1952). Thus, action research consisted of active participation by those who had to carry out the work in the exploration of problems that they identified. Following the investigation of the problems, the group makes decisions on the actions to be taken, monitors them and keeps note of the consequences (Adelman, 1993). The group decides whether a programme or strategy has achieved its objectives and in the course of its discussions identifies newly presented issues or problems. As Lewin himself observed, 'No action without research: no research without action.'

Lewin and his co-researchers classified their work into types of action research:

a   Diagnostic, which is designed to produce a needed plan of action;
b   Participant, in which it is assumed that the members of the affected community who were to help to effect a cure must be involved in the research process from the beginning;
c   Empirical, which is primarily concerned with keeping records and gathering experiences in day-to-day work, ideally with a succession of similar groups;
d   Experimental, which calls for a controlled study of the relative effectiveness of various techniques in nearly identical situations. (Marrow, 1969: cited in Adelman, 1993)

It is clear from Lewin's work that his emphasis was on process rather than outcomes in participatory research. He believed that action research could inform social planning and action.

In Britain, Elliott (1978) founded the Classroom Action Research Network (CARN), and since then, a great deal of work has been done by its members. This has now been expanded to form an international network for action research by teachers. It is not surprising that action research has become an influential movement in support of teacher professional development. Although it has a long history in education, only recently has it been considered as an important vehicle for preparing reflective teachers (Zeichner, 1987). In action research, the teacher adopts the role of the researcher in the classroom. The goal is that the teacher acquires and/or seeks to perfect his or her understanding of the teaching process and the skills necessary to accomplish it. Elliott (1981) viewed the process as 'the study of a social situation with a view to improving the quality of action within it'.

Cohen and Manion (1989) stated that there are many definitions of action research and argued that 'usage varies with time, place and setting'. They went on to say that action research is situational, usually collaborative and also participatory and self-evaluative. They offered a conventional definition as a 'small-scale intervention in the functioning of the real world and close examination of the effects of such intervention'.

Troyna and Carrington (1990), emphasizing the benefits of an action research approach in education, stated that it provides '. . . invaluable data on, for example, the influence of situational constraints (school ethos, phase, type, ethnic composition) on such innovations, it would also serve to remind researchers of the varied institutional constraints under which teachers currently work'.

Watt and Watt (1993) defined action research as 'a systematic inquiry by collaborative, self-critical communities of teachers, which takes place in schools. It is pursued out of a desire or need to improve educational knowledge and practices'.

A review of various writings on action research suggests that 'action' is an integral ingredient of the research process which can be seen as an evolving discipline within the educational context.

Altrichter (1993) identified two main strengths in action research. Firstly, it provides a framework of justification and orientation for those professionals who wish to develop their practice in a socially responsible way. Secondly, by relating the 'context of use (application)' and the 'context of discovery and justification' in a coherent image of the research process, action research provides a more realistic understanding of what rigorous research means in practice.

We opened this brief introduction by noting that for some time action research suffered from the reputation of being a soft option. Some people still assume that it is an easy way of conducting classroom research. Nixon (1981) argued that, on the contrary, it was an extremely challenging form of inquiry in which the classroom teacher was the key agent. He wrote:

> Action research is an intellectually demanding mode of inquiry, which prompts serious and often uncomfortable questions about classroom practice. It requires a willingness on the part of teachers to learn about their classrooms, and a desire to develop themselves professionally.

Action research embodies a whole range of practices drawn from across different disciplines. Within the educational context, it aims to help students, teachers and others sharing a common concern and then to design action to improve the situation they live in. It should be emphasized that action research is not a technique of data collection or data analysis. It tends to integrate various approaches and techniques into a framework. It is 'the study of a social situation with a view to improving the quality of action within it' (Elliott, 1981). In its approach, action research shares with other approaches the need for careful systematic planning and the selection of methods appropriate to the nature of the information required.

In the field of education, action research has been employed in curriculum, professional, and policy development, as well as institutional improvement. It has certain essential features: testing ideas in practice as a means of increasing knowledge about the curriculum, teaching and learning. The desired outcome is an improvement in the teaching/learning situation. As Kemmis and McTaggart (1988) wrote, an essential characteristic of action research is that it 'provides a way of working which links theory and practice into one whole: ideas-in-action'.

The Experimental Method of Research

The experimental method is often regarded as the 'scientific' approach to research. As has been seen in the earlier sections of this chapter, historical research studies of past events are conducted primarily for gaining a clearer understanding of the present, and, in descriptive research, attempts are made to determine the nature and degree of existing conditions. In experimental research, through manipulating an experimental variable, attempts are made to determine how and why a particular condition or event occurs. This manipulation is deliberate and systematic. So, for any experimental study, there has to be an independent variable that is manipulated by the researcher under highly controlled conditions.

The experimental method has its roots in the natural sciences. Within the social sciences, it has been applied chiefly by psychologists, but there are indications that its use is becoming more widespread in sociology and other disciplines. The strong influence of psychology and the behavioural sciences on educational research is most clearly evidenced in the use of experimental designs in the investigation of educational problems. Thorndike (1924) was one of the early investigators who extended the experimental method into education.

One of the main functions of experimentation is to generalize the factor or the variable relationship so that they may be applied outside the laboratory to a wider population. However, in the social sciences, it is not always possible to adopt the same methodologies and strategies as used in the natural sciences. One of the reasons is that conducting experimental research can be extremely costly and time-consuming. Moreover, in educational research, we are concerned with human behaviour which is most difficult, and at times impossible, to control and manipulate. Critics of experimental research contend that experimental studies relating to education lack realism and that results obtained have little practical significance to the classroom setting. Admittedly, the control of the independent variable and outside factors is difficult when dealing with human behaviour. This is not to say, however, that the problems are impossible to overcome. The experimental method has been utilized with varying degrees of success in education, where, within certain limits, it is sometimes possible to control significant influences to an extent.

In experimental research, all variables or factors identified as relevant to the problem under study are controlled or held constant while the impact of one or more variables is deliberately manipulated (e.g. a particular teaching method), so that its effect may be assessed. In other words, it involves the deliberate manipulation of certain stimuli or treatments by the experimenter and the observation and analysis of how the behaviour of the subject is affected or changed. In its simplest form, an experiment has three components: the independent variable, which the experimenter deliberately and systematically manipulates during the course of the experiment, the effect produced by the manipulation of the independent variable is called the dependent variable; all the variables except the independent variable are kept constant. An essential element of the experimental design is the development of the experimental and control situation prior to the actual experiment. We shall examine these and other concepts used in experimental research in a moment.

Experiments are typically designed to produce results that can be applied to groups other than those which participated in the experiment. Therefore, a crucial decision in the design of an experimental research project is the selection of those individuals who are to take part in the experiment. It is necessary that both the initial and the final discussion of any experiment should include information about the way in which the subjects were chosen and some indication of the groups to whom the findings might be reasonably applied.

Experiments in education can be conducted either in a classroom situation (a natural setting) or in a laboratory. In a laboratory, situation factors or variables can be controlled adequately, whereas experiments in a natural setting are less susceptible to control because of the many unknown and floating variables. It is true that educators prefer to undertake experiments in the classroom setting, arguing that, if one wants to know how to influence pupil learning in that setting, one should conduct experiments in the classroom. The most difficult task for the researcher, however, is to apply strict experimental methods and strategies to educational problems by controlling the extraneous variables while manipulating the independent variable.

There is no single, simple formula which can be prescribed for conducting experimental research under controlled conditions. However, there are a number of essential steps in experimental design which require close attention by the research worker. They are:

1   The investigator should, first of all, identify the problem and define it clearly. The source of the problem may emanate from personal experience, from reading the relevant literature, or from discussions with other educators or social scientists. For example, the researcher may feel on the basis of experience that students who are taught by the discussion method have a better understanding of controversial issues than those taught by the lecture method. A literature search may provide the basis for reformulating initial ideas as well as for forming new ones. Thus, definition of a problem involves the evaluation not just of the concepts to be utilized, but of the propositions and theories as well.

2   The investigator should then formulate an hypothesis or hypotheses in clear and unambiguous terms. In some cases, this or these may be best stated in the form of the null hypothesis (see the Glossary). He or she may even wish to simply pose broad questions at the initial stage.

3   The experimenter should identify as many variables as possible which are likely to affect the understanding of students with regard to controversial issues, and should decide which of these are to be manipulated. This process must be completed before the experiment begins. In moving from problem definition to experimental design, the implications of the general research objectives must be outlined in order to make decisions on specific procedures.

4   The next step is to make a list of all possible non-experimental variables that might contaminate the experiment. The investigator has to decide how best to control them.

5   The researcher's next step is to select an experimental design which constitutes the blueprint for the collection and analysis of the data. It is also important to keep in mind the limitations of the experimental design selected for the application. The development of a research design,

however, does not necessarily move the investigator toward more highly structured techniques.

6   At the same time as the researcher considers the design for the experiment, he or she must consider the sample of subjects who will be involved in the study. Questions such as the size of the sample, their ability, age, sex, and so on will have to be decided. It will also be necessary to decide how to obtain representative samples of the chosen population, how to divide these subjects into groups (the experimental and control groups) who will be treated differently and then compared. In assigning subjects to groups for the experiment, investigators must adopt a system that operates independently of their personal judgment and of the characteristics of the subjects themselves. (See Chapter 8 for a discussion of some of the problems in the area of sampling.)

7   The next task of the investigator is to decide about the tests, techniques or instruments to be used to evaluate the outcome of the experiment. If existing tools are not satisfactory, new tests will have to be developed in accordance with the requirements of the research design. These tests must be evaluated by reference to the concepts of reliability and validity (see the Glossary).

8   The procedures for data collection should be outlined. In order to ascertain that the experimental methods will work, it is always advisable to conduct a pilot experiment with a small group of subjects. This trial experiment will enable the investigator to test the instruments and/or techniques as well as the research design.

9   At this point, the scene is set to conduct the final experiment in a well-planned way. The statistical or null hypothesis, whichever has been formulated, must be stated at this stage.

10   Finally, the data obtained should be processed and analysed in order to produce an appraisal of the effect which is assumed to exist. The application of an appropriate test of significance will be necessary to determine the degree of confidence that can be placed on the results of the experiment. In light of these, the confirmation or rejection of the hypothesis/es is likely to be stated in terms of probability rather than certainty. Most social scientists accept this, but they are also aware that this type of methodology has only minor applications in the study of many educational problems in the classroom context.

Terms Used in Experimental Research Design

An experiment involves the comparison of a particular treatment (the independent variable) with a different treatment or with no treatment. In a simple conventional experiment, two groups of individuals are required. These are referred to as the *experimental* and *control groups*. As will be considered more fully presently, the two groups are matched as nearly or closely as possible. The 'experimental group' is exposed to the influence of a particular treatment; the 'control group' is not. It should be remembered that the control group is basically similar or comparable (but not necessarily, identical) to the experimental group. Observations or measurements are then made to determine what change or changes have occurred in the experimental group as compared with the control group.

Experiments are not always designed to make a treatment/non-treatment comparison. In other words, the control group is not an essential ingredient in the experimental model. There are many situations in which researchers are concerned with comparing the efficiency of two types of instructional method. For example, in an experiment exploring the relative efficiency of the lecture method as compared to the discussion method in teaching humanities to students, there are really no experimental and control groups. In this example, each group is subjected to a different treatment. The treatment refers to the method of teaching, perhaps lecture versus discussion. On the other hand, if a researcher is investigating the impact of a new curriculum programme on pupils' critical thinking, the control group becomes an essential element in the experimental design. In this case, the hypothesis will be formulated to find out whether the group exposed to the new curriculum programme shows superior critical thinking skills to the group which had not had that exposure. Pupils participating in the new programme will form the experimental group and others who do not take part will be treated as the control or non-experimental group. The decision about whether or not to employ a control group is not only about the researcher's judgment but is dictated by the type of hypothesis being investigated.

It must be emphasized that whether an experimental design uses a control group (receiving no treatment) or two experimental groups (each receiving a different treatment) the research worker must try to make the two groups equivalent in respect of the factors that may influence the dependent variable, except for the factor or factors chosen as the independent variable. In practice, it is extremely difficult to select two groups from the population who are equivalent or comparable in all respects. However, various methods of equating the different groups are employed and we shall briefly consider some of them that are used in educational research.

Randomization is perhaps the simplest and most economical way of assigning individuals to groups. This can be achieved by a pure chance selection of subjects from a given population. The procedure involves assigning individuals to the experimental and control groups in such a way that the two groups are reasonably similar.

If two groups are required for the study, randomization can be achieved by drawing names from a hat. When more than two groups are required, a table of random numbers can be employed. The principle of randomization is based on the assumption that differences between groups will tend to cancel each other out. This assumption is more sustainable in the case of large groups than when smaller groups are used.

Randomization attempts to provide an effective method of eliminating bias that might otherwise enter into the experimental design and of minimizing the influence of extraneous variables. However, it is up to the researcher to decide, depending upon the circumstances, as to when and what kind of randomization should be used. He or she is the only person who is in a position to ascertain whether subjects should be selected randomly, or/and individuals should be randomly assigned to different treatments, or/and experimental treatments should be randomly assigned to selected groups.

Matching is another procedure for equating groups. This is done by selecting pairs or groups with similar characteristics and assigning one of each to the experimental group and the other to the control group. Perhaps this is not the most efficient procedure of equating individuals in the experimental and control groups. There are various problems associated with this method. First, matching is a complex task. In order to make the groups as comparable as possible, it is necessary to match them on a number of characteristics. The researcher should have a large number of individuals in the initial pool because the matching process usually results in a number of them being excluded because a matching subject is not available. Thus, the final group (or groups) may not adequately represent the population, from which it has been drawn.

Another problem in this procedure is that in many studies the researcher is not sure about which characteristics are relevant and, hence, about which variables need to be matched. Because of this uncertainty, research workers in the field of social sciences, particularly in education, are often faced with the problem of deciding what variables should be controlled or minimized.

A number of procedures have been utilized to match individuals or equate groups. Each seems to have various limitations and problems associated with it. Many writers suggest that this method should be avoided unless absolutely essential. We believe, however, that it should be left to the judgment of the researcher to decide about the most practical and appropriate procedure to be used in his or her particular situation.

Because of the problems in randomization or matching techniques, a statistical method known as *analysis of covariance* (ANCOVA) is sometimes used to equate the groups on certain relevant variables identified prior to the investigation. This method tries to eliminate initial differences on several variables between the experimental and control groups by covariance techniques. In this method, pre-test mean scores are used as covariates. Analysis of covariance is often useful for educational research, especially in the classroom setting. Researchers who wish to use this method are strongly recommended a specialist handbook on statistical techniques used in educational research, such as Peers (1996).

In the *repeated measures* design, each subject takes both pre- and post-tests and thus, differences between groups can be eliminated as a source of error. The advantage of this method is that only a few subjects are required for the study because several measures can be used for each subject. One main assumption in this design is that no differential transfer of training occurs at the post-test stage as a result of the pre-test. Therefore, differences between the experimental and the control groups can be eliminated. The most difficult part of the repeated measurement design is its inability to control or eliminate the influence of such extraneous variables as instrumentation, specific events between the first and second testing, maturation, and tools or instruments, that are outdated and/or were developed in a different cultural setting.

The experimental condition, introduced in experimental research, is often referred to as the *treatment*. A treatment is a type of independent variable which the researcher manipulates in an attempt to ascertain its relationship to observed phenomena. In the simplest type of educational study, differences between the presence or absence of a particular condition or individual behaviour are explored, and this would require a comparison between two levels (absence or presence) of a particular treatment. There may be more than one independent variable in a particular study, although all are not essentially manipulated by the experimenter. There are also more complicated experimental designs involving a multitude of independent variables (treatments) and the researcher may be interested in studying the interaction of these treatments. For example, if the treatment is a teaching strategy using a pack of teaching materials, the researcher may wish to explore not only the effect of teaching on student learning but also the effects on the learning process of varying amounts of exposure to the teaching strategy and the material. In this case, the researcher has to manipulate both the type and amount of treatment.

In an experimental study, variables are the characteristics that are manipulated, controlled or observed by the experimenter. The variable that is deliberately and systematically manipulated (a teaching method, for example) so that its effects may be measured, assessed or observed, is called the *independent variable*. The effect produced or the change in behaviour that results from the manipulation of the independent variable is called the *dependent variable*. In other words, the dependent variable is that characteristic which is affected or influenced by the treatment (the independent variable), that is, the outcome of the experiment. In most educational research programmes, the dependent variable is the measured change in pupil behaviour attributable to the influence of the independent variable. It should be mentioned that, depending on the type of experimental design, there may be more than one dependent variable, just as there may be more than one independent variable.

There are many types of educational research in which it is notoriously difficult to establish the relationship between the independent and dependent variables. One of the crucial reasons is that certain floating variables which cannot be controlled may have a significant influence on the outcome. Such variables intervene between the treatment and the effect. For example, in a computer assisted learning experiment, the researcher is interested in determining the effect of immediate feedback upon student learning. He or she knows from the experience of other studies that there are certain factors which may affect the relationship, even though they cannot be observed directly. These *intervening variables* may be fatigue, boredom, anxiety, and so on. However, the researcher must not ignore the possible existence of such variables and efforts should be made to minimize their influence through careful design of the experiment.

Extraneous variables are those uncontrolled variables (e.g. the subjects' environments or personality characteristics) that hinder attributing all differences found in the dependent variable to the independent variable. These variables are not explicitly taken into account in the research design. Many educational research findings are of questionable validity because no attempt has been made to minimize the effect of extraneous variables. There is no denying the fact that it is impossible to control or eliminate the influence of all extraneous variables, particularly in educational research.

The term 'extraneous', as used in this context, can perhaps be best explained by means of an illustration. A researcher wished to study the effectiveness of three methods of teaching about race relations. In order to do this, 60 year 10 pupils were selected. The researcher was unable to randomize or control such variables as teacher competence or enthusiasm or prejudice. The criterion of effectiveness was attitude change measured by scores on a standardized test. At the end of one school term, the attitude scores of the three groups were compared. It would seem clear that many extraneous variables (e.g. differences in teachers in this example) precluded valid conclusions about the relative effectiveness of the independent variables which were three teaching methods. Statistical methods exist that can be used to estimate the extent to which the resulting difference between the three methods of teaching about race relations can be considered to be reliable and not simply a result of differences between the teachers involved.

As mentioned earlier, in social science research (including educational research) conducted outside the laboratory, many extraneous variables are present in the environment or are generated by the experimental design. Although these variables cannot be completely eliminated or controlled, the research worker must try to identify as many variables as possible so that he or she is able to exercise sufficient control to make the findings interpretable. Campbell and Stanley (1963) have provided researchers with an excellent characterization of experimental validity. According to them, there are two types of experimental validity — internal and external.

Internal validity deals with such questions as: 'Did the treatment really make a difference to the dependent variable?', 'How can the investigator be sure that it was the experimental treatment that made a difference in the outcome between the groups?' *External validity* is concerned with the generalizability or representativeness of the research findings. It provides an answer to the question, 'How far can the research findings be generalized?' That is, to which populations, samples, situations, events or experimental variables can the observed, assessed or measured effect be generalized?

The questions concerning internal validity cannot be answered by the researcher with any confidence unless the research design provides sufficient control of extraneous variables. He or she must therefore attempt to determine whether the changes in the dependent variable were not influenced by extraneous and uncontrolled factors. The extent to which this objective is achieved is a measure of the internal validity of the experiment. It must be recognized that the attainment of both internal and maximum external validity is considered as the most skilful experimental design even though, in practice, it is extremely difficult to achieve.

Campbell (1957) identified a number of extraneous variables that must be controlled. We shall consider some of these variables which can affect the internal validity of the experiment. The interactive effects of these factors with the treatment can affect the external validity of the experimental findings. The following factors seem to pose a threat to the internal validity:

- History — in a conventional pre- and post-test design, some external event or situation beyond the control of the researcher may have a favourable or disturbing effect upon the performance of the subjects. The appearance of these extra-experimental uncontrolled factors is referred to as the confounding effect upon the treatment. If this confounding effect is a specific event, action or situation, it is called history.
- Maturation — individuals change in many different ways over a period of time and the possibility exists that these changes may be confused with the influence of the experimental treatment being studied. Thus, maturational effects are systematic and orderly over a period of time. It is true to say that, in certain situations, it is difficult to determine whether the improved performance over a period of time is due to the experimental variable, to maturation, or to an interaction of the independent variable with maturation.
- Testing — the process of pre-testing prior to the experiment may influence the performance on post-test. There are other problems associated with testing. Tests may make the subjects more aware of any hidden purposes of the researcher and may act as a stimulus for change.
- Instrumentation — in many studies, unreliable and/or outdated tools or techniques are used to describe aspects of human behaviour. This presents a threat to the validity of an experiment. If inaccurate or inconsistent observational techniques are used, a serious element of error is introduced. If interviewers are used to study behavioural changes in subjects, changes in their criteria over a period of time may provide unreliable and invalid information.
- Regression — statistical regression is a phenomenon that sometimes functions in a pre- and post-test design and makes the results difficult to interpret. Testees who score highest at the pre-test stage are likely to score relatively lower at the second test, whereas those who score lowest on the pre-test are likely to score higher at the post-test stage. In a pre-test post-test design, there is a normal regression towards the mean. The researcher should be able to recognize the effect of this regression in the interpretation of results.
- Bias in the selection of subjects — the selection of subjects is the most important aspect in a piece of experimental research. As pointed out earlier, some form of randomization is essential in order to evaluate properly the influence of the treatment variable. Selection bias may be introduced in the experiment if, for instance, intact classes are used as experimental or control groups. However, if randomization is not possible, matching can be used to make the groups more comparable.
- Experimental mortality — mortality, or loss of sample, is another extraneous variable. Supposing that experimental and control groups were equal to begin with, if any subjects drop out of one group during the experimental

period, the researcher may not be able to know what kinds of members dropped out and this loss may affect the outcome of the study. That is, any differences between the experimental and control groups on the post-test may be attributable to the biased composition of the samples. In a long term study, the loss of subjects is fairly common. In smaller and shorter studies, student absence on the day of a test critical to the experiment can cause complications.

• Contamination — this is a type of bias introduced when the experimenter has some previous knowledge about the individuals participating in the study. This knowledge of participant characteristics may affect the objectivity of the researcher's judgment. In educational research, contamination can be minimized if outside observers are utilized to assess or rate the subjects without any prior knowledge of their traits or characteristics.

Types of Experimental Design

As noted earlier, experimental research is concerned with studying relationships between independent and dependent variables. Selection of a particular experimental design should be determined by the purposes of the study, the type of variables to be manipulated, the way the variables are to be manipulated and the circumstances under which the experiment is to be conducted. The design should clearly state how subjects are to be chosen for the experimental and control groups, the way extraneous variables are to be controlled and the type of statistical techniques to be used for analysing the data.

There are many different types of experimental designs available which can be utilized by researchers. In the section that follows, we outline a few simple experimental designs that have proved useful in educational research.

In *the single-group design*, a reliable form of pre- and post-testing is necessary. Broadly, it consists of three stages. The first stage is the administration of the pre-test measuring the dependent variable. In the next stage, the experimental treatment, or the independent variable, is applied. At the third or final stage, a post-test is applied, again measuring the dependent variable. The amount of change from pre- to post-test is obtained and a statistical technique is applied to ascertain whether the change, if any, is significant. Thus, this design uses a single group which is tested twice. The following is a paradigm for this design:

Pre-test	**Independent variable**	**Post-test**
Test 1	X	Test 2
	(treatment)	

This design has a number of weaknesses. The researcher, by examining the overall performance on the pre-test and the post-test, assumes that any gains between the two testing situations are attributable to the experimental treatment. As mentioned earlier, it is extremely difficult for the researcher to determine whether the change or gain between the pre- and post-test is produced by the experimental treatment or by pre-testing, the instrument used, statistical regression, maturation, extraneous variables, and so on. Because of the absence of a control group, it cannot be ascertained whether the above-mentioned factors have influenced the outcome of the experiment. Thus, the design may lack internal validity. Although the single-group design does not meet all the requirements for 'scientific' experimental methodology, it is often used for preliminary research, or when it is impossible to obtain a control group.

In the *two groups design* (post-test only), both control and experimental groups are used. The two groups are equated by randomization. At the conclusion of the experiment, the dependent variable is measured. No pre-test is given. The mean test scores of the experimental and control groups are subjected to a t-test. The assumption is that, since the subjects are randomly assigned to the experimental and control groups, the two groups will differ only to the extent that random samples from the same population differ. The design is shown below:

Group	Pre-test	Treatment	Post test
Experimental	—	X	Test
Control	—	—	Test

This design is widely used in educational research, because of its efficiency in terms of time and economy. Randomization is one of the main strengths in the design which gives reasonable assurance about the statistical equivalence of the two groups prior to the experiment. The influence of extraneous variables should be balanced in the two groups. The design may be susceptible to low internal validity because of experimental mortality. A major limitation of this design is that it cannot assess change.

In the *classic design* (pre-test post-test control group design), the experimental and control groups are often equated by randomization and hence the problem of selection bias is minimized. If the researcher is in any doubt that the groups are not comparable, analysis of covariance can be used to adjust for any initial differences between the groups. Pre-tests are administered prior to the application of the treatment. At the conclusion of the experiment, the groups are re-tested. The difference between the pre-test and post-test is obtained for each group and these difference scores are compared by subjecting them to a t-test in order to ascertain whether the treatment produced a greater change than no treatment. Thus, the design allows the researcher to study change over a period of time. The design is as follows:

Group	Pre-test	Treatment	Post-test
Experimental	Test 1	X	Test 2
Control	Test 1	—	Test 2

Although this design has strong internal validity, making generalizations from the results introduces some problems. That is to say, the main concern is about external validity. Since both the experimental and control groups are pre-tested, it is not known whether or not the same findings would be obtained from other individuals who were selected from the same populations but who were not pre-tested. The problem, therefore, is not lack of control, but of generalization. There is always a possibility of an interaction occurring between the pre-test and the experimental treatment. For example, if a pre-test increases or decreases the subject's sensitivity to the treatment, then the findings may be unrepresentative of the impact of the experimental variable on the unpre-tested population from which the experimental sample was drawn. The problem becomes obvious in such studies as those concerned with attitude change, values, and so on. It should be mentioned that the pre-test effects are largely dependent on the nature and dimension of the study. For instance, in a piece of research concerned with racial attitudes, the effects of pre-testing may be more marked than in a study concerned with cognitive abilities. Another shortcoming of this design is that control subjects are likely to be contaminated by experimental subjects. Although the control group is not exposed to the experimental treatment, they will have the opportunity of interacting with the experimental subjects between the pre- and post-tests. For example, in a school-based study, experimental and control group subjects meet in many situations except when the experimental pupils receive specific treatment.

In *two or more experimental groups design* studies, the researcher is concerned with two or more experimental groups whose performance has to be compared with the control group. One of the most popular of such designs is the randomized groups design, which involves the random assignment of individuals to each of the experimental groups as well as to the control group. A design for three experimental groups and one control group is shown below:

Group	Pre-test	Treatment	Post-test
Experimental 1	Test 1	X	Test 2
Experimental 2	Test 1	X	Test 2
Experimental 3	Test 1	X	Test 2
Control	Test 1	—	Test 2

Let us assume that the independent variable is a film aimed at improving race relations in society. The length of the film varied between the three experimental groups. An attitude test is administered to all four groups before and after the experimental manipulation, to which the control group is not exposed. The test data can then be analysed by comparing the change at the post-test stage in the three experimental groups with that manifested in the control group. In this way, the researcher can compare the effects of different degrees of exposure to the film. This design has similar weaknesses to that of the classical design.

Solomon (1949) developed the *two control group design*, which is an extension of the classical design described earlier. In it, there are two control groups and one experimental group. Subjects are randomly assigned to the three groups. The advantage of this design becomes evident in situations where the pre-test is expected to interfere with the experimental manipulation. The second control group is not pre-tested but is exposed to the experimental treatment. Their post-test scores are then used to determine the interaction effect. Thus, the Solomon design of a pre- and post-test experiment with two control groups is aimed at providing both an estimate of the magnitude of any such interaction and an estimate of the effect of the experimental treatment alone. The design is as follows:

Group	Pre-test	Treatment	Post-test
Experimental	Test 1	X	Test 2
Control 1	Test 1	—	Test 2
Control 2	—	X	Test 2

In the *Solomon four group design*, there are two control groups and two experimental groups. Individuals are randomly assigned to the four groups. The effects of the pre-test are controlled because only one control and one experimental group are given pre-tests but all four groups are post-tested. Expressed in the same format as before, we have:

Group	Pre-test	Treatment	Post-test
Experimental 1	Test 1	X	Test 2
Control 1	Test 1	—	Test 2
Experimental 2	—	X	Test 2
Control 2	—	—	Test 2

It should be noted that, although the third group is exposed to the experimental manipulation, it functions as a control group. One of the strengths of the four group design is that it can make several comparisons to study the impact of the independent variable. Since only one half of the groups are pre-tested, the investigator can ascertain the impact of the pre-test; he or she can determine the effect of the treatment in both the pre-test and non pre-test situations, as well as assess the interaction effects of pre-test and experimental treatment. The main limitation of this design is the problem encountered in implementing it in the practical situation. The researcher requires sufficient time and resources to conduct two experiments simultaneously — that is to say, one with pre-tests, and one without pre-tests. There can also be the problem of locating enough subjects needed for this type of design.

The experimental designs described so far take into account only one variable at a time. In other words, the researcher systematically manipulates one independent variable in order to produce an effect on the dependent variable. However, very often in the educational field, the researcher is interested in studying the effect of two or more variables simultaneously. In such cases a *factorial design* is employed. This type of design employs two or more independent varibles and each is varied in two or more ways. Thus, in a factorial design, the researcher manipulates two or more variables simultaneously, in order to study the independent effect of each variable on the dependent variables, as well as the effects due to the interaction among the several variables.

Factorial designs have been developed with varying levels of complexity. The simple one is the 2 × 2 design. The number of digits shows the number of independent variables being studied. The numerical value of the digits shows the number of levels for each independent variable. Suppose that the researcher is interested in comparing the effectiveness of two types of teaching strategies (discussion and lecture method) on pupil learning in the humanities in secondary schools. His experience suggests that the effects of these methods may be different according to the length of time spent, for example, whether lessons are say, 60 minutes or 30 minutes in length. Thus, in this experimental design, there are two experimental treatments (discussion and lecture methods) and two conditions of learning (one hour lessons and half hour ones). There are then four combinations of variables.

The researcher assigns the subjects randomly to one of four experimental groups. Group 1 is involved in 60-minute lessons of discussion; group 2 in 30-minute lessons of discussion; group 3 is assigned to 60-minutes of lecture, and group 4 to 30 minutes. At the end of the school term, pupil learning in the humanities (the dependent variable) is assessed by means of a standardized test. In this design, each of the two independent variables has two values. The factorial design 2 × 2, for assessing the effects of two methods of teaching on pupil learning is shown below. Remember that a 2 × 2 design requires four groups of subjects:

Time spent each week	Method of teaching	
	Discussion	**Lecture**
60 minutes	X	X
30 minutes	X	X

The four cells represent the scores of the four groups on the dependent variable, i.e. the humanities achievement test. By using this design, the researcher can first determine the main effects of the two independent variables (discussion and lecture methods) and then the main effects on the achievement scores of time spent each week.

There are a number of advantages in the use of the factorial design. First, the researcher can treat as independent variables what would otherwise be regarded as extraneous variables. Secondly, many independent factors can be considered simultaneously in a single study, which can result in savings in effort and work on the part of the researcher. Thirdly, the factorial design claims to have high internal validity. Fourthly, the interaction effects of many variables can be studied at the same time which is often essential in educational research.

The factorial design can, of course, be extended to achieve more complex experiments. For instance, an experiment using four teaching strategies, with subjects of three ability levels and five age groups would be represented as 4 × 3 × 5 factorial design. As the number of experimental treatments is increased, the number of experimental groups required also increases, since all kinds of one independent variable are considered in combination with all kinds of the other independent variables. However, such an experiment becomes very complex because a great many factors need to be manipulated or controlled simultaneously. Moreover, it is true that the complex statistical analysis involved can now be handled by computers, but the data have to be presented in a form acceptable to the computer and this, in itself, can generate a great deal of work that can be both laborious and tedious. It is advisable that beginners in educational research should try to answer their questions with the simplest possible designs consistent with the issue being investigated.

Sometimes, the researcher is compelled to depart from the strict rules of experimental design, because administrative conditions, limited resources, or the like, restrict what is possible. For example, the researcher might seek to assign year 10 pupils at random to three separate groups to be exposed to three different teaching strategies. However, the school may not permit this, saying that the pupils have already been assigned to different classes for teaching purposes. Under these circumstances, the researcher cannot conduct a 'true' experiment, although he or she may still do a study that comes close to being an experimental research project. Such research studies are called *quasi-experiments*. The term, first introduced by Campbell and Stanley (1963), has been widely used in the social sciences. In quasi-experiments, the conditions are taken as they are found in naturally occurring contexts. The 'true' experiment, on logical grounds, necessarily yields more certain knowledge and understanding than the quasi-experiment, and whenever possible, should be carried out in preference to the quasi-experiment.

References

ADELMAN, C. (1993) 'Kurt Lewin and the origins of action research', *Educational Action Research*, **1**, pp. 7–24.

ALTRICHTER, H. (1993) 'The concept of quality in action research: Giving practitioners a voice in educational research', in SCHRATZ, M. (ed.) *Qualitative Voices in Educational Research*, London: Falmer Press.

ANDERSON, G. (1994) *Fundamentals of Educational Research*, London: Falmer Press.

BARNES, J.B. (1960) *Educational Research for Classroom Teachers*, New York: G.P. Putnam's Sons.

BARZUN, J. and GRAFF, H.F. (1970) *The Modern Researcher*, New York: Harcourt Brace.

BEARD, R.M. (1969) *An Outline of Piaget's Developmental Psychology*, London: Routledge and Kegan Paul.

BECKER, H.S. (1968) 'Observation: Social observation and social case studies', in SILLS, D.L. (ed.) *International Encyclopedia of the Social Sciences*, Volume II, New York: Macmillan.

BERELSON, B. (1952) *Content Analysis in Communication Research*, Glencoe, ILL.: Free Press.

BORG, W.R. and GALL, M.D. (1983) *Educational Research: An Introduction*, (4th edition), New York and London: Longman.

BURGESS, R.G. (1983) *Experiencing Comprehensive Education: A Study of Bishop McGregor School*, London: Methuen.

CAMPBELL, D.T. (1957) 'Factors relevant to the validity of experiments in social settings', *Psychological Bulletin*, LIV, pp. 297–312.

CAMPBELL, D.T. and STANLEY, J.C. (1963) 'Experimental and quasi-experimental designs for research on teaching', in GAGE, N.L. (ed.) *Handbook of Research on Teaching*, Chicago: Rand McNally and Co.

CHALL, J. (1967) *Learning to Read: The Great Debate*, New York: McGraw Hill.

COHEN, L. and MANION, L. (1989) *Research Methods in Education*, 3rd edition, London: Routledge.

DOUGLAS, J.W.B. (1967) *The Home and the School: A Study of Ability and Attainment in the Primary School*, England: Panther Books Ltd.

EISNER, E.W. (1979) 'The use of qualitative forms of evaluation for improving educational practice', *Educational Evaluation and Policy Analysis*, **1**, 6, pp. 11–19.

ELLIOTT, J. (1978) 'What is action research in schools?', *Journal of Curriculum Studies*, **10**, pp. 355–57.

ELLIOTT, J. (1981) *Action-research: A Framework for Self-evaluation in Schools*, TIQL-Working Paper No. 1, Mimeo, Cambridge.

ENNIS, R.H. (1975) 'Children's ability to handle Piaget's propositional logic: A conceptual critique', *Review of Educational Research*, **45**, pp. 1–14.

FOWLER, F.J. (1993) *Survey Research Methods*, 2nd edition, Newbury Park, California: Sage.

GUILFORD, J.P. (1967) *The Nature of Human Intelligence*, New York: McGraw Hill.

HAMMERSLEY, M. (1994) 'Ethnography policy making and practice in Education', in HALPIN, D. and TROYNA, B. (eds) *Researching Education Policy*, London: Falmer Press.

HAMMERSLEY, M. and ATKINSON, P. (1992) *Ethnography: Principles in practice*, London: Routledge.

HAMMERSLEY, M., SCARTH, J. and WEBB, S. (1985) 'Developing and testing theory: The case of research of pupil learning and exams', in BURGESS, R.G. (ed.) *Issues in Educational Research*, London: Falmer Press.

HITCHCOCK, G. and HUGHES, D. (1989) *Research and the Teacher*, London: Routledge.

HÚSEN, T. (1967) (ed.) *International Study of Achievement in Mathematics*, New York: John Wiley and Sons.

JAHODA, M., DEUTSCH, M. and COOK, S. (1951) *Research Methods in Social Relations*, New York: Holt, Rinehart and Winston.

KEMMIS, S. (1982) 'Seven principles for programme evaluation in curriculum development and innovation', *Journal of Curriculum Studies*, **14**, 3, pp. 221–40.

KEMMIS, S. and MCTAGGART, R. (1988) *The Action Research Planner*, Geelong: Deakin University Press.

KOHLBERG, L. (1964) 'Development of moral character and moral ideology', in STEVENSON, H. (ed.) *Child Psychology*, 62nd Yearbook, National Society for the Study of Education: University of Chicago Press.

KOLUCHOVA, J. (1972) 'Severe deprivation in twins: A case study', *Journal of Child Psychology and Psychiatry*, **13**, pp. 107–14.

LEWIN, K. (1946) 'Action research and minority problems', in *Journal of Social Issues*, **2**, pp. 34–6.

LEWIN, K. (1952) 'Group decision and social change', in SWANSON, T.M., NEWCOMB, M. and HARTLEY, E.L. (eds) *Readings in Social Psychology*, New York: Holt.

LYND, R.S. and LYND, H.M. (1937) *Middletown in Transition*, New York: Harcourt, Brace and World Inc.

MARROW, A.J. (1969) *The Practical Theorist: The life and work of Kurt Lewin*, N.Y.: Basic Books.

MAYKUT, P. and MOREHOUSE, R. (1994) *Beginning Qualitative Research: A Philosophical and Practical Guide*, London: Falmer Press.

NEWSON, J. and NEWSON, E. (1965) *Infant Care in an Urban Community*, Harmondsworth: Penguin Books.

NEWSON, J. and NEWSON, E. (1970) *Four Years Old in an Urban Community*, London: Allen and Unwin.

NEWSON, H. and NEWSON, E. (1978) *Seven Years Old in the Home Environment*, Harmondsworth: Penguin Books.

NIXON, J. (1981) *A Teacher's Guide to Action Research*, London: Grant McIntyre.

PEERS, I.S. (1996) *Statistical Analysis for Education and Psychology Researchers*, London: Falmer Press.

PLATT, J. (1988) 'What case studies do?', in BURGESS, R.G. (ed.) *Studies in Qualitative Methodology*, Volume 1, London: Jai Press.

RICE, J.M. (1897) 'The futility of the spelling grind', *Forum 23*, April and June, pp. 163–72, 409–19.

RIST, R.C. (1975) 'Ethnographic techniques and the study of an Urban School', *Urban Education*, **10**, 1, pp. 86–108.

RUNYAN, W.M. (1982) *Life Histories and Psychobiography*, New York: Oxford University Press.

RUSK, R.R. (1912) *Introduction to Experimental Education*, London: Longman.

RUTTER, M., MAUGHAN, B., MORTIMORE, P. and OUSTON, J. (1979) *Fifteen Thousand Hours: Secondary Schools and Their Effects on Children*, Shepton Mallet: Open Books.

SCHRATZ, M. (1993) (ed.) *Qualitative Voices in Educational Research*, London: Falmer Press.

SOLOMON, R.L. (1949) 'Extension of control group design', *Psychological Bulletin*, XLVI, pp. 137–50.

SPINDLER, G. (1970) *Being an Anthropologist*, New York: Holt, Rinehart and Winston.

SPRADLEY, J. (1980) *Participant Observation*, New York: Holt, Rinehart and Winston.

STAKE, R.E. and DENNY, T. (1969) 'Needed concepts and techniques for utilizing more fully the potential of evaluation', in TYLER, R.W. (ed.) *Educational Evaluation: New Roles, New Means*, 68 Yearbook of the National Society for the Study of Education, Part II: University of Chicago Press.

TERMAN, L. and ODEN, M.H. (1959) *The Gifted Group at Mid-life*, Stanford: Stanford University Press.

THORNDIKE, E.L. (1924) 'Mental discipline in high school subjects', *Journal of Educational Psychology*, **15**, pp. 1–22, 83–98.

TRAVERS, R.M.W. (1978) *An Introduction to Educational Research*, 4th edition, New York: Macmillan.

TROYNA, B. (1994) 'Reforms, research and being reflexive about being reflective', in HALPIN, D. and TROYNA, B. (1994) *Researching Education Policy*, London: Falmer Press.

TROYNA, B. and CARRINGTON, B. (1990) *Education, Racism and Reform*, London: Routledge.

VERMA, G.K. (1980) *The Impact of Innovation*, Evaluation of the Humanities Curriculum Project, England: CARE: University of East Anglia Press.

WALKER, R. (1981) 'On the uses of fiction in education research', in SMETHERHAM, D. (ed.) *Practising Evaluation*, Driffield: Nafferton.

WATT, M.L. and WATT, D.L. (1993) 'Teacher research, action research: The Logo action research collaborative', in *Educational Action Research*, **1**, 1.

WEIS, L. (1992) 'Reflections on the researcher in a multicultural environment', in GRANT, C.A. (ed.) *Research and Multicultural Education*, London: Falmer Press.

WERNER, O. and SCHOEPFLE, G. (1987) *Systematic Fieldwork*, Volume I: *Foundations of Ethnography and Interviewing*, Beverley Hills, CA: Sage.

WEST, D.J. (1969) *Present Conduct and Future Delinquency*, London: Heinemann.

WILLIAM, D. and BLACK, P. (1996) 'Meanings and consequences: A basis for distinguishing formative and summative functions of assessment', *British Educational Research Journal*, **22**, 5.

WOLCOTT, H. (1988) 'Ethnographic research in education', in JAEGER, R.M. (ed.) *Complementary Methods for Research in Education*, Washington, DC: American Educational Research Association.

YOUNG, P.V. (1966) *Scientific Social Surveys and Research*, Englewood Cliffs, New Jersey: Prentice Hall.

ZEICHNER, K. (1987) 'Preparing reflective teachers: An overview of instructional strategies which have been employed in preservice teacher education', *International Journal of Educational Research*, **11**, pp. 565–75.

Chapter 6

Research Tools in Education

The previous chapter sought to characterize three main approaches to research in education. As was pointed out, those approaches could not be viewed as discrete ones, there being, in some cases, a fair degree of overlap between them. It was further pointed out that there was an even greater overlap between the research tools used. This was increasingly the case, because of the complexity of research design in more recent times. The present chapter seeks to address the research tools used in education, to consider their strengths and weaknesses, and to relate them to the approaches with which they are primarily, if not exclusively, associated.

Documentary and Content Analysis

This tool is most frequently employed in descriptive studies, although it may form part of any kind of research. It has been described as '. . . a research technique for the objective, systematic and quantitative description of the manifest content of communication' (Berelson, 1952) and, although this definition is over 40 years old, it has not been significantly improved upon by more recent researchers.

Content analysis is conducted to analyse documentary information. It 'refers to the systematic description of the contents of documents' (Anderson, 1994). According to Anderson, there are four common uses for content analysis:

- to describe the relative frequency and importance of certain topics;
- to evaluate bias, prejudice or propaganda in print materials;
- to assess the level of difficulty in reading materials;
- to analyse types of errors in students' work.

It simply means that content analysis involves counting concepts, words or occurrences in documents and presenting them in tabular form. It might be said that there are five main traditions which have utilized documentary sources in their work: historical studies, literacy studies, quantitative context analyses, ethnographic studies, and personal documentary research (Platt, 1981).

The content analysis technique can be applied to any form of communication. The raw materials are usually in written form, but radio and television programmes, pictures, tape-recordings of interviews, lessons or conversations, music, or anything which 'communicates' are all susceptible to its use. It lends itself to a wide range of research objectives. As such, it is a valuable tool in educational research (Bell, 1987). Since it can also provide valid results at various levels of sophistication in use, it is also an attractive tool for many post-graduate students. In its simplest form, it can provide frequency counts of things like spelling errors in the written work of students in schools. The teacher can analyse the work that a class has produced in free writing exercises and assemble a list which shows the most frequently misspelled words. Armed with this information, the teacher can employ remedial strategies designed to correct these errors. Publishers engaged in creating reading schemes for young children have conducted research to discover the most frequently used words in English at various ages as part of their strategy to make the stories accessible to young readers. Of course, some care has to be exercised in relying on the results of even these simple studies.

Children may well be uncertain how to spell the word that they would use for preference, and so use a less appropriate one about which they are more confident. Many schools encourage the use of personal dictionaries and some pupils may look up a word about which they are uncertain. This produces the correct result but does not necessarily mean that they will be able to spell it correctly next time. Many readers will have a group of words about whose spelling they remain uncertain, as has the writer; we have come to depend on the word processor's spelling checker to solve the problem. Most young children lack this useful facility, however, and their use of the easier alternative conceals the weakness from the teacher/researcher. It can also affect other objectives the teacher might have. Suppose, for example, the teacher was also interested in the extent of the pupils' active vocabulary and was using the same raw materials for the study. The use of the less appropriate but easier word would suggest that the pupils had a more restricted vocabulary than was really the case. Similarly, the work done by the publishers did not always have the looked-for results. The words the children read were certainly ones they were likely to recognize. Their carefully calculated repetition possibly helped the children to recognize and learn how to spell them. Unfortunately, the stories constructed from those words were sometimes so boring that no child with a lively mind would want to spend time reading them. Content analysis can also be used for a variety of more sophisticated tasks. For example, it could enable a researcher to show how and to what extent history textbooks used in British secondary schools changed their assessment of Japan between 1939 and the present day.

After the researcher has defined his or her research objectives, the first task will be to find the materials required for the study. In the case of the example suggested above, locating the textbooks will be time-consuming but not too difficult. In addition, whilst there is likely to be a good number of them, each book will be unlikely to devote more than one chapter to the matter under consideration. They will also have useful indexes so that the researcher can quickly find his or her way to the relevant passages and confidently ignore the rest. Let us suppose, however, that the intended project was to conduct a content analysis of children's comics produced over the same period with a view to discovering how they represented Japan to their readers. The volume of material to be found — all the comics printed over the last 60 years — is dauntingly large. Leaving aside the question of whether it would be possible to locate them all, the sheer volume of material is likely to be unmanageable.

It is necessary in cases like this to devise a plan by which the material can be sampled. Much the same considerations apply to this as to a sample for conducting a survey. The researcher has to be alert to the dangers of using an unrepresentative sample since this would bias the study's findings and damage them, probably fatally. The researcher might well decide to focus on the comics produced by one or two publishers, or perhaps on ones that were intended for a specified age range of readers. Even then, he or she may still be faced with more than can be managed in the time and with the resources available. It then becomes necessary to sample the materials. This can be done in a variety of ways but, essentially, it involves looking at issues of each title which are selected by a pre-determined scheme. This might be the first issue of each month or, by using a table of random numbers, selecting a sample of editions of manageable size from each year of publication. A further strategy is to set a particular time frame, for example, 'British comics published between 1945–55'. Ideally, the 'start' and 'end' years ought to be linked to related significant events, perhaps in terms of history or the politics of relations between the two countries, thus helping to provide a rationale for the time frame selection.

Once these decisions have been made, it will be necessary to develop a system for identifying and classifying the content. The form of this and the categories adopted will depend on the research objectives of the study. However, to pursue the example of the children's comics a little further, it is possible that the research will be interested in such matters as the extent to which notions of the exotic east existed and persist; the portrayal of the Japanese as enemies in World War II and the extent to and manner in which these perceptions were modified in the decades following it; crucially, perhaps, whether the Japanese were still perceived as enemies in an ongoing economic war in much the same way as they were in the shooting war, and so on.

Content analysis studies rely heavily on statistical procedures to summarize the data and make interpretations possible. The most favoured approach is to use frequency counts of specific usages found in the materials studied and their relative proportions. So, for example, the frequencies of words clustering round concepts like 'strangeness', 'cunning', 'cleverness', 'ruthlessness', 'bravery', 'ingenuity' and their antonyms would be arrived at and used to support the researcher's findings.

The examples used above have assumed quite large scale studies because they have provided opportunities to introduce matters such as sampling. The method is equally suitable for small scale studies and might profitably be considered by post-graduate research students. As Borg and Gall (1983) observed, books, periodicals and other documents are usually more accessible than human subjects, the data can be analysed directly from the page without having to collect it first through inter-views or other processes and there is a reduced danger of bias in its collection and interpretation.

Case Study

A case study approach in educational research is likely to be personal. For example, an in-depth study of teaching and learning is likely to unravel opinions and behaviours of teachers, students, administrators and others and expose them to unusually intense scrutiny (Borg and Gall, 1983). For this reason, all case study research has a special obligation to provide legal and ethical protection to the subjects. A study of ideas, beliefs or actions in an educational institution can be seen to be an invasion of privacy and publication of the findings can create tensions between colleagues, students and the general public. The use of fictitious names is a not uncommon device for creating an air of 'realism' without compromising the identity of individual institutions or people. *Hightown Grammar* (Lacey, 1970) is a classic example.

Case study is an umbrella term for a whole range of research techniques or methods. It has been widely used in many disciplines. It is much more than a description of an individual, event or situation. It is primarily concerned with the interactions between various events and situations. As Nisbet and Watt (1984) pointed out, 'sometimes it is only by taking a practical instance that we can obtain a full picture of this interaction'. Although interviews and observations are the most commonly used methods in case studies, other techniques can also be employed depending on the nature of the inquiry. For most people, the main characteristic of case study is its concentration on a particular instance in order to reveal the ways in which events or situations come together to create particular types of outcomes (Hitchcock and Hughes, 1989).

One of the strengths of a case study is that it allows the researcher to focus on a specific instance or situation and to explore the various interactive processes at work within that situation. Large scale quantitative studies can be very effective in identifying the outcomes of, for example, a major innovation in the curriculum but such studies do not readily lend themselves to exploring the interactive processes involved in the introduction of that innovation. Critics of case study work point to the fact that information obtained by this method cannot be generalized and that there is always a danger of the findings being distorted as a result of unrecognized biases in the researcher. Its supporters stress the meaningfulness of the data, gathered as it is from the interaction between people and events in their natural environments. Claims have been made that, if a case study is carried out systematically and rigorously, the interactive processes that it reveals can be generalized. However, it needs to be emphasized that the case study is one of the more difficult methods to use in educational research. Since education is a process, it is necessary to employ a case study approach that is process-oriented, flexible, and adaptable (Anderson, 1994).

A case study is a detailed study of an individual or a group — however that group may be defined — or an event. The emphasis in case study is on explanation, keeping in mind the issue being explored. To be of any value, a case study involves the collection of very extensive data on the person or group being studied. The kind of data and the methods of collection will depend on the nature of the case being studied. In educational research, the three most common forms of case study are observational, historical and clinical studies.

An observational study is commonly concerned with the in-depth study of an institution, usually a school; a classroom; or a group of children defined by some common characteristic, their ethnicity perhaps. The approach has much in common with ethnographic studies. Like them, it is time-consuming since its prime value lies in the richness of the data that are accumulated and that can only be acquired as a result of long and painstaking observation and recording followed by subsequent analysis. It is also unlikely that the researcher will begin with a hypothesis to be tested, though it may be that following analysis of the data, one or more hypotheses will be generated which will repay further investigation using other research techniques. It also suffers from similar drawbacks, chief among which is its lack of generalizability. However carefully the subject or subjects of the study are selected, there can be no guarantee that they are typical of other, apparently similar subjects. It is therefore dangerous to draw general conclusions from a case study. Nor can a case study be truly replicated: another group may appear to be very similar but it will not be identical.

Historical case studies usually chart the progress of an educational institution, frequently chosen from schools that have achieved prominence or notoriety. Such studies are heavily dependent on documentary evidence, although it may be possible to supplement this with interview materials. Clinical case studies are usually concerned with the problems of individuals and are usually undertaken by psychologists. However, a teacher might engage in a case study of a child with behavioural problems in an attempt to discover the root causes of the child's problems. In case study, various types of evidence are collected and hence it embraces the whole range of formal and informal instruments, from questionnaires to observation schedules (Anderson, 1994).

Surveys

The survey has come to be one of the most widely employed tools in educational research. It is a form of planned data collection for the purposes of explaining or answering questions as a guide to action. It is favoured by both post-graduate and professional researchers alike as a means of gaining information. It depends on the proposition that data obtained from a sample of the population under examination will be generalizable to the whole 'population' (see the Glossary). In conducting a survey, the researcher will probably employ questionnaires and, probably, interviews. In this way, the results from one form of data will help to inform and refine the other data, so that the conclusions drawn are meaningful, precise and representative. These are considered in the next two sections of this chapter. Alternatively, the survey may be of documentary evidence. For example, a study might be made of a sample of schools from a Local Education Authority to determine truancy rates for specified groups of students. As a means of obtaining data, the survey has much to commend itself to the researcher. The information collected is controllable and focused on the research issues. It also comes in readily quantifiable form and well-tried and comprehensive computer software has been developed to enable statistical analyses, which were once both complex and time-consuming, to be made quickly and painlessly.

There are various types of survey, as discussed in the literature. The most simple one is the census type of survey where the views of a representative sample on a specific issue/issues are obtained and then inferences are made about the population as a whole. It should be remembered that such surveys simply tell us how many members of the population hold a certain view on a particular issue. The findings do not tell us 'why' members hold particular views. The purpose of such surveys may be described as essentially fact-finding. An illustration of the 'goal' of surveys can be offered by reference to election polls. It is possible to find out the popularity of political parties by monitoring the opinion of people at various stages of time.

Surveys cannot provide a causal connection; they can simply indicate associations and therefore researchers must be careful in their analysis and conclusion of the findings. At this point, it is necessary to note that much educational research involving surveys, certainly at post-graduate level, involves samples drawn from children and young people at school. This has some advantages for the researchers. For example, the subjects are potentially more accessible and controllable than if they were adults. On the other hand, it presents them with additional responsibilities and obligations. These aspects are important and are dealt with in Chapter 7.

For most educational researchers, the object of the survey is to discover things about their sample population as it is at the time, although this information may, of course, include subjects' recollections of the past or expectations for the future. This factor may have some impact on the nature of the survey and the means by which the data are collected. What needs to be borne in mind is that the perceptions and experiences of the people making up the sample can change over time. The speed of these changes will vary depending on the nature of the information sought and the ages of the respondents but, as a general principle, the data collection should be conducted in as short a time as can be managed to avoid the risk of external events over which the researcher has no control influencing responses, while the survey is in progress. For example, if a survey was in progress to discover the problems foreseen by headteachers arising from growing class sizes and the government were to announce that it had established a target of no more than 25 pupils per class in primary schools, the responses of those participating in the survey before and after the announcement would almost certainly be very different.

The nature of the sample to be surveyed will depend on the objectives of the study for which it is designed. For example, the study might be concerned with the attitudes of 16-year-old school leavers towards work, their career ambitions and expectations. For this, it will be necessary to build up a representative sample and then to construct a suitable questionnaire. Another study might wish to find out how the attitudes to work, career ambitions and expectations of adolescents and young people change over time. This can be approached in two ways.

For practical reasons, the commoner approach is to draw up a sample which contains groups of respondents at various ages — perhaps 12-, 15- and 18-year-olds, to construct a questionnaire containing the same items for all of them and then to see how their responses differ with age. The obvious weakness of this approach is that, however much care is taken to select respondents who are similar in each group except for their ages, there is always the possibility that hidden differences between the groups will materially affect the findings. Theoretically, a longitudinal survey will avoid this problem.

In a longitudinal survey, the researcher constructs a sample of 12-year-olds (frequently referred to as a 'cohort') and administers the questionnaire. This is repeated with the same group when they are 15, and again at 18, using the same questionnaire. By using the same respondents at each age the problems arising from the previous approach are avoided. Unfortunately, other problems replace them. It is difficult to keep track of the individual members of the cohort. Their parents move out of the district, perhaps out of the country, and take their children with them. In spite of his or her best endeavours, the researcher will lose contact with them. Even if they all stay in the district, those who leave school at 16 and go perhaps to Further Education Colleges may well prove to be so elusive that the researcher can no longer find them. Finally, the whole process of data collection lasts for six years and few organizations are prepared to commit themselves to funding studies over such a period.

Questionnaires

For post-graduate research students and for professional researchers alike, the questionnaire is often a vital tool in the collection of data. If it is well-constructed, it can provide data economically and in a form that lends itself perfectly to the purposes of the study. It therefore makes sense to ensure that, as far as possible, the questions it asks will provide the information sought, that the respondents are able to answer all the questions, and that as many of them as possible complete it.

Questionnaires can be of two kinds: those designed for self-completion and those for assisted completion. The latter assumes that the researcher or a field worker will personally ask the respondent the questions and fill in the answers given. The former is designed for the respondent to complete himself or herself with no researcher present. In educational research, questionnaires for self-completion are the most widely used form, and this dictates much of what follows, although many of the considerations apply equally to both kinds.

The first step in constructing the questionnaire is to review the objectives of the study and the intended function of the questionnaire within it. If the nature of the study is such that the survey is, for all practical purposes, the only data gathering tool to be employed, the task is somewhat simplified. The objectives will provide a touchstone against which the first draft of the questionnaire can be tested. Every question should be justifiable and it should be possible to explain how the responses will be analysed and used. Care should also be taken to ensure that, so far as can possibly be foreseen, the questions cover all aspects of the study: few events are more depressing in the researcher's life than when it is discovered, long after the data collection has been completed, that important data have not been collected, because the necessary question was not asked.

On the other hand, in designing a questionnaire, the researcher must be wary of making excessive demands on the people for whom it is intended. A questionnaire intended for completion by students in school time will be unwelcome by the school, however worthy its purpose and however interested the school may be in the research, if it is likely to take more than half an hour for the average student to complete it. However, once a school has agreed to cooperate with the researcher, the response rate and the number of valid responses will be high. Postal survey questionnaires are even more of a problem. In the nature of things, the people to whom they are addressed are likely to be busy and have many responsibilities. Completing questionnaires sent to them by researchers will come low on their list of priorities. In designing the questionnaire, the researcher should make every effort to ensure that the demands made are the minimum consistent with the research objectives.

Considerations like this often result in a trade-off between the possible and the desirable in terms of the size of the questionnaire. It has to be assumed that the sample to be surveyed has been carefully constructed to represent the whole population (see the Glossary). It is therefore very desirable to have as high a response rate as possible. Obtaining very full responses from only a small proportion of the sample renders the research findings suspect. The few who respond are likely to be untypical of the whole population: they may well be a small minority group with strongly held views on the matter being investigated that are the opposite of those of the majority.

Not all surveys are totally dependent on the questionnaire. Many also make use of interviews with a proportion of the sample. In this case, a decision has to be made about the functions of the two data gathering exercises. Is the purpose of the interview to collect data which are supplementary or complementary to those obtained through the questionnaire? If they are to be supplementary — that is to say, if the interviews are to cover much the same ground as the questionnaires but at a much greater level of detail — this may affect the number and nature of the questions in it. If they are to be complementary to the questionnaire — that is to say, if they are to cover a different but related aspect of the study — then the questionnaire will have to be constructed as if it was the sole instrument.

Questions fall into two types: the 'open' and 'closed'. Of the two, closed questions are the more commonly used, not least because they are easier to code for subsequent analysis. A closed question is one expressed in a way that allows a limited number of options for the respondent to select. For example, in a questionnaire seeking to find out what games or athletic activities children played and how often they did so, a closed question might take the following form. (It is assumed that in an answer to a previous question the respondent said he was a swimmer.)

About how often do you take part in swimming? Please tick the box that is right for you.

Once a week or more often	¦ ¦
About once a fortnight	¦ ¦
About once a month	¦ ¦
Less often than once a month	¦ ¦

Closed questions are not restricted to matters of fact, they can be, and very often are, used to find out the opinions of the respondent. Such questions are often expressed as a statement to which the respondent is given an opportunity to agree or disagree with at various levels of enthusiasm. When a scale of possible responses are provided as in the following example it is known as a Likert Scale. The Likert Scale is one of the most useful question forms. The scale is named after Rensis Likert who developed this format in 1932. In its most popular format, the respondent is presented with a sentence and is asked to agree or disagree on a three, five, or seven-point scale. The five-point scale is the most practical for most common purposes. In a study of adolescent attitudes towards sexual equality, an item such as the following might be included. (In the questionnaire, the boxes 1–5 would have the following headings: Strongly agree; Agree; Uncertain; Disagree; Strongly disagree.)

	1 2 3 4 5
It is more important that boys rather than girls should go to university	¦¦ ¦¦ ¦¦ ¦¦ ¦¦

Closed items need to be framed with some care to ensure that it is possible for the respondents to give an answer that properly reflects their situation or perception.

Although some flexibility of response is often desirable, the researcher may want to force a positive agreement or disagreement from the respondent. This can be the only option if, for example, the question is dealing with very grey areas of attitude or behaviour and the researcher suspects that a high proportion of the respondents would tick the 'uncertain' box. Whilst being uncertain is a perfectly legitimate response and could be of value to a study with one set of objectives, the findings of a different study with other objectives might be so blurred by uncertainty as to have little value.

Open questions, on the other hand, allow the respondent to answer in as much detail as he or she wishes without any prompting. For example, let us suppose that the questionnaire had established that the respondent used to take an active part in some games but had now stopped. It is important to the study to find out why. It would be difficult to construct a question which provided all the possible reasons that might account for this, so an open-ended question is the only option. This might be something like the following:

Please write down why you stopped playing those games. (Please take your time over this answer and give your reasons in detail. Continue your answer on the blank page overleaf if necessary.)

The problem with this kind of question arises when coding the responses for analysis though the difficulties are often more apparent than real. The researcher will usually find that the responses can be reduced to a manageable number of response types.

It is also worth considering structuring open-ended questions by asking respondents to state, for example, their 'three *main* factors/reasons'. This makes data recording easier, since it will give more shape to the response patterns from the sample, without restricting individual choice of factors/reasons stated. Such a strategy is particularly useful when dealing with younger or less articulate respondents. It may also help them from spending a long time on one answer and perhaps running out of time and thus not answering later and equally important questions.

However carefully the questions have been constructed, it is often useful to find somebody who corresponds to the group for whom the questionnaire is intended and ask him or her to complete it and to make any comments on it. This will often reveal ambiguities or other problems that have to be dealt with. Finally, the questionnaire should be pre-tested on a group similar to the sample for which it is destined. This need not be large: a dozen or 20 is usually adequate. For this purpose, it is helpful to print the questionnaire in such a way that the respondents have room to write their comments, problems and suggestions for possible improvement. A careful study of their answers to the questions should be made. It may be found that answers to a question are very unexpected. This may be because the researcher's preconceptions were incorrect, but it may also mean that the question was misunderstood or the range of answer options not appropriate. It is important for the researcher to discover which of these alternatives applies. It is also a final opportunity to check that the questions provide all the data that are needed and were expected, and to take whatever action is necessary if they do not.

Probably the only contact the researcher will have with the members of his or her sample will be through the questionnaire. It is therefore important that it makes a good impression. Potential respondents are more likely to take seriously a document that has been carefully and attractively produced than one that looks as if it has been casually thrown together. They are in no position to judge its inherent intellectual quality and they may well take the view that, if it was not worth the researcher's time and effort to produce it attractively, it is not worth their time to complete it. The following guiding principles (based on suggestions by Borg and Gall, 1983) have been found to help in optimizing the response from the sample:

1   Make the questionnaire look attractive. Use whatever devices available to achieve this. For example, use a well-designed cover page. If the research budget will stretch to it, have it professionally designed and printed. If your questionnaire falls into definable sections, use different coloured paper for each section. Use good quality paper.

2   Organize the questionnaire into a logical sequence, so that related items are grouped together. Use headings to tell the respondent what each group of questions is about, or what their purpose is.

3   Lay out the questions so that they are as easy as possible to read and to complete.

4   Do not hesitate to give clear instructions in **BOLD** type wherever it may be thought necessary, so that the respondents are not left wondering what it is that they are expected to do.

5   Use examples to demonstrate how to complete items wherever you think the respondents may have a problem. (Be careful, however, that your examples do not prompt them to provide what may be perceived to be the 'correct' answer.)

6   Begin your questionnaire with the items that are most easily answered, so as to build up the respondents' confidence.

7   Do not leave the most important questions until the end. By this time, whatever the length of the questionnaire, the respondents will be intent on finishing it and may answer them more casually than would be wished.

8   Precede the questions by a statement about the nature of the research; what it seeks to achieve and the benefits that will flow from its successful completion. Make it clear to the respondents that their cooperation is vital to its success, and express your gratitude for it. If it is for postal use, put the name and address of the person to whom it is to be returned. You will have included a self-addressed, stamped envelope for return, of course, but it is not unknown for them to become separated from the questionnaire and mislaid, or lost.

     The statement should also give assurances to the respondents on the subject of anonymity. This is particularly important when they are asked to write their name on the questionnaire as may be the case in a postal survey or if the researcher intends to follow up the questionnaire by interviewing a proportion of the respondents.

9   At the end of the questionnaire, express your thanks to the respondents for cooperating in the study by completing it.

As was observed above, much educational research involving surveys uses children and young people in schools as its subjects and once arrangements with the schools have been made, response rates are excellent. Postal surveys are a different matter entirely. Initial response rates of under 20 per cent of the sample are not uncommon. As we have seen, this is not good enough and has to be improved. As an 'insurance' against a low return rate, it is well worth considering increasing the numbers in your 'target' population. It is basically true to say that a larger sample is likely to be more reliable than a small one.

Each questionnaire is naturally accompanied by a letter and considerable care should go into its composition. This letter should contain the following items:

1   Explain the purpose of the study to which the questionnaire relates.

2   Point out the importance of the study. For a professional researcher, this is likely to be connected with its outcomes. The same may also apply to the post-graduate researcher, but he or she need not be afraid to tell the respondents that three years of his or her life hang on the successful outcome of this survey.

3   If the members of the sample are likely to be members of a professional association, it may be worthwhile to obtain its endorsement of the study, in which case the fact should be included in the letter. A statement such as 'The objects of the study have been supported by the NUT' (a UK teachers' association) may persuade some teachers to cooperate who might otherwise reach for the waste paper basket.

4   Provide a date by which it is hoped the completed questionnaire will be returned. At the same time, it will do no harm to ask for its completion and return to-day, if possible.

5   Repeat the assurance of confidentiality given at the beginning of the questionnaire and explain that all information will be anonymized in any report arising from the study.

6   Write the salutation in by hand using the name of the respondent. 'Dear Sir' or worse, 'Dear Sir or Madam' in print is less likely to encourage cooperation than a handwritten 'Dear Mr Smith'. You should also sign each letter individually, for the same reason.

By the specified date, it will be possible to see how many responses have been obtained. If, as is likely, the proportion is too low, it will be necessary to send a follow-up letter — similar to the first but modified appropriately — with another copy of the questionnaire to those who have not replied. A second follow-up letter may be necessary to get the response rate up and if matters are desperate, a third, though it is widely accepted that appeals beyond the first follow-up decrease rapidly in effectiveness.

Interviews

Where the object of a questionnaire survey is to produce quantitative data, interviews are normally used to obtain qualitative data. It is common for the two tools to be used in the same study: the questionnaire providing what are often called the 'hard data', and the interviews making it possible to explore in greater detail and in depth some particularly important aspects covered by the questionnaire (supplementary) or related topics which do not lend themselves to the questionnaire approach (complementary). The interview method also forms a significant part of the ethnographer's repertoire of investigative procedures (Brenner, 1981). Thus, the interview is often used in survey research, case-study and ethnographic research.

Powney and Watts (1984) defined an interview as 'a conversation between two or more people where one or more of the participants takes the responsibility for reporting the substance of what is said'. It represents an interaction between three elements: the interviewer, the interviewee and the context of the interview including the issues/questions raised in the interview. Thus the role of the interviewers is a demanding one as they have to ask questions, record answers and to try and keep the interview session interesting and worthwhile for the interviewees.

A major problem with interviews is that they are heavy consumers of resources. Whilst the researcher can get on with other useful work while respondents are filling in questionnaires in their schools or offices or homes, the interview requires his or her presence or that of a field worker who also has to be paid. In addition, it is normal for the interviewer to go to the interviewee so that, in addition to the time spent on the actual interview there is the time and expense taken up by travelling to be considered. It is all the more important, therefore, to make the best use possible of the time spent in actually conducting the interview.

Interviews fall into three categories. There is the 'structured' interview in which the interviewers have a list of prepared questions from which they cannot deviate. Since this is effectively an assisted questionnaire we shall say no more about them.

At the other extreme, there is the 'unstructured' or 'open-ended' interview in which the researcher has some broadly defined objectives but allows the interviewee a great deal of freedom in his or her responses. Indeed, the researcher positively encourages him or her to explore at depth issues within those broad research objectives that are of interest to the interviewee. Typical users of the open interview are psychologists dealing with issues about which the interviewee feels very sensitive. To the outsider, it might be difficult to determine who is in charge of the process, the interviewer or the interviewee. Responses to questions reveal attitudes or further lines of inquiry which the interviewer had not previously considered. In many cases, depending on the interviewer's skills, a rapport can be established between the interviewer and the interviewee which results in revelations obtainable in no other way.

Powerful though the approach may be, it is not without its disadvantages. In the end, the researcher has to make an assessment of the subject's responses and that assessment may well be coloured by the rapport that has been developed between the two. Another important factor is the nature of the preconceptions, beliefs, attitudes and so on, that the interviewer brings to the assessment. It is unlikely that another researcher would ask the same questions or follow the same lines of questioning as the interview developed, still less that he or she would make the same assessment of the data provided by the interview. In other words, the validity and reliability of the subsequent analysis of the interviews are open to question. Fortunately for the educational researcher, since these interviews are of indeterminate length and can extend over many sessions, they are seldom employed in educational research, as the approach is not normally suited to gathering the kinds of information desired.

Between these two extremes lies the 'semi-structured' interview. Since there is a continuum between the two extremes, the extent to which a semi-structured interview is structured varies from case to case. The thing that gives such an interview a structure is normally called the interview schedule and the process of its construction resembles in many ways that of the questionnaire.

The first stage is to return to the objectives of the study. If, as is often the case, the interviews are being designed for use in conjunction with other data gathering tools, it will be necessary to ensure that the interview is designed so as to fulfil its proper functions and not merely to replicate evidence already collected. In this connexion it is worth noting that there are advantages in postponing the design of the interview schedule until the questionnaire data have been collected and analysed. These results often provide the researchers with valuable information and insights, not to mention surprises, which they will wish to investigate further. It is this that the interview is best fitted to do, since it provides the researcher with an opportunity to explore at a depth and a degree of detail aspects such as the motivation governing the behaviours of the interviewee that are far beyond the scope of the questionnaire.

As we have seen, a schedule is important to ensure that the interview makes good use of time and resources, ensures that the data gathered are relevant to the study's objectives and that opportunities to collect data essential to its successful outcome are not lost. They also ensure that, within the limits allowed by the structure of the schedule, a balance is struck between allowing the variety of responses from one interviewee to another and reasonable consistency in the interviewer's approach. This last consideration is particularly important when the researcher is not acting alone but is one of a team, or employing a team of fieldworkers.

Generally speaking, if the researcher is acting alone, the schedule will take the form of a statement of what the next part of the interview is going to be about followed by a general question. The opening question will be followed by a number of supplementary questions acting as a reminder to the researcher to ensure that all the foreseen aspects of the issue are covered. Of course, and this is the beauty of interviews, interviewees do not respond in foreseeable ways and the researcher will have to be ready to invent further questions as the interview proceeds to explore in depth the issue of interest. When this part of the interview has been completed, the process is repeated. The schedule is made up of a series of opening statements, primary questions and supplementaries. If the researcher is one of a team, rather more elaborate measures will be needed to ensure that reasonable consistency is combined with freedom of response by the interviewee.

Fowler (1993) suggested five aspects of interviewer behaviour that researchers should attempt to standardize: the way they present the research objectives and the task; the way questions are asked; the way inadequate answers are probed by the interviewer; the way answers are recorded; and the way interpersonal aspects of the interview are dealt with.

One way of doing this is to adopt a format for the schedule which looks rather like a flow chart. This will be the job of the principal researcher. An example appears as Figure 6.1. This example is taken from a study undertaken by the senior author for The Sports Council Research Project and shows how one section of the interview was planned. Since there were eight fieldworkers drawn from eight ethnic groups conducting the interviews, the balance between consistency and freedom was particularly difficult to achieve. Clearly, a sole researcher would not need to develop a schedule as complex as this example for use in the field. However, the work of designing the schedule with its primary and supplementary questions ready for use will involve these sort of considerations in its construction (see Figure 6.1).

If possible, interviewees should be selected from the same sample as was used for the questionnaire. In an ideal world, the selection would be governed by the same considerations as those for the sample as a whole, although in practice this is not normally possible.

Figure 6.1: Extract from an interview schedule

Can we talk about the sort of physical activities you take part in now?
Either You told us that you play [write in the activities]

Or You told us that you aren't taking part in any activities at the moment. Is that still true?

IF TAKING PART IN ACTIVITIES
One of the things we are very interested in finding out is <u>why</u> people play games.

[For each activity] ↓
What do you think your <u>main reason</u> is for playing [activity]?

Are there any other reasons?
If **necessary, prompt:** Lots of people say it's to do with things like:—
— Health and fitness
— The game/activity itself
— Having fun with your friends
— Liking to be on the winning side
— Getting out of the house.
Probe to get to the real reason
↓
Do you think seeing games on TV encourages you to play them?

YES　　　　　　　　　**NO**
↓　　　　　　　　　　　　↓
What are they?　　　How did you manage?
Did anyone help you?

YES　　　　　NO
↓　　　　　　↓
Who were they?　How did you get
　　　　　　　　back into
What did they　games then?
do to help?　　　↓
↓　　　　　　　　↓
　　　　　　　　↓
Do you think your　↓
friends had the same　↓
problems?　　　　　↓
↓　　　　　　　　↓
Some people tell us they generally play with others of the same ethnic group. Other people say they play in mixed teams. Which would you really prefer?

MIXED　　　**SAME**
↓　　　　　　　↓
Do you think that's　Why is that?
true for your friends?　Do you think your
　　　　　　　　friends feel like that?
Why do you prefer it?　↓
Have you always
preferred it?　　↓
↓

IF NOT TAKING PART IN ACTIVITIES
Could we start by asking why you have stopped?
[**Refer back to school activities. Try to identify the main reason for stopping each activity.**]
Try something like —
You told me just now that you played [*name* game] at school. Why did you give it up?

Probe — e.g. Lots of people have told us it's because of things like —
— I didn't have friends to go with, or
— I was too busy at work, or
— I didn't know how to get going on my own.
What was <u>your</u> real deep-down reason?
[***Allow time for a considered response. Don't be*** satisfied with a quick answer if you suspect it's not the *real one.*]

When you see people on TV swimming or playing games and obviously enjoying themselves, don't you ever think 'They seem to be enjoying themselves, I wonder if I would?'

YES　　　　　　　**NO**
↓
But you never followed it up?
↓
Do you think you might one day?

Check responses to Q30. <u>Explore any negative responses, e.g.</u>
You said here that when you were watching TV and saw people involved in sport and other physical activities, that you thought it was wrong for people to behave like that. Could you tell me more about that?　←　←　←　←

Many people tell us that they play games in order to stay fit because it helps them to remain healthy. Does this sound sensible to you?

YES　　　　　**NO**
Do you do anything that might help
you to keep fit and healthy?
↓
Go to Section D

DON'T CARE
↓
Do you think your friends
feel like that?
↓
↓

→ **Go to Page 5** ←

Figure 6.1:   (Cont)

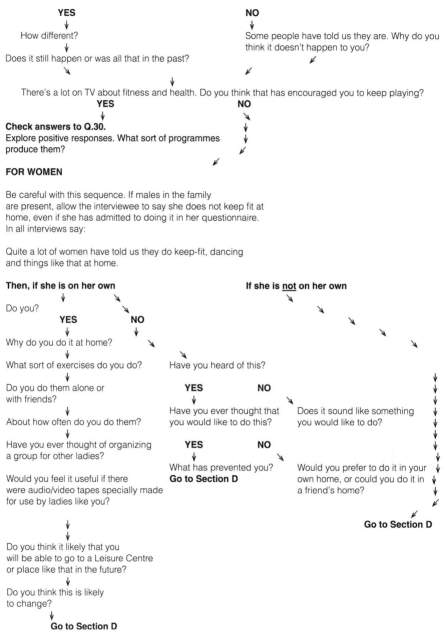

When you play, do you ever feel that you are treated differently from other players because you are [**name** *ethnic group*]?

YES
How different?
Does it still happen or was all that in the past?

NO
Some people have told us they are. Why do you think it doesn't happen to you?

There's a lot on TV about fitness and health. Do you think that has encouraged you to keep playing?

YES
Check answers to Q.30.
Explore positive responses. What sort of programmes produce them?

NO

FOR WOMEN

Be careful with this sequence. If males in the family are present, allow the interviewee to say she does not keep fit at home, even if she has admitted to doing it in her questionnaire. In all interviews say:

Quite a lot of women have told us they do keep-fit, dancing and things like that at home.

Then, if she is on her own
Do you?
YES   **NO**
Why do you do it at home?
What sort of exercises do you do?
Do you do them alone or with friends?
About how often do you do them?
Have you ever thought of organizing a group for other ladies?
Would you feel it useful if there were audio/video tapes specially made for use by ladies like you?

If she is not on her own

Have you heard of this?

YES   **NO**
Have you ever thought that   Does it sound like something
you would like to do this?   you would like to do?

YES   **NO**
What has prevented you?   Would you prefer to do it in your
Go to Section D   own home, or could you do it in
                          a friend's home?

Go to Section D

Do you think it likely that you will be able to go to a Leisure Centre or place like that in the future?
Do you think this is likely to change?

Go to Section D

Source: Verma et al. (1991) Unpublished Report for Sports Council, Manchester.

Before conducting the interview, the researcher should deal with some important preliminaries. The first of these is to thank the interviewee for agreeing to the interview. The second will be to give assurances of confidentiality and anonymity: that, in the event of part of the interview appearing in a report or publication, it will be presented in such a way as to make attribution impossible. Some brief but relevant background data on the interviewee is useful so that a profile of the interview sample can be drawn up, to facilitate comparison with that of the questionnaire sample.

It is also necessary to arrive at an agreement on how the interview is to be recorded. From the point of view of the researcher, a tape recording is likely to be the favoured option, since it not only provides a record of the interviewee's actual words but the inflections of his or her voice which can be an additional and valuable source of information. It also means that the researchers will be able to give all their attention to the interview process and concentrate on the interviewee's expressions and body language when responding to questions. Such observations obviously provide clues in framing the next question. When asked, most people agree to this. If they do not, the researcher must accept their decision and make do with taking notes.

If agreement over tape recording is reached, the researchers should tell their subjects that they are not obliged to answer questions if, for any reason, they do not wish to do so, and that it is possible for them to terminate the interview at any point. On the other hand, the researchers should make it clear that words spoken will not be deleted but must remain as part of the record of the interview.

These formalities should not be taken lightly and never omitted. They are there for the benefit and protection of both the subject and the researcher. Once dealt with, the interview can go ahead. Some researchers believe that the presence of a tape recorder can inhibit the subject's responses. We have to say that, in our experience this does not happen. Indeed, people's lack of inhibition is often a matter of surprise as they make statements which, in the wrong hands, would result in — at best — their being disciplined or dismissed and in some cases render them liable to action in law. We mention this to add force to what follows. The assurances of confidentiality must not be taken lightly. Tapes of interviews must be kept in a secure place. If they are transcribed, the audio-typist must be trustworthy and made aware of the status of the materials which are being worked with. Once the study is completed, the tapes should be wiped or destroyed.

Whichever type of interview is employed, a number of problems need to be thought through by the researcher at an early stage. The following checklist published in a BERA Newsletter provides a useful guide:

1   Kind and context of interview
    What is the rationale for using interviews?
    What kind of interview is it?
    How is the interview structured?
    How much flexibility does the interviewer have?
    What is the length, location and occasion of the interview?

2   Characteristics of the interview participants
    (a) Interviewees
        Who and how many people are involved?
        What is the basis for their selection and how was the selection made?
    (b) Interviewers
        Who and how many people are involved?
        What experience of interviewing do they have?
        What is their relationship to the main research?
        What is their status and relationship to the interviewees?
3   The purpose of the interview
    What are interviewees told about the purpose of the interview?
    Is this understanding shared with the interviewer?
    Who will have access to the data collected and is it negotiable?
4   The method(s) of data collection
    How strictly controlled is the method of asking questions?
    How are responses recorded?
    What other methods of data collection are being used and what is the relative weighting between the methods?
5   Analysis and reporting of data
    Who analyses what?
    How are the interviewers concerned with the analysis?
    How many analysts are there and how are disagreements resolved?
    Are full transcripts used?
    What basis is used for filtering the data?
    What level of uncodeable data is tolerated?
6   Sorting of results
    How are the outcomes of the interviews being evaluated?
    What access may the academic community have to raw data?

(Powney and Watts, 1984)

In the structured interview, and even more so in the semi- or unstructured interview, much depends on the personality of the interviewer and the circumstances of the interview. Being interviewed is a voluntary activity on the part of the subjects and they are likely to be affected by the circumstances and nature of the interviewer to the extent that their answers may be as full as the interviewer could wish for, minimal or effectively non-existent.

Critics of the interview approach say that the collection of data by interview involves a complex set of social relationships that can contaminate the final product. The social relationship may result in the distortion of the information supplied as well as being open to unconscious bias on the part of the researcher in assessing it. The fact remains that interviews can yield rich material unobtainable in any other way, and which can support or be supported by other data from questionnaires or standardized test responses. The interview is wonderfully adaptable and flexible. A trained, experienced and skilful interviewer can probe responses, investigate feelings, motives, experiences and attitudes which no other investigative technique can reach.

Observation Techniques

The observational method is a tool for collecting information without direct questioning on the part of the researcher. This method is often used in combination with other techniques. For example, if the interview is not a structured one, the investigator's observations of the respondent's behaviour may be a help in formulating questions and in interpreting the meaning and significance of the respondent's answers to questions in the interview.

The distinction between structured and less structured observational techniques is analogous to that between structured and unstructured interviews. The less structured observational technique may be classified into two broad types: participant and non-participant observation. The distinction has to do with the role of the observer within the situation and the extent to which the observer adopts the role of member of the group being studied.

As its name implies, non-participant observation is a method of obtaining information in which the researcher observes and records activities but plays no part in them. An extreme example of this would be one in which the researcher, unknown to the children, observed a class from another room by using closed circuit television (CCTV), or through an observation window disguised as a mirror. More commonly, however, in the absence of these devices, the researcher sits in the classroom and, as unobtrusively as possible, makes observations and records them. Some time should be spent in the classroom before starting work to allow the pupils time to grow accustomed to the researcher's presence. Depending on the age of the children being observed, the presence of a stranger is likely to affect their behaviour in ways that will make the observations unreliable. How long this preliminary stage lasts will be dependent on many factors outside the researcher's control — the age of the children, the work they are engaged in and the ability of the class teacher to engage them in it, to suggest but three — as well as the purposes of the study. However, the researcher's ambition will be to become functionally invisible to the children — to become a temporary classroom fitting which they will first ignore and then forget about. Once this, or something like it, has been achieved, the non-participant observation can begin.

As with interviewing, the researcher will have made serious preparations for the observational sessions and for much the same reasons: they are expensive in researcher time; they usually involve travelling costs and time; and there must be some consistency in the objectives of the observation — especially if more than one researcher is involved or more than one class is being observed. These preparations involve the construction of a schedule of the observations to be made. As with the interview schedule, the items on it will be determined by the objectives of the study for which the observations are to be made. Suppose, for example, the study has to do with the relations between pupils and teacher in a multi-racial classroom.

The research hypothesis might be that a white teacher is liable to interact differently as between white children and those from other ethnic origins. The sorts of data the researcher will be looking to collect might include the following:

1 In the course of a lesson, how were questions distributed between white children, Afro-Caribbean children, South Asian children and Chinese children? (It might be possible for the researcher to be more precise in defining 'South Asians' and specify Indian, Pakistani and Bangladeshi.)
2 When asking the question, did the teacher smile at the pupil or not?
3 How did the teacher respond to the answer? With a smile? Neutrally? With dissatisfaction?
4 When asking a question, did the teacher address the class as a whole and then select one child to answer it?
5 If the question was intended for a specific pupil, did the teacher use the pupil's name, or point?
6 How did the teacher respond to questions from the pupils?
7 How did the teacher respond to trivial but irritating behaviour on the part of pupils?

It would be easy to continue along these lines. However, once the array of questions covering the important aspects of teacher/pupil relationships have been formulated, it will be necessary to convert them into a form that will enable the observer to record each event as it happens, quickly, accurately and in a way that makes it possible to quantify the types of interaction between the teacher and the various groups of children that make up the class.

In this example, the schedule is likely to fall into three main areas: teacher questions, teacher instructions and pupil questions. Under the heading 'Teacher Questions' there will probably be a grid something like the following:

```
      1  2  3  4  5  6  7  8
Q1.  |  |  |  |  |  |  |  |  |
Q2.  |  |  |  |  |  |  |  |  |
Q3.  |  |  |  |  |  |  |  |  |
Q4.  |  |  |  |  |  |  |  |  |
```

Column 1 would record the ethnic origin of the child asked the question; column 2, whether the teacher smiled or not; column 3 how the teacher responded to the question; column 4, whether the teacher used the pupil's name, or not; column 5, whether it was correctly pronounced, or not; column 6, whether the pupil was a boy or a girl; column 7, whether the pupil was the first in the class to be asked that particular question or was second or third; whether, if the question had been addressed to the whole class, the pupil had volunteered an answer or had been selected by the teacher. At the end of the lesson, the observer will have a mass of data in a form that will readily lend itself to analysis and will provide objective information on the defined interactions between the teacher and children by ethnic origin.

In this example, the observer's task is demanding in terms of the need for sustained concentration, but essentially simple. All the observations, except one, are either positive or negative: the pupil was either of this or that ethnic origin, was a boy or a girl, was addressed by name or not, and so on. Some judgment is required in deciding whether the teacher smiled or not and the schedule might make provision for this by building in a range of scores from, say, 0 (certainly not) to 4 (very positive). There are clear benefits in keeping the number of observations of each event down to a manageable number and in ensuring that as many observations as possible are effectively either 'yes' or 'no'. In a lively classroom, events can follow each other very rapidly and it can quickly become very difficult for the observer to keep up with them, particularly if there are many observations to be made of each event and a number of the observations require a judgment of their quality or intensity.

If, because of the demands made by the objectives of the study, this sort of simplicity is impossible, it may become necessary to adopt alternative techniques. In these sorts of cases, CCTV comes into its own since the lesson can be recorded and the events of interest to the researcher studied at — relative — leisure. Where this is not possible the commonest device is to sample events by using a watch and recording observations of events every so many minutes thus making it possible for the observer to maintain a full record during the agreed periods.

At its best, non-participant observation can and does provide the researcher with valuable, quantifiable data. As with any other technique, however, it is not without its problems. Perhaps one of the most difficult of these arises from the obvious need to have the cooperation of those observed. In the above example, the researcher wished to discover if the teacher behaved differently towards children from differing ethnic origins. Clearly, it would be necessary to get the permission of the headteacher and teachers concerned to make the observations. If the teachers know the intentions of the researcher, they are virtually certain to behave untypically. If, for example, the teachers believe that the researcher suspects that they are likely to address more questions to boys than girls, to white children than ethnic minority children, or to South Asian than Afro-Caribbean children and to adopt a friendlier approach to all white children than to all ethnic minority children, they would be scarcely human, if they did not make particular efforts to demonstrate that this did not happen in their classes.

In obtaining permission from the headteacher, it will be necessary for the researcher to tell him or her what the purposes of the research are. The headteacher will want to know, and it would clearly be unethical to attempt to conceal the real reasons for the request to observe lessons. If the headteacher expresses an interest, it then becomes necessary for the researcher to point out the necessity for the teachers concerned *not* to know why their lessons were to be observed. It requires little imagination to sympathize with the headteacher's position. How is the headteacher to persuade colleagues to agree to the researcher's presence in their classes if they are to be kept in ignorance of the objectives of the study? The issues are sensitive and despite the researcher's assurances about confidentiality and anonymity, the headteacher may well have residual worries about what the proposed research will uncover. It is not uncommon for researchers to be given access to classrooms on the understanding that they provide the schools concerned with a brief report of their findings. What is the headteacher to do if provided with evidence that some teachers are treating some children less favourably than others on the basis of their ethnic origin? It would be understandable if, at this point, the headteacher decided that, however worthy the intentions of the research, the potential problems were more than he or she was prepared to contemplate.

Other Devices

Under this heading are included all the vast array of published tests, inventories and so on, employed in educational research. It is for the researcher to select those, or the one, most suitable in the light of the objectives of the study. It is outside the scope of this book to itemize those currently available — one publisher alone lists 65 psychological tests of potential interest to educational researchers — still less would it be possible to discuss their applications. We therefore restrict ourselves to a few general comments.

Tests generally fall into two types, 'norm-referenced' or 'criterion-referenced'. Norm-referenced tests compare an individual's performance to those obtained from a population of a similar age and background. Criterion-referenced tests seek to establish whether or not a person is capable of a task or set of tasks. The best known example of this type is the Standard Assessment Test (SAT), used in schools in England and Wales to test the attainment of pupils at the designated Key Stages. Neither type is inherently 'better' than the other: they perform different functions and which is chosen will depend on what the researcher is seeking to discover.

For example, if it is desired to test reading ability, the researcher may want to know how a child or class of children aged 10 or thereabouts compares with other children of the same age, and to do this might decide to use the NFER Reading Test Series. This test has been nationally standardized and norm-referenced. The scores from it will be a product of comparing the performance of the particular class being investigated with those expected from children of a similar age nationally. Another researcher might also be interested in reading ability but wish to discover the commoner problems children encounter in learning to read. He or she might then use NFER's Test of Initial Literacy which identifies particular areas of need: a different test, constructed on different lines for different purposes.

In selecting a test or tests, the researcher should ensure that they meet two important criteria: *reliability* and *validity*. They have been touched on before in this book but they are so important that we make no apology for returning to them here. In educational contexts, 'reliability' refers to the degree of accuracy with which the test measures whatever it is that it measures (remember the speedometer in Chapter 2). Information on the reliability of a test is normally supplied with the test. A common method of establishing reliability is to test the same group of people on two occasions separated by a few weeks. The results of the two tests are then correlated. This provides what is called the 'test–retest reliability'. Another way of establishing a test's reliability is the 'split half' method. In this, the scores obtained from taking comparable halves of the test (for example the odd and even items) are used to determine the correlation between them. The important question of how reliable a test should be to make it trustworthy for its intended purpose is difficult to answer. A well-constructed test of achievement or cognitive ability might be expected to have a reliability in excess of 0.90. One designed for use in areas such as personality and attitude is acceptable with much lower reliability. This is not because the standards of those working in these areas are lower but because the problems of measurement are greater. Reliability, then, is essentially about the accuracy of the tool used to measure something: is the ruler exactly a metre long? Validity is a more difficult issue.

'Validity' refers to how appropriately a test goes about what it is supposed to measure. A test cannot be considered valid unless it is highly reliable. Typically, establishing the validity of a test requires professional judgment. There are various types of validity. The most common of these are *content, concurrent, construct,* and *predictive* validity. 'Content' (or 'face') validity could be seen as referring to how appropriate a test is judged to be as a means of testing what students ought to know after doing a particular unit or module. This judgment would be based in part on the extent to which the test gave adequate coverage of the unit's content whether expressed in terms of knowledge and/or skills to be acquired. 'Concurrent' validity refers to the extent to which a test is judged to be in keeping with other established tests considered to be valid measures of the same attribute or trait. 'Predictive' validity refers to the extent to which scores on the test can be shown to 'predict' performance. For example, scores on IQ tests can sometimes be shown to correlate highly with success in later public examinations. 'Construct' validity is judged by the extent to which scores on a test of some well-defined attribute are shown to correlate highly with known differences among subjects in the samples being tested. It should be emphasized that validity is a complex topic and the type of validity required varies according to the nature of what the test is seeking to measure. Furthermore, although reference has been made to 'professional judgment', this should not be that of the researcher! In the case of a school-type test, evidence of validity might be sought by reference to independent judges who are expert in that field of the curriculum and its testing.

Care has to be exercised in selecting norm-referenced tests to ensure that the people the researcher intends to use them on are as nearly as possible the same as those for whom the tests were designed. This is because the results of the test are expressed in terms of a comparison between those obtained from the subject and those obtained from a large number of other people. Suppose, for example, the researcher has formulated the hypothesis that Muslim adolescent girls in British schools are likely to have lower self-esteem than their white British peers. It will be necessary to apply the same test on both groups if a comparison is to be made. Clearly, such a test must be 'culture-free'; that is to say, the responses to the items in the test must have the same meaning for both groups. If the test were to include items such as:

I enjoy going to parties and meeting boys
I enjoy dressing up and going to discos

the chances are that the two groups would give different responses to these state-ments which might indicate that the white British group had higher self-esteem than their Muslim peers. A moment's thought suggests that such a finding would be very suspect. The problem arises because the test had been standardized on a population that excluded Muslim girls, and so its results were not valid for them. A test would have to be found consisting of items that provided both groups with equal opportun-ities to respond in ways that demonstrated their self-esteem. Such a test might not be easy to find and the researcher would have to face the possibility that some other way of testing the hypothesis would have to be adopted.

Publishers of norm-referenced tests (NFER and Moray House in the UK, for example) provide details of the population on which the test has been standard-ized. These may include the age range, social class, gender, ethnicity and coun-try of origin. As the example above shows, it is important for the researcher to ensure that the test used is appropriate for the group or groups on which it is to be used.

Most psychological tests are norm-referenced and it as well for the researcher to be aware of at least one of the major criticisms of psychological tests as a whole. The criticism revolves about the concept of reliability. These tests are designed to measure something and by measuring it a concept develops to account for what is being measured. The classic example of this process is the concept of general intelligence. The French Ministry of Public Instruction set up a commission in 1904 to define educational subnormality so that children who needed special treatment could be placed in special schools. The members of the commission found it very *difficult* to arrive at a satisfactory definition of intelligence. One of its members, Alfred Binet adopted the following approach in an attempt to arrive at an answer. He went out into schools armed with a huge number of questions which children were asked to answer. At the same time, he asked their teachers which of the children were, in their view, intelligent and which were not. The questions which did not discrimin-ate well between the two groups were rejected; those that did were retained. These formed a battery of items which became the first IQ test. Children who were reckoned to be intelligent did well in it; those who were less intelligent did not.

The essence of the criticism that can be made, and often is, lies in the fact that the *concept* of general intelligence grew out of a measuring process. Normally, concepts exist and devices are invented to measure them: watches came into exist-ence in order to measure time for example. The concept of intelligence was arrived at by precisely the opposite process and the problem is that no satisfactory answer has been given to questions, such as 'What is being measured? Does intelligence have any existence outside the piece of paper giving the result of an IQ test?'. It is a sobering thought that, from 1944 to the adoption of comprehensive schools in Britain, the futures of millions of children were largely determined by tests which suffered from this logical flaw.

Standardized tests cover a wide range of aspects of individuals' behaviour, traits, aptitudes and skills: self-esteem and intelligence, as previously considered, personality, psychological states (such as stress and anxiety), motor skills (such as manual dexterity, and hand-to-eye coordination), particular aptitudes (such as musicality and creativity), and so forth. It is obviously not possible in a chapter like this to go into detail on these. Many of the points made, however, about self-esteem and intelligence testing, their strengths and limitations, would apply equally to these also albeit in varying degrees.

The usefulness of standardized tests is easy to underestimate when beginning on research. However, such tests, if chosen wisely, can be very helpful in establishing the reliability and validity of the data collected in one's study. The theme of the standardized test does not have to be immediately related to the main topic of the research. A standardized test may well be useful to determine the degree of comparability between one's samples on some particular attribute. For example, a study into the effectiveness of a particular set of teaching/learning materials, might well be enhanced by being able to compare pupil performance on an assessment test given at the end of the programme to measure the gains made by pupils, against their performance on a standardized reading test. This might help to demonstrate that the materials worked particularly well with 'average' readers or 'weak' ones, rather than the 'more able'.

It is often very difficult to be sure whether the sample drawn from one school is really comparable with that drawn from another school, even if both schools operate in similar areas and enjoy similar local reputations. A standardized test can help to confirm the essential similarity of the samples drawn from different sources, since the performance by subjects on it can be compared with the established norms, published in the manual accompanying the test. It is also useful if one can demonstrate a strong correlation between performance on one's main instruments with that on the standardized test. Such a result helps confirm the reliability and validity of the findings.

With many of such tests, however, especially if they are paper and pencil ones, there can be 'problems' of equivalence, if the test, despite its impressive reliability and validity credentials, was developed and standardized on a population from another cultural setting. The wording of items may make particular cultural assumptions about the subjects which may not really be valid in the setting in which one is proposing to use it; equally, the norms established for particular age groups in one setting may not be equally valid in another. This necessitates careful investigation of the claims made for particular standardized tests in terms of the populations for which norms have been established, and comparison with other ones dealing with related areas. There are also the same logistical issues, considered earlier when looking at self-esteem and intelligence tests, relating to costs of using the test, whether or not specialist training is a pre-condition of use, and so on. At the end of the day, a judgment has to be exercised, which may involve compromise. However, it is well worth spending time, checking out the suitability of the inclusion of a standardized test or tests within the research design.

References

ANDERSON, G. (1994) *Fundamentals of Educational Research*, London: Falmer Press.

BELL, J. (1987) *Doing Your Research Project*, Milton Keynes: Open University Press.

BERELSON, B. (1952) *Content Analysis in Communication Research*, Glencoe, ILL: Free Press.

BORG, W.R. and GALL, M.D. (1983) *Educational Research: An Introduction*, 4th edition, New York and London: Longman.

BRENNER, M. (1981) 'Survey Interviewing', in CANTER, S. and CANTER, D. (eds) *Perspectives on Professional Psychology: Current Developments in the Applications of Psychology*, Chichester: John Wiley.

FOWLER, F.J. (1993) *Survey Research Methods*, 2nd edition, Newbury Park, CA: Sage Publications.

HITCHCOCK, G. and HUGHES, D. (1989) *Research and the Teacher*, London: Routledge.

LACEY, C. (1970) *Hightown Grammar: The School as a Social System*, Manchester: Manchester University Press.

NISBET, J. and WATT, J. (1984) 'Case study', in BELL, J., BUSH, T., FOX, A., GOODEY, J. and GOULDING, S. (eds) *Conducting Small-scale Investigations in Educational Management*, 2nd edition: Harper and Row Publishers, in association with The Open University (Chapter 5).

PLATT, J. (1981) 'Evidence and proof in documentary research: Some specific problems of documentary research', in *Sociological Review*, **29**, 1, pp. 31–52.

POWNEY, J. and WATTS, M. (1984) 'Reporting interview: A code of good practice', in *Research Intelligence*, BERA Newsletter, **17**.

VERMA, G.K. and CHAN, Y-M. (1996) *The Cultural Identity of Chinese Adolescents in Britain*, Report to the Leverhulme Trust, London.

VERMA, G.K. et al. (1991) *Sport and Recreation with Specific Reference to Ethnic Minorities*, Report to Sports Council, Manchester.

Chapter 7

Educational Research Planning

In planning a study, a number of tasks tend to go on at the same time. These include the selection of the research problem, its definition and a review of the literature dealing with the area of interest within which the study is to be situated. It is clearly impossible to deal with all of these issues at the same time without getting hopelessly confused. In spite of the fact that they are really concurrent activities, we deal with them consecutively, beginning with selection and definition.

Selection and Definition of the Problem

Note the phrase that heads this section: 'selection and definition of the problem' — particularly the last word in it. Leedy (1993) in common with many, many others, makes the point that research is not about discovering facts, it is about recognizing and formulating the problem which the research will seek to solve. However the study is subsequently conducted, whether it is qualitative or quantitative, ethnographical, experimental, eclectic, large- or small-scale, if it does not address a problem and seek to solve it, then it is not, strictly speaking, research.

For those who are employed to spend much of their time as researchers, the main problem is likely to be best expressed by the question, 'What, of all the possible issues shall I explore next?' This is because each piece of research is likely to suggest further possible studies. Thus, using the knowledge and experience gained in previous research projects, they will find the selection of the next subject for study a matter of resolving conflicting interests and priorities rather than looking for something to do and faced with a blank sheet of paper on their desk in front of them. For a would-be researcher, on the other hand, the selection and definition of the research project present problems which must be successfully overcome if the study is to be brought to a successful conclusion.

As with almost any human activity involving decision-making, the process is difficult because so many factors have an impact on the outcome. The next few pages are concerned with trying to identify those factors and to show how they must be taken into account if the outcome is to be a well-conceived research project. The first and very important factor must be the inclination of the researcher: what aspect of education is of interest to him or her?

There is, or ought to be, a sense of excitement at the beginning of a research project. Will the hypothesis turn out to be correct? What unexpected information will be revealed? What preconceptions will be shown to be inaccurate? What unforeseen problems in its conduct will occur? With this sense of excitement should also be a pleasurable anticipation at the thought of the next year, or two, or three, being spent in exploring an aspect of education that is of real interest. This excitement revisits the researcher as the study progresses, data accumulate and start to form patterns whose meanings become increasingly clear, some expected, some less so. Then the time comes to make the final analyses and reflect on what has been discovered, to bring together all the data in their various forms and weigh their importance, significance and reliability and draw conclusions that are balanced and dispassionate.

However, between these high points, there are long periods of very demanding work interspersed with problems: some schools have new headteachers who are not as sympathetic to the research as the previous ones were and will not allow access to their students. Real disasters may occur: tapes with three days of vital interviews, recorded with subjects in a city 100 miles away, may go mysteriously 'missing', and the interviewees almost certain to be unwilling to be re-interviewed! All may turn out well in the end, the tapes being found subsequently in the box of tapes that have already been transcribed, or in the box of blank tapes! (This emphasizes the need to keep careful records, not just a written record, but also to label cassettes and their plastic cases.) Unless the researcher is really interested in the subject of the study, the problems, disappointments and sheer hard work involved will combine to make his or her life miserable.

For the professional researcher, the matter is complicated by mundane but important considerations, such as the need to persuade a funding body to provide a grant which will make the project possible. Secretaries of State for Education and their advisers often have their own priorities which are reflected in the willingness with which they provide funding for research in one field and withhold it from another. Indeed, as we observe later in this chapter, government-sponsored research projects have increasingly taken the form of a series of instructions, specifying the research problem, the methodology to be employed and the time scale to be observed. On the basis of this, researchers are invited to bid for the work.

This practice has caused widespread resentment among educational researchers since it takes away from their independence as scholars. However, although government is the prime source of research funding, there are other sources — notably a large number of charitable trusts — which, between them, provide money to fund research on a wide range of issues. A would-be researcher can avoid a great deal of wasted work and disappointment by ensuring, at an early stage, that the projected study is one that has a realistic chance of finding a sponsor.

The fact, however, remains that there must be a pre-existing interest in the area to be researched. The next step is to refine that general area of interest so that it becomes a manageable subject of study. Let us suppose, for example, that the researcher has been caught up in the interest, expressed in 1996 by church leaders, parents and politicians, in moral values and the role that schools have in inculcating them. He or she has now to construct a hypothesis within this area. If the subsequent research is to be of value, it must conform to the following criteria:

(i)   It must be capable of clear statement,
(ii)   It should be stated in terms that indicate a relationship between variables,
(iii)   It should be testable.

The researcher might be tempted to form a hypothesis such as: 'Children whose parents are regular church-goers have a greater moral sense than those who do not.' This meets criteria (i) and (ii) but not (iii). What is meant by 'a greater moral sense'? As a term, it depends for its meaning on a consensus of opinion between the writer and the reader. So many aspects of human thought, motivation and behaviour are involved that no instruments exist capable of measuring them, even if the aspects could be adequately defined. The hypothesis, as expressed, is incapable of being tested and hence cannot be verified or rejected as incorrect.

The reseacher might well then try to reformulate the hypothesis and might think along the following lines. There is a substantial minority of schools in Britain which are church foundations and remain within the state education system as either voluntary-aided or voluntary-controlled schools. Of these, the voluntary aided schools retain most strongly the characteristics of their church foundation. Most of them have explicit statements in their prospectuses about their educational object-ives as regards their intentions to foster beliefs and behaviours consistent with their church origins. Some of these schools make it a condition of accepting pupils that their parents are practising members of a particular denomination, though many do not. Would it be possible to formulate a hypothesis around the moral values held in high esteem, comparing the different types of church schools, and county schools (those with no church affiliations)?

At this point, a little preliminary research would be necessary. A sample of schools would be selected, their prospectuses obtained and an analysis undertaken of their expressed objectives in moral education. It might be that a consistent pattern began to emerge in which the various schools were seen to express common objectives related to their church origins. The researcher might then think, 'Parents who place a high value on moral education try to send their children to church schools.' This has some advantages over the first hypothesis, but the moral values are still undefined except in terms of the schools' prospectuses. There is also the problem that some of the church schools might, because they are selective, have a strong local reputation for being schools that achieve very good academic results. There is plenty of anecdotal evidence that some parents start to attend church only when they realize the possible academic advantages to their children, and for no other reason. And, again, there is no obvious way of testing the hypothesis.

Another possibility that might occur to the researcher is that children at schools which emphasize moral education ought to be better behaved than children at schools that do not. Most schools have codes of discipline which are based on generally accepted principles. Perhaps it might be possible to use school records on the assumption that those schools which take moral education seriously will have fewer problems with the pupils. Unfortunately, this breaks down because some schools are better at record-keeping than others and some schools draw on populations in which most of the parents share the school's assumptions, even if some do not.

It is also at least possible that schools keen on inculcating strong moral values will take action and record transgressions and remedial treatments more frequently than others that take a more relaxed view of their responsibilities.

So the search will have to continue until a hypothesis is arrived at which meets the necessary criteria for eventual success. This example was selected to illustrate two things. First, there are some areas that are properly the business of education and present interesting questions but which are not very amenable to research. As Travers (1978) observed, schools have to help children to develop the values inherent in their society. He came to the conclusion that 'What research programmes cannot do is to define the values that should underlie a school programme'. The second was to show how difficult it can be to construct a hypothesis that will serve as a secure basis for subsequent research.

As we have seen earlier, there are approaches to educational research which do not depend on formulating a hypothesis and testing it. The researcher with an interest in moral values might frame an ethnographic study in which he or she observed the behaviours of children in school, their teachers and parents. As we have seen, such a study does not require hypotheses: on the contrary, it requires an open mind to make unbiased observation possible. It can be a precursor to the formulation of hypotheses, however, and it may be that, in the literature search, the researcher will discover such a study from which a hypothesis on some aspect of the observations can be formulated which will meet the required criteria.

Another way of formulating a research problem is to construct a question, or more commonly, a series of linked questions which the research will seek to answer. These questions serve in some respects the same purpose as the hypothesis: they focus the researcher's mind on the problem and make it possible to think purposefully about what research tools might be employed to arrive at their answers. As with the hypothesis, their formulation is of great importance since they will determine the whole nature and conduct of the study and will, in large measure, decide its value. Good research questions will share some common characteristics. They will:

- Go to the heart of the research problem being addressed;
- Be simply and clearly expressed; and,
- Be answerable, using the tools at the researcher's disposal.

To attempt an analogy, in a number of respects they are to a research study what the rules are to a game. They will guide the actions of the researcher, determine the equipment to be used and establish the nature of the research outcomes.

As well as the criteria discussed above, other, more mundane, but important considerations enter into the selection of a research project. One of them will be the resources available to the researcher. For students framing the subject of an MPhil or PhD thesis, recognition of limited resources must form an essential element in deciding what they will attempt. In some scientific disciplines, it is not uncommon for a PhD student to be one of a team of researchers working on a major project. In educational research, this is almost unknown. Normally students will be working alone, learning how to do research, conducting their own study, writing it up and submitting their thesis at the end of three years. Whilst their universities will provide essential services like libraries and computing facilities, the students have to meet many expenses — travelling, consumables, small pieces of equipment for example — out of their own pocket. Factors like this have a real effect on the nature of the subject matter selected for research and the way the study is conducted.

For professional researchers, the situation is different. They will have selected and defined the problem to be addressed, worked out appropriate methodologies for the collection of data, devised strategies for their use and carefully costed the project as part of their preparation for seeking funding. The challenge for them lies in persuading a funding body that what they propose is worth doing, that the way they intend to do it is sound and can be managed and that the funds requested are, in the circumstances, reasonable. However, even they might have to ask themselves if a set of research questions which implied a five-year longitudinal study of 2,000 children in two countries at a cost of, say, £750,000, might not be sensibly discarded and replaced by others which could be answered more cheaply.

This leads us to another consideration in the selection of a research problem by an individual researcher. Big problems are not usually manageable because of their complexity. The objective of a researcher should not be to make a discovery that will change the world, it should be to add a small brick to the edifice of knowledge. For the research to be good research, that brick must be well-made. Research is a cumulative business and workers build on the results of previous studies, so it is the duty of the researchers to ensure, as far as possible, that their findings are reliable and valid.

Literature Review

In practice, the above activities coincide with, or at least overlap, the literature review. The object of this is to discover what researchers in the area chosen have been, and are, doing and also to clarify the problem or issue to be researched. By reading their work, it is possible to identify and avoid problems and pitfalls which might otherwise make themselves known too late in the study.

More positively, careful and critical reading of research reports might well enable a researcher to identify possibilities for further research which had been overlooked or not pursued by the original researcher. Indeed, it is very common for researchers themselves to conclude that further work is necessary or desirable on a particular aspect of the subject that has been investigated and to say so in their reports. It is surprising, perhaps, how seldom this opportunity is seized upon. An individual researcher looking for a matter to investigate should take hints like these very seriously; they are useful opportunities to pursue a project within a well-defined research context.

It might be thought that a prime purpose of reviewing the literature would be to ensure the avoidance of inadvertently repeating a previous study. Certainly it is as well to avoid repetition by inadvertency. However, there is nothing *per se* wrong in deliberately and consciously repeating a study, particularly if some doubt exists about an aspect of its methodology which might have affected the results. For example, it might be that a crucial instrument that was responsible for generating a large quantity of data could be shown to be, or is suspected of being, unsuitable for the purposes for which it was used; or perhaps a better, or more appropriate one has since been devised. Then again, it might be that the original study was conducted in, say, the USA and you wish to test its validity by replicating it in Britain.

Another possibility that might present itself is that you find a report of a small-scale, limited study that could lend itself to a larger-scale treatment with, perhaps, some additional variables. Another reason for replicating a study is the effect of the passage of time. Societies are dynamic and can change substantially over a generation. For example, in one of the earliest studies of the Chinese in Britain, Ng (1968) found that most wished and intended to return to China. A recent study of Chinese adolescents in Britain found that very few had any such intention (Verma and Chan, 1996). On the contrary, they spoke of their parents' descriptions of the hardships of life in China and were very clear that what they wanted to do was to succeed in school and find good, well-paid jobs in Britain.

The actual process of identifying the literature relevant to the proposed study has been greatly simplified by the development of computerized databases that are now accessible through libraries. In a rapidly developing technology such as this, it would be pointless to go into detail about the mechanics of the process, what it is capable of and how to get the best out of it. The chances are that the details will be out of date well within the lifetime of this book. Librarians are invariably helpful and will be very happy to pass on their expertise when, or if, it is needed.

A problem that can arise with the use of computerized databases is a consequence of their virtues of size and accessibility. Researchers can find themselves drowning in a sea of data. This should obviously be avoided. Although technology changes and improves, certain well-established problems remain. These were identified by Borg and Gall (1983) who provided a useful list of mistakes which can be made in reviewing research literature. Since technology may change but human fallibility remains more or less constant, we include some of them here:

1   Because of the desire to get on with the actual study, the literature review is too hurried. This can result in overlooking previous studies that would have improved the project.
2   Too much reliance is placed on secondary sources.
3   Too great a concentration when reading the literature on the findings at the expense of the methodology employed and the instruments used. Since these papers have been written by successful researchers, they should be treated as opportunities to learn something of the research process as well as the results.
4   Failure to define carefully the topic limits. If it is too broadly defined, there is simply too much to read as carefully as is needed. If it is too narrowly defined, important papers may be omitted and the project may be impoverished.

5   Too much (or too little) material in the form of extracts from research papers and so on, copied on to note cards.

Preparation of the Research Plan

Once the researcher has worked through the stages discussed above and has arrived at a hypothesis to be tested or research questions to be answered, it becomes necessary to devise a plan of action which will map out the processes involved in order to achieve his or her objectives. As was seen in Chapter 5, many approaches are open to an educational researcher, and in Chapter 6 we dealt with some of the tools available. Taken together, they provide almost endless possibilities for differing research plans, so this section will necessarily concern itself with general principles that it would be well to observe.

Most research projects fall into four phases which correspond to the nature of the work to be done at various times during the study. The research plan reflects this. However, like most plans, it suggests that one group of activities always precede and are completed before the next group begins. In real life, this does not always happen: activities tend to overlap and merge.

Phase I

An early part of the study will be the literature search, since this forms a vital part of the identification and formulation of the research problem. The hypothesis or research questions will largely determine what has to be done. Let us suppose that the study requires the use of a questionnaire, a standard psychological test and some interviews, and that these are to be employed on a sample of adolescents in schools. As soon as possible after this point, provision should be made to make initial contact with schools to find out if, in principle, they would be willing to cooperate by allowing access.

Bearing in mind what has already been said about the construction of a questionnaire in Chapter 6, this will have to be drafted, piloted and revised as necessary. A coding scheme will then have to be devised so that the data it provides can be converted into a form suitable for computer analysis. It is a good idea at this stage to code up the information gained from the pilot to make sure that the scheme works.

It is then necessary to make a decision about the best psychological test. There is a substantial array of such tests available for almost every eventuality. In making the selection the following questions might be helpful:

1   Does the test meet the requirements of the study as expressed in its aims and objectives?
2   Has it been standardized on an appropriate population?
3   Has it been successfully employed in studies by other researchers in circumstances similar to your own?

4 Am I qualified to use it? (Many, though by no means all, psychological tests are restricted in their use to trained psychologists.)

5 Can I afford it?

If the answer to all these questions is a firm 'Yes', the instrument chosen should work well for the study.

Decisions will have to be made about the type of interview to be used and an early draft made. If it is desirable and possible to delay a final draft until the data from the questionnaire and tests are in, it will nonetheless be necessary to indicate the lines of questioning envisaged, even if these are subsequently amended or added to. It is now possible to review all the data-gathering materials, set them against the objectives of the research and check that, between them, they will produce all the data that are necessary for the purposes of the study.

Since the study calls for a sample, this will have to be constructed. We stress again here that, if the results of the study are to be safely generalizable to the whole population, great care must be taken to ensure that the sample is as exactly representative of the population as can be managed. Sampling is considered in Chapter 8 where the problem of establishing the desirable size of the sample is addressed.

The next stage of the plan is to set out where the sample is to be found and the methods to be adopted to find them. In the case of this study, they are children and the intention is to gain access to them through their schools. A word of caution may be appropriate here. Schools exist in large numbers and it may be supposed that headteachers will enthusiastically support suitable research projects and facilitate access to their staff and children. As Maruyama and Deno (1992) warn, some may, but many will not. It has to be said that one of the side-effects of the 1988 Education Reform Act (NCC, 1989) with its increased workload on headteachers and teachers has been to reduce the time they are prepared to devote to the needs of researchers. However well-disposed headteachers may be, they may refuse to cooperate because of the added workload that the study will place on the staff. This problem may be avoided if the researcher's budget runs to buying in a supply teacher to free up staff time. Other obstacles may not be so easily overcome.

Phase II

This part of the plan sets out the practical arrangements for contacting the schools, gaining access to the students and making arrangements for the administration of the questionnaires, tests and interviews.

Phase III

At this point the data are all in and the researcher sets out the work to be done on them. Questionnaire data and test results have to be coded and the necessary analyses carried out on them. These will need to be specified at this stage. This ensures that the researcher has a clear picture of what needs to be done with the data and provides an opportunity to reflect on the intended course of action. He or she can relate the statistical analyses to the aims of the study and ensure that those that are proposed are those that are required. If the interviews were recorded, they will need to be transcribed.

Phase IV

Analysis of all data completed, the report of the study has to be written up. As well as clarifying the mind about what needs to be done, the research plan fulfils another valuable function. Most studies have to be completed within a specified time. For many studies this is because there is a contract between the researcher and a grant-awarding body which specifies the date on which the report is to be submitted. For post-graduate research students, it is the expectation on the part of the university that the thesis will be ready for examination after two or three years. Even for those free from these external constraints, it helps to ensure that their time will be spent as productively as possible. The preparation of a research plan makes it possible for the researcher to estimate the length of time each activity will take and so embark on the study with reasonable confidence that what is proposed can be managed within the time available.

For this reason, it is important that the time allotted to each activity is realistic and that allowance is made for delays that in the real world are inevitable. For example, any study which depends on the cooperation of administrators and managers has to take account of the fact that they are busy people for whom requests from researchers are time-consuming interruptions in their more important business. In a study requiring headteachers' permission and the cooperation of class teachers to work with children, weeks can go by before a decision is made. This is bad enough even when the decision is a positive one, but there can be no guarantee that it will be so. It will then be necessary to start negotiations with another school with further delay. Facts like this have to be taken into account in making the research plan and should be reflected in it. In the example of research planning given above, it may have been noted that initial contact with schools was an early item to be undertaken as soon as the main purposes of the study were known. This was to ensure that as much time as possible was made available for both the headteachers and the researcher to come to an agreement.

Many post-graduate students report when returning from their fieldwork that 'dead time' was their biggest problem. The 'dead time' to which they refer is time spent waiting in schools between interviews or between administering questionnaires with one group and another; or time spent travelling from school to school. Invariably, despite careful planning, this takes longer than they expected. All sorts of factors contribute, problems with transport, teacher absence, a local holiday or special event meaning that the subjects from whom data are to be collected are unavailable, and thus require re-visiting the school on another day.

It is sensible to allow as much time as can be managed for the final analysis and writing up. Except for the most brilliant and incisive minds, time spent on reflecting on the data, looking at them from differing angles, considering their relationship with each other, dwelling on the interpretations that can be placed on them, seeking to make sense of unexpected findings, is time well spent. For most researchers, insights and perceptions only come after lengthy periods of contemplating the research findings and, in fairness to the researchers and their sponsors, time should be set aside to allow this to happen.

It is also well worth spending some time, considering the best order in which to present the findings, so that the reader can follow these readily. It is sometimes tempting merely to follow the order of the items in the questionnaire, from which the findings are taken, rather than to arrange the findings, perhaps in terms of addressing the main research questions. Once the data are ordered in that fashion, it is a matter of considering the sequence in which the least repetition occurs. What is the best sequence of presenting the findings, so that the reader who was not present during the data collection, can best follow? It sometimes helps to consider beginning with a descriptive approach to give the reader a platform from which to follow a subsequent more detailed analysis which is better understood in the broad context of the findings. It is also worth experimenting with ways in which data are to be presented, i.e. in table or chart/graph format. A little time spent exploring the types of graph which a computer spreadsheet package can generate from a data table can help inexperienced researchers to decide which medium of presentation is best suited to their purposes.

All this planning needs to be done as part of the study's conception. Stouthamer-Loeber and Van Kammen's (1995) words neatly sum up the value of careful planning and the benefits that it brings:

> Planning may be viewed as the reduction of uncertainty about what is feasible so that later surprises are prevented as much as possible. Good planning leads to a study that delivers high quality data that are relevant to the aims of the study and are produced on time and within budget. Many early decisions are irreversible and influence the future course of the study and the use of available funds. Needless to say, these decisions have to be made with care.

Ethics and the Research Process

As Burgess (1989) observed, 'Within educational research there has been a great deal of discussion and debate about the ethical issues that face researchers in general and ethnographical researchers in particular.' Since children and schools play a large part in the lives of many educational researchers, this section begins by considering the researcher's obligations towards them.

A great deal of educational research uses children and adolescents as the subjects of studies. It is clearly important that they should be protected from any ill-effects that might result from a proposed study, unless it can be demonstrated that these will be trivial by comparison with the anticipated benefits for others. Fortunately, most research involving children and adolescents takes place in schools and headteachers are properly very careful to ensure, before giving their permission, that the rights of the children in their care are safeguarded. However, it would be wrong for researchers to assume that they as researchers have no responsibilities in this matter but that it is for the headteacher to act as their ethical guardians. In some countries, it may be necessary, or advisable to obtain permission from the Ministry of Education, and/or the local regional education office, before approaching head-teachers in individual schools.

Consent by a headteacher to research involving children is only valid if it is informed consent. It is important to remember that children and young people in their classrooms are not free agents. With few exceptions, they will tend to do what their class teachers expect of them. When told that a lesson, or part of a lesson, is to be taken up with completing a questionnaire or a psychological instrument for a researcher, they are not in an easy position to refuse. The same applies to their involvement in an experimental procedure, or any other aspect of research. They cannot assess the value of the study. They cannot make judgments in advance on the likely effects the treatment will have on them, nor can they withdraw from it once it has been started. There is an unavoidable element of coercion in their par-ticipation in the research and this can only be mitigated by obtaining their implied consent through the headteacher. If the headteacher is to come to an informed decision on their behalf, what information should the researcher provide?

The governing principle should be that the headteacher should be treated as if he or she was being asked to take part personally in the research. The British Educational Research Association has published *Ethical Guidelines* (BERA, 1992) covering a range of research issues and we use those under the heading of 'Respons-ibility to the participants' as the basis for the advice which follows. (The paragraph numbers are taken from the original.)

7 Participants in a research study have the right to be informed about the aims, purposes and likely publication of findings involved in the research and of poten-tial consequences for participants, and to give their informed consent before par-ticipating in research.

It is unlikely, though not impossible, that the headteacher will object to the aims or purposes of the study. Where objections are raised, they may result from misgivings about the value of the research. This is most likely to occur when the study means that students will be occupied for substantial periods of time in com-pleting questionnaires or other research instruments or being interviewed to the detriment of their normal programme. (Another possible reason for 'rejection' may be that, despite the merits of your study, the school is already, or has recently been, engaged in research and the headteacher judges it unwise to disrupt the school's work further by agreeing to participate.)

Another possible problem arises if the subject of the research is one which is perceived as sensitive. Studies concerned with issues relating to race or ethnicity, for example, are prone to this problem. Headteachers are rightly anxious to ensure that the research will not provide ammunition for racist propaganda and will require reassurance on this point. They are also likely to require convincing that any procedures, questionnaires, interviews or instruments employed in the conduct of the study will not cause distress to the students from ethnic minority groups, or to their parents.

They will certainly be concerned about the publication of the findings. The normal conventions of publication result in findings being anonymized so that neither the school nor any of its pupils can be identified. For the majority of studies, this presents no problems but there are occasions when only qualified anonymity is possible. For example, the study might propose to compare the academic performances of girls in all-girls secondary schools with those in mixed schools in a named county. If there are only two all-girls schools, readers of the published findings, especially those with local knowledge, might find it fairly easy to identify the schools involved and the headteachers and staff working in them. In circumstances like this, the researcher must be honest and say that whilst every effort will be made to ensure anonymity it won't be guaranteed absolutely. It may be that the way the findings will be presented does, in fact, ensure anonymity, but it will be for the researcher to convince the headteachers concerned that this is possible and to carry this through to publication, even if, by doing so, the research paper is weakened.

> 8   Care should be taken when interviewing children and students up to school leaving age; permission should be obtained from the school and, if they so suggest, the parents.

Headteachers may well ask for a copy of the interview schedule. If the planned interviews are semi-structured but only the key questions have been devised, they may ask what sort of follow-up questions are intended. The researcher must, of course, be honest about these and not use the interview as an opportunity to follow a line of questioning that has not been disclosed. It would, for example, be unethical whilst conducting interviews in the course of a study on home–school relationships to include, unbeknown to the school, a line of questions which sought to expose the possibility of the preferential treatment of white middle-class parents compared to that of working-class Pakistani parents.

At the time of the interview, children and young people should be given the same assurances as any other subjects. The procedures before conducting interviews were covered in some detail in Chapter 6 and should be gone through with students in schools.

> 9   Honesty and openness should characterize the relationship between researchers, participants and institutional representatives.

The above reinforces what has recently been discussed. Concealment of purpose and attempts to deceive schools as to the conduct of a piece of research are dishonest and unethical. There are, however, grey areas in this, as in almost all aspects of human activity.

In studies of behaviour, for example, if the subjects of the research know what the researcher is seeking to observe, they will probably behave untypically and the research will be flawed. When discussing non-participant observation in Chapter 6, we gave the example of a study which sought to determine if teachers behaved differently to students from different ethnic origins. There is an obvious danger that teachers, knowing what the observer is there for, will be very careful to relate in the same way to children from all ethnic groups. Even if that is what they normally do, the research will have no value because their actions will be self-conscious. In that example, the researcher, very properly, said what the real purposes of the observation were and put the burden of the decision, whether to allow it to happen, on the headteacher's shoulders.

The headteacher was then faced with three alternatives:

(i)   To agree to the study and get the agreement of the teachers to allow their classes to be observed without being told what the purposes of the observation were;

(ii)   To agree to the study and get the agreement of the teachers by misleading them about its true purpose; or

(iii)   Not to allow the research to be undertaken in the school.

We suggested in Chapter 6 that (iii) would be the most likely outcome. From the point of view of the researcher, the important thing is that the headteacher was told what the real purposes of the observation were. However worthy the motives, it would have been unethical to gain entry to the classrooms by dishonestly claiming, for example, that the observations were not to record the differential behaviour of male and female teachers towards boys and girls in their classes.

10   Participants have the rights to withdraw from a study at any time.

This applies to headteachers acting on behalf of students in their schools, as to everyone else.

11   Researchers have a responsibility to be mindful of cultural, religious, gendered, and other significant differences within the research population in the planning, conducting, and reporting of their research.

Most intending researchers are well-aware of the pitfalls and problems associated with research in the fields of gender, culture, religion, ethnicity, and the like. However, problems can arise in studies that have apparently no connexion with them because the sample includes children whose parents are members of a minority group sensitive to issues which present no problems to members of the white majority. Headteachers and teachers are likely to be sensitive to these issues and may well reject questionnaires or interview schedules or procedures which raise them. By the time this happens, it is probable that the study will be too far advanced to permit an easy revision of the offending items. It may be possible to negotiate successfully for access through another school, although the same problem may arise again. It is far better to be aware of the dangers from the outset and design the study accordingly.

As well as dealing with the researcher's responsibility to the participants, BERA's ethical guidelines cover a range of other ethical considerations related to research. A major consideration in its decision to draw up and publish these guidelines was concern over the increasing tendency of the DFE (Department for Education, as it then was) and other governmental agencies to assume control over the nature, objectives, conduct and dissemination of the findings of educational research and evaluation which they funded. The Introduction to the Guidelines makes this clear:

> Such a concern must be seen in a context where involvement in funded research is now viewed as a major indicator of the quality of schools and departments of education in higher education, and where central government now controls access to large amounts of funding for research in a field which it increasingly views as its policy domain. In this context, there is a great temptation for educational researchers and their institutions to accept sub-optimal contractual conditions which compromise the canons of intellectual inquiry in a free society. These conditions tend to impose restrictions on the freedom of researchers to publish and disseminate their findings. But there is also increasing evidence of a tendency to impose restrictions on the conduct of the inquiry itself, e.g. on the questions to be addressed and on methods of data collection and analysis. (BERA, 1992)

Much of the above is effectively dealt with in the following, paragraph 16 of the guidelines:

> Educational researchers should not agree to conduct research that conflicts with academic freedom, nor should they agree to undue or questionable influence by government or other funding agencies. Examples of such improper influence include endeavours to interfere with the conduct of research, the analysis of findings or the reporting of interpretations . . .

The relationship between a researcher and his or her funding agency is a delicate one and cannot be compared with that which exists between a purchaser and supplier of goods or services. It is reasonable for the funding agency to expect that the researcher will be properly diligent in pursuing the study, be professionally competent to do so and conduct the study in accordance with the agreed aims and objectives using the methods to achieve them agreed between them. In those respects, there is little difference between the researcher and sponsor on the one hand, and the purchaser and supplier on the other. The differences arise from the fact that the findings of the research are unforeseen: there would be no point in undertaking it if they were already known. It can be argued, therefore, that the sponsor is buying a process, not a product. In addition, those findings and their interpretation exist independently of the report in which they are expressed as part of the normal contractual obligations of the researcher to the sponsor.

Historically, these problems were accommodated by effectively limiting the rights of sponsors to demanding proper diligence and competence in conducting the research, collecting the data and arriving at a reasonable interpretation of them, using the funds allocated to it responsibly and supplying a report. The data and results of the research and the right to publish them were held by the researcher. The fact that BERA's ethical guidelines include the following paragraphs suggests that attempts have been made, notably by government and its agencies, to change that contractual relationship:

14   The data and results of a research study belong to the researchers who designed and conducted the study unless alternative contractual arrangements have been made with respect to the data or the results or both.

15   Educational researchers should remain free to interpret and publish their findings without censorship or approval from individuals, or organisations, including sponsors, funding agencies, participants, colleagues, supervisors, or administrators . . .

An extended consideration of this issue is beyond the scope of this book. However, it must be said that researchers have ethical obligations not only to the subjects of, or participants in, their studies, but also to the research community, and to the world of education generally. It is their duty to resist the attempts, clearly implied in BERA's guidelines, from whatever sources, to use data selectively, amend their interpretation, or prohibit publication.

References

BERA (1992) *Ethical Guidelines for Educational Research*, Edinburgh: British Educational Research Association.

BORG, W.R. and GALL, M.D. (1983) *Educational Research: An Introduction*, New York: Longman.

BURGESS, R.G. (1989) (ed.) *The Ethics of Educational Research*, London: Falmer Press.

LEEDY, P.L. (1993) *Practical Research Planning and Design*, 5th edition, New York: Macmillan.

MARUYAMA, G. and DENO, S. (1992) *Research in Educational Settings*, London: Sage.

NATIONAL CURRICULUM COUNCIL (1989) *An Introduction to the National Curriculum*, York: NCC.

NG, K.C. (1968) *The Chinese in London*, Oxford: Oxford University Press.

STOUTHAMER-LOEBER, M. and VAN KAMMEN, W.B. (1995) *Data Collection and Management: A Practical Guide*, London: Sage.

TRAVERS, R.M.W. (1978) *An Introduction to Educational Research*, New York: Macmillan.

VERMA, G.K. and CHAN, Y.-M. (1996) *The Cultural Identity of Chinese Adolescents in Britain*, Report to the Leverhulme Trust, London.

Chapter 8

Statistical Concepts and Educational Research

In this chapter we look at some of the statistical concepts and tools that are used in educational research. What follows does not pretend to be anything but a brief introduction to this field. As educational research has developed during this century, many tools and techniques for the statistical manipulation of data have been introduced to enable researchers to arrive at, or test the validity and reliability of, their conclusions. These have made possible the use of experimental procedures, the results of which would not otherwise have been possible to validate. The description and explanation of many of these techniques are outside the scope of this chapter. What follows is an attempt to introduce some of the commoner concepts.

As the chapter proceeds, some mathematical formulae are used to show how various calculations are made. For readers with a background in mathematics these will cause no difficulties. For those without that advantage we would simply say 'Do not worry too much about them.' The advent of powerful statistical programmes for computers means that they will do the calculations for you. The important thing is that you realize what the implications of these concepts are and understand the significance of the results which computers will supply in interpreting the results of your study. We begin by introducing the concept of *normal distribution* and the related *normal curve*.

The Normal Distribution and the Normal Curve

A girl says that, whilst playing in the playground, she tossed six coins together three times and, each time, six tails turned up. Could it happen? Is it likely that there was something unusual about the coins, or that she cheated? A 9-year-old boy, given a vocabulary test at school, scores 144. The average score at his age is 100. Is he very exceptional? In a test of spatial imagination given to the third year of a middle school, the average score for a group of boys was 67 and that for girls was 59. Is such a difference likely to occur by chance, or does it indicate a real difference in their average achievement? Two teachers in a school say that they compared an individual method of teaching with class teaching; when tested at the end of term, their pupils did better in the topics they learned by individual methods. Can this result be trusted to the extent of recommending the new method to their colleagues, or is further investigation needed? These are just a few of the questions that statisticians or research psychologists might be asked. In order to answer them, they must be familiar with theoretical distributions which enable them to say what the probability of each result is.

Let us return to the example of the girl and her coins. Is there a theoretical distribution which arises when coins are tossed? Unless a coin is biased there is an even chance that heads or tails will turn up. If two coins are tossed together, there are four possibilities: both turn up heads, the first turns up heads and the second tails, the first turns up tails and the second heads, or both turn up tails. Using H for head and T for tail, the four possibilities are HH once, HT twice and TT once. Similarly, when three coins are tossed together there are eight possibilities, i.e. HHH; HHT, HTH, THH, HTT THT, TTH, TTT. The frequencies of these possibilities may be written as in Table 8.1.

Table 8.1: *Probability and the 6-coin test*

Possibility	3H	2H 1T	1H 2T	3T	Total
Frequency	1	3	3	1	8

A pattern of possibilities is beginning to appear which can be extended by simply adding adjacent pairs of numbers in the line above, keeping 'all heads' to the left and 'all tails' to the right. It is shown in Figure 8.1 for up to 6 coins, but can be continued indefinitely.

Figure 8.1: *Probability and the 6-coin test*

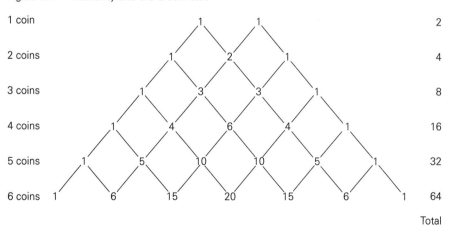

The last line in the triangle gives the theoretical distribution, or 'expected frequencies', when six coins are tossed together. If the six coins are tossed together 64 times, we expect on average that 6 heads will appear together once, 5 heads and 1 tail six times, 4 heads and 2 tails 15 times, 3 heads and 3 tails 20 times, 2 heads and 4 tails

15 times, 1 head and 5 tails six times, and 6 tails once. This is expressed in another way in Table 8.2.

Table 8.2: Probability and frequency and the 6-coin test

Possibility	6H	5H1T	4H2T	3H3T	2H4T	1H5T	6T	Total
Frequency	1	6	15	20	15	6	1	64
Probability	1/64	6/64	15/64	20/64	15/64	6/64	1/64	1

The probability of each event is calculated by dividing each frequency by the total. Thus the total of the *probabilities* of all these events is 1.

It is already possible to answer the question 'What is the probability of a girl tossing six coins at once three times with all the coins turning up tails?' The probability that the girl would toss six tails together once was 1/64, i.e. once in 64 times. The probability that she would do so three times in succession was $(1/64)^3$, i.e. 1/262,144 which is less than once in a quarter of a million tosses. In other words, the probability that this event would occur by chance is less than one in a quarter of a million. It is very unlikely indeed. The triangle of expected frequencies which can be extended indefinitely is known as Pascal's triangle. The mathematician Blaise Pascal (1623–62) discovered it at the age of 16 following a question put to him by the Chevalier de Méré who, like most aristocrats of the time, enjoyed gambling. From this discovery has developed the use of *parametric statistics* based on the study of the normal curve.

Staying a little longer with tossing coins as the example, Table 8.3 sets out the distribution for 10 coins in the same way as Table 8.2 did for six.

Table 8.3: Probability and frequency and the 10-coin test

Distribution	10H	9H1T	8H2T	7H3T	6H4T	5H5T	4H6T	3H7T	2H8T	1H9T	10T	Total
Frequency	1	10	45	120	210	252	210	120	45	10	1	1024
Probability	$\frac{1}{1024}$	$\frac{10}{1024}$	$\frac{45}{1024}$	$\frac{120}{1024}$	$\frac{210}{1024}$	$\frac{252}{1024}$	$\frac{210}{1024}$	$\frac{120}{1024}$	$\frac{45}{1024}$	$\frac{10}{1024}$	$\frac{1}{1024}$	1
To 3 dec. places	0.001	0.010	0.044	0.117	0.205	0.246	0.205	0.117	0.044	0.010	0.001	

It can be seen that the chances of tossing 10 coins and getting 10 heads or 10 tails are 1/1024, i.e. once in 1024 attempts. Equally, it is possible to use the Table to calculate the probability of tossing, say eight or more heads: using fractions it is:

$$\frac{45 + 10 + 1}{1024} = \frac{56}{1024} = \frac{7}{128}$$

or to 3 decimal places, $0.044 + 0.010 + 0.001 = 0.055$.

That is to say, it may be expected to happen a little more often than once in 20 times.

Another way of representing the contents of Table 8.3 would be as a column graph as in Figure 8.2.

Figure 8.2: Normal distribution and the 10-coin test

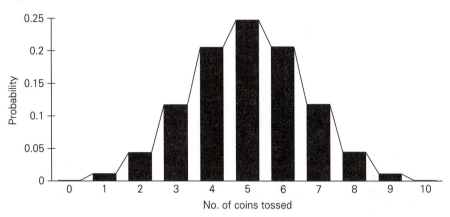

It can be seen that the tops of the columns lie approximately on a curve and that the area under the curve is equivalent to that of the columns. However, to obtain the probability of 8 or more heads by using the curve we need to obtain the area under the tail of the curve from 7.5 to 10.5. Since tables of areas under the normal curve are obtainable in books, they are often used to obtain probabilities in large distributions. Although laborious, it would be possible to work out the probabilities if 100 coins were tossed together. If the result were represented in a column graph, the tops of the columns would form an almost perfect curve known as the 'normal curve'.

Many distributions of measurements of human beings such as heights, weights, sizes of shoes, gloves or hats, the distances individuals of the same age and sex can throw a ball, and so on, fit very well to the normal curve. So do many educational and psychological test scores, although in the case of standardized tests, this may be partly because educationists and psychologists designed them to do so.

Before we can make use of the normal curve in order to say how exceptional a pupil's score is as compared with other children of the same age, we need to turn his or her score in a test into a *standard score*. To do this we must first obtain the *mean* and *standard deviation* for the distribution of scores.

Taking a simplified example initially: in six tests, a boy obtains marks of 36, 49, 52, 60, 65, 74. The mean (or average) score is defined as the total of the scores for all the tests divided by the number of tests, i.e. the boy's *mean score* is $\frac{336}{6} = 56$.

Deviations of the scores above and below the mean are as follows:

Score   52   49   65   36   60   74
Deviation from 56   −4   −7   9 −20   4   18   Total = 0

Squared deviation   16   49   81   400   16   324   Total: 886

∴ mean squared deviation from the mean (*the variance*) $= \dfrac{886}{6} = 147.67$

Having obtained the variance by squaring the deviation (which gave us 147.67 in this example) the 'standard deviation' is arrived at by finding the square root of 147.67 which is approximately 12.2. It is now possible to arrive at the 'standard score' in each subject by using the formula $z = \dfrac{x - m}{s}$ where z is the standard score, x is the original score, m is the mean score and s is the standard deviation.

When the scores in different normal distributions are treated in this way, it has the effect of reducing them all to similar normal distributions having mean of zero and unit standard deviation. This makes possible comparisons between, say, distributions of examination scores originally having different means and different spreads. In the case of our example, the standard scores in each subject work out as follows:

Original scores   52   49   65   36   60   74
Standard scores   −0.33   −0.58   0.74   −1.65   0.33   1.49

It is now possible to show how standard scores and the normal curve work in practice by giving some examples.

Example 1: The normal curve
For the normal curve, and therefore approximately for all normal distributions,

about $\dfrac{2}{3}$ of the scores (68.26%) lie in the range $m \pm s$

about $\dfrac{19}{20}$ of the scores (95.44%) lie in the range $m \pm 2s$

about 998 scores in 1000 (99.74%) lie in the range $m \pm 3s$

Figure 8.3:   Normal distribution and the standard deviation

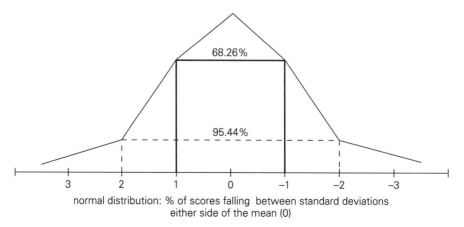

normal distribution: % of scores falling between standard deviations
either side of the mean (0)

This is shown in Figure 8.3. If information concerning, say, a standardized test of arithmetic achievement gives the mean score for 8-year-olds as 60 and the standard deviation as 12, then, for the entire population, or a large representative sample, about two-thirds (67 per cent) can be expected to gain scores in the range 48–72, about nineteen-twentieths (95 per cent) in the range 36–84, and almost all in the range 24–96.

Example 2
Since many achievements in, for instance, reasoning, reading vocabulary, arithmetic, and so on, seem to be distributed normally, this has an interesting bearing on the range which can be expected in 'mixed ability' classes.

As an example, scoring of individual tests in the Terence-Merrill tests of intelligence (largely of reasoning), the scores obtained can be expressed as mental ages. A 6-year-old who passes all the six tests for 6-year-olds, four of the tests for 7-year-olds and three tests for 8-year-olds has a mental age (MA) of 7 years 2 months, (using each test as two months after the base year). A child whose *mental age* is the same as his chronological age is said to have an *Intelligence Quotient* of 100. The standard deviation in terms of quotient points is given as 16. For this, therefore, nearly all IQs will lie between $100 \pm 3(16)$ i.e. 100 ± 48 or between 52–148. What does this imply in terms of 'mental age'? Since 16 is about a sixth of 100, at 6 years, the standard deviation is about one year (a sixth of 6 years) and almost all 'mental ages' will, therefore, lie in the range 3–9, i.e. a range of 6 years. Similarly at 12 years, the standard deviation will be about 2 years and consequently almost all 'mental ages' will then lie in the range 6–18 years, a range of 12 years. Table 8.4 shows results in more detail.

Table 8.4: IQ scores and mental age

IQ		52	68	84	100	116	132	148
Approx. MA	6 yrs	3	4	5	6	7	8	9
in years and at	8 yrs	4	5.4	6.8	8	9.4	10.8	12
months	10 yrs	5	6.8	8.4	10	11.8	13.4	15
	12 yrs	6	8	10	12	14	16	18

Since reading and other achievement 'ages' follow a similar pattern, it is not so surprising, perhaps, that some children at 9 years are found to have reading ages not much higher than 6 years. Whilst such ranges undoubtedly raise problems for teachers of mixed ability classes, the lowest scoring group (more than two standard deviations below average) are usually in special schools or receive specialist help in class. Further, the school catchment area tends to limit the range of achievement amongst the children each school receives. This wide range is not necessarily a convincing argument for giving up mixed ability teaching. Where this is used well, it has been found not to handicap able children whilst having good effects on the motivation and skills of the less able; in effect, the achievement range is reduced by a movement upwards at the lower end.

Example 3: How achievements in different subjects can be compared
In a mathematics test having mean score 50, and standard deviation 16, a boy scored 74. In an English test, with mean score 48 and standard deviation 10, he scored 65. In which subject did he do better?

$$\text{Standard score (maths)} = \frac{74 - 50}{16} = \frac{24}{16} = 1.5$$

$$\text{Standard score (English)} = \frac{65 - 48}{10} = \frac{17}{10} = 1.7$$

Although his raw score was lower in English than in maths, when the distributions are equated it is evident that he did rather *better* in English than in maths.

Example 4
To answer the second question near the beginning of the chapter (Was the 9-year-old boy who scored 144 in a vocabulary test exceptional?), we need to know the standard deviation of the scores for 9-year-olds. If it is 17, then the boy's standard score is $\dfrac{144 - 100}{17}$. To obtain the probability of obtaining such a high score we use tables of areas under the normal curve. Using a simplified table of areas under the normal curve, see Table 8.5, the probability of a score so high as 2.59 is about 0.006; i.e. only 6 in 1000 9-year-olds would be expected to do so well.

Table 8.5: *Standard scores and the normal distribution*

Standard score	Probability area under the normal curve
0.00	0.500
0.25	0.401
0.50	0.309
0.75	0.227
1.00	0.159
1.25	0.106
1.50	0.067
1.75	0.040
2.00	0.023
2.25	0.016
2.50	0.006
2.75	0.003
3.00	0.001
4.00	0.0000317
5.00	0.000000287

Testing Populations and Large Samples

The discussion of normal distributions so far applies to large populations, where the population is the whole group of people under consideration, e.g. all 9-year-old school children, all 5-year-olds in their first term at school, all entrants to universities in 1997, and so on. Often, these populations are too large to be studied *in full*: it would be too time-consuming and expensive. However, entire populations are sometimes studied if an enquiry is considered sufficiently important — such as the 10-yearly census of the population — and is generously staffed and funded. Bodies such as the Scottish Educational Research Council (SERC), the National Foundation for Educational Research (NFER) and the Department for Education and Employment (DfEE) have sometimes obtained funds for studies on a very large scale.

Concern that children should achieve a high standard in basic skills has also led a number of local authorities to test substantial samples of children, or all children, in their areas. It is, of course, very important that these tests should be well chosen. Many are likely to be norm-referenced and so need to have been standardized fairly recently on a similar sample of children. Since educational methods are changing, children can be expected to show rather different strengths and weaknesses from those of their predecessors. If tests are selected which are unsuitable, they can give very misleading results. Their administration, too, is important, for if they are administered incorrectly, results are no longer comparable with those of the standard population. Moreover, if an administrator, teacher, or local politician misunderstands what the test measures, he or she may reach unsound conclusions when interpreting results.

A standardized test is one in which the procedures, apparatus and scoring have been predetermined. Usually there are standard ways of putting questions, detailed directions to administrators which must be clearly followed, instructions as to time to be allowed for each page, when to turn over or to wait, the method of indicating answers, and so on. Indeed, every administrative condition which affects performance must be specified if the test is to be regarded as standardized. In addition, norms may be given which show means and standard deviations for different age groups, for boys and girls separately and, sometimes, for children attending different types of school. This enables psychologists and teachers to compare a child's performance with those of others. In criterion-referenced tests, this is not possible, but children's performances can sometimes be assessed by comparing their performance in terms of specified skills mastered.

Even when using standardized tests, the results of any one child can be expected to vary on different occasions. Interestingly, the sex or ethnic origin of the tester may influence results: children usually perform rather better with a tester of their own sex and origin. In addition, of course, children cannot be expected to perform at their best when they are tired, hungry or emotionally disturbed. The environment, too, may affect results if ventilation or light is poor, or if extraneous noise or the size of a hall makes listening to instructions difficult. For these reasons, more faith can be put in high marks than in low ones.

In England and Wales, the introduction of a National Curriculum which arose out of the 1988 Education Reform Act, requires formal testing of (almost) all children at the end of the four Key Stage at 7, 11, 14, and 16. Although results are reported in terms of 'level' attained, these provide useful baseline data. Results are published in, among other ways, in the form of league tables, showing the standards reached by individual school, local education authority (LEA), as well as nationally.

Whatever, the form of testing, familiarity with test conditions, or with the kind of test items, may also considerably affect a child's score. For instance, in testing 7-year-olds with a group 'intelligence' test, their headteacher found IQs for Max and Barbara of 95 and 98, respectively. Earlier conversations with them suggested that these scores did not do them justice. When tested individually by a research worker using an interesting variety of test items and in a situation where instructions could be clarified, Max obtained an IQ of 137 and Barbara an IQ of 128. This makes the difference between seeming about average and demonstrating exceptional ability. A teacher who accepted the group test IQ would have been seriously misled.

Younger children and those retarded for any reason are more likely to display their full abilities when with one sympathetic adult. But a highly intelligent girl of 12, unpractised in group test technique, spent so long trying to solve a few difficult items that she failed to complete the test and so gained an IQ of 105. Retested with an individual test, her IQ was 165, and, in a different group test, after she had been instructed to omit difficult items until the end, her IQ was 160. These quotients are quite unusually high; the test in which she was not adequately briefed was wholly misleading and could have had serious consequences for her future. Certainly, in the past, when such tests were routinely used to determine the kind of education children were to receive after the age of 11, the lower score would have denied her a place at Grammar School.

A few additional concepts will be introduced here. When preparing norm-referenced tests of achievement the test development team not only excludes confusing or ambiguous items but also calculates measures of *item difficulty* and *item discrimination*. In simple terms, item difficulty is derived from the proportions of those tested obtaining the correct answer for an item. This is then used to compare the differences in the proportions of correct responses for each other item. Item discrimination relates to the power of individual items to discriminate between, for example, high, medium and low achievers, as determined by their performance on the test as a whole. Knowledge of difficulty level and discrimination indices helps the test developers to decide on the best order in which to arrange the items, usually beginning with some easy ones to help those being tested to feel comfortable.

It is from results in group tests constructed by using items which have been subjected to item analysis before final selection and then been standardized on a carefully selected sample, that tables of norms are prepared showing how different scores compare with chronological ages. In this way it is possible to say that a child aged 9 years 6 months performs like an average child aged 8 years 6 months in reading, but achieves the score of average children of 10 years 3 months in mathematics.

Sampling from a Population

A great deal of educational research is conducted using samples drawn from the population being studied. One of the most difficult questions to answer is 'How large need the sample be to make reliable generalizations about the population as a whole?' In practice, two considerations tend to dominate the process of arriving at a decision. The first is the number of sub-divisions (often referred to as 'cells') that will be required for statistical analysis. Suppose, for example, that a study of South Asian adolescents' attitudes towards higher education is being planned. Perhaps the researcher is concerned to find out if their attitudes at various ages change differentially in the three main ethnic groups, how they differ from their white British peers and whether any changes could be attributed to differing cultural values. The sample might be built up as shown in the grid which follows:

Figure 8.4: Grid for a sampling frame

Ethnic Origin	Boys: ages			Girls: ages			Total
	12–13	14–15	16–17	12–13	14–15	16–17	
Pakistani							
Indian							
Bangladeshi							
White British							

This grid contains 24 cells and, in practice, it is desirable to have 30 or more subjects in each cell so the sample size would need ideally to be at least 720. If the researcher suspected that not only age but religious belief had an effect on attitudes, this would obviously lead to greater complexity and a larger overall sample size. However, as will be seen shortly, other considerations than simply adequate cell sizes are also involved.

Statisticians have developed techniques to arrive at theoretical sample sizes for different population sizes at various levels of certainty. Table 8.6 is taken from Anderson (1994) and shows how small those minimum sample sizes can be, particularly if an error rate of 5 per cent is considered acceptable. The Table also makes clear the fact that very small populations of 100 or so require proportionately very large sample sizes (79 at a 95 per cent level of certainty) whilst populations of 5,000 or more require proportionately very much smaller samples. As the numbers in the population rise, the required minimum sample size scarcely increases at all, even at a 2 per cent level of tolerable error. It is for this reason that national

Table 8.6: Confidence levels and sampling

Confidence level	Required sample for a tolerable error at:			
	5%	4%	3%	2%
Population				
100	79	85	91	96
500	217	272	340	413
1000	277	375	516	705
5000	356	535	879	1622
50000	381	593	1044	2290
100000	382	596	1055	2344
1000000	384	599	1065	2344
25000000	384	600	1067	2400

Source: Anderson, 1994, Fundamentals of Educational Research, London, Falmer Press.

surveys conducted by polling organizations such as MORI can be so confident of their findings even though only about 1,600 people have been questioned. The statistics behind the calculations which lead to these surprising numbers are outside the scope of this book.

The important thing to remember at all times about a sample is that a sample is only a sample. If it is to produce results that can be reliably generalized, it must, as nearly as possible, replicate in miniature the whole population which it represents as well as being of adequate size. This means that the researcher has to define very carefully the way the sample has been constructed. To return for a moment to the example of the study involving South Asian adolescents and their attitudes towards higher education: what would the researcher have to be careful to ensure in defining the sample?

Clearly, it would be essential to ensure that the sub-samples taken from each group were, as far as possible, comparable. The results of the study would be valueless if, for example, substantial numbers of Indian and white British respondents were drawn from selective schools (where the expectations were that *all* students should aim for entry to university), whereas the majority of respondents from other ethnic groups were drawn from inner-city comprehensive schools (where the expectations were that unemployment or, at best, a course at a further education college lay ahead of their students). The findings would then simply show that adolescents who attended selective schools with high academic expectations had different attitudes towards higher education from those who did not — a scarcely surprising outcome — whilst any attempt to relate the findings to values forming part of their different cultures would be impossible. Thus, to achieve comparability and ensure that differing attitudes (if any) could be related to cultural values, the sample for all ethnic groups would have to be drawn from similar schools.

It is now possible to return to the sample grid and fill in some numbers. Most research apart from work undertaken by government ministries, is locally based and, for convenience, it is assumed that this study is to be conducted in London. As has been seen, minimum sample sizes are related to the size of the population being studied. The 1991 census showed that there were, to the nearest thousand, 13,000 Indian males and females aged between 15–19, 4,000 Pakistanis, 5,000 Bangladeshis and 15,000 white British living in London (Storkey, 1991). A sample shown in Table 8.7 would therefore be adequate at a 5 per cent level of tolerable error.

Table 8.7: Cell size and sample grid

Ethnic Origin	Boys: ages			Girls: ages			Total
	12–13	14–15	16–17	12–13	14–15	16–17	
Pakistani	120	120	120	120	120	120	720
Indian	130	130	130	130	130	130	780
Bangladeshi	120	120	120	120	120	120	720
White British	130	130	130	130	130	130	780

Constructing a sample frame such as the above as part of a research project involving the use of questionnaires and, perhaps, interviews, is an important part of the planning for any research project. However, not all samples are under the control of the researcher as that one was. Researchers are often faced with data acquired as a result of procedures over which they had no control and have then to determine whether or not the apparent meanings they convey are real or not, in terms of their being typical of a wider population.

Suppose, for example, the researcher is asked whether the assessments made by two teachers of the same 10 essays differed significantly. The word 'significantly' here means that the researcher has to discover whether the differences between the two teachers in scoring the essays were attributable to chance variations or were the result of genuine differences in the teachers' standards or opinions. Their scores are set out in Table 8.8.

Table 8.8:   Test scores: Inter-marker variations

Essay	A	B	C	D	E	F	G	H	I	J
Mark (Teacher 1)	2	3	4	5	5	5	6	6	7	9
Mark (Teacher 2)	0	1	3	6	4	5	7	3	8	9

The answer to that question can be arrived at by applying the 't' test to the scores. It starts from an hypothesis concerning the expected or true state of affairs: *the null hypothesis*. In this instance, since the teachers would be expected to agree, the null hypothesis is that the mean difference between the teachers' marks is zero.

Calculation

Total

$d = difference\ (Mk1 - Mk2)$ 2 2 1 1 1 0 1 3 1 0   12
d^2 4 4 1 1 1 0 1 9 1 0   22

Mean difference $= \dfrac{12}{10} = 1.2$

Estimate of $\sigma = \sqrt{\dfrac{1}{9}\sum(d - m)^2}$

$\qquad = \sqrt{\dfrac{7.6}{9}}$

$\dfrac{\sigma}{\sqrt{N}} = \dfrac{\sqrt{0.84}}{\sqrt{10}} = \sqrt{0.084} = 0.29$ (approx.)

useful equivalents:

$$\sum(d - m)^2 = \sum d^2 - Nm^2 = \sum d^2 - \frac{T^2}{N}$$

$$\sum(d - m)^2 = 22 - \frac{144}{10} = 22 - 14.4 = 7.6$$

$$t = \frac{m - \sum}{\sigma/\sqrt{N}}$$

where $\sum$ is the expected mean difference, i.e. zero, and $\sigma/\sqrt{N}$ is the standard of the mean.

$$t = \frac{1.2}{0.29} = 4.1 \,(\text{approx.})$$

Probability tables of t show that this is very high, see Table 8.9.

Table 8.9:   t-test table values

Confidence level	0.10	0.05	0.02	0.01	0.001
degrees of freedom					
1	—	—	—	—	—
5	—	—	—	—	—
6	1.94	2.45	3.14	3.71	5.96
9	1.83	2.26	2.82	3.25	4.78
10	1.81	2.23	2.76	3.17	4.59

For 10 pairs of marks (9 degrees of freedom)

The probability that t = 3.25 or higher is 0.01, i.e. one in 100.
The probability that t = 4.78 or higher is 0.001, i.e. one in 1000.
Since 4.1 lies between 3.25 and 4.78, we conclude that so great a difference between the teachers marks is improbable unless they genuinely differ in standards or opinions. The difference is said to be significant.

The concept of *degrees of freedom* is closely related to the number of observations, in general, the number of observations minus the number of constraints put on the system. This will be recognized from experience of examples. If two distinct samples are to be compared, e.g. girls' and boys' marks in a mathematics test, a different formula for 't' is available. Degrees of freedom in the comparison are given by (number of girls + number of boys – 2). To anyone lacking experience in statistics, it is tempting to think that a difference in mean score between two samples is necessarily meaningful. But if samples are small, the difference between them needs to be quite large to be significant when tested by the 't' test. Use of the test enables us to say whether the difference obtained is quite likely to occur by chance, or whether it is significant, i.e. it is improbable. In the latter case, the difference may be due to some underlying cause which deserves further investigation.

If populations differ, comparisons should be made with caution. In a letter to *The Times* in 1978, a comparison was made between the performance of comprehensive schools, grammar schools, and independent and the then direct grant schools, as to the success of their pupils in obtaining two A-levels. The figures given were 6 per cent, 30 per cent and 35 per cent, respectively. I do not remember where the writer claimed to have obtained the figures, but he certainly concluded that the latter schools were better. It must be remembered, however, that comprehensive schools took almost 100 per cent of the population (with the exception of very backward and, usually, of very able children). Grammar schools took, on average, the top 20 per cent, and the last group, which is more mixed, took pupils on the whole from the top 10–15 per cent of the population. Since 30 per cent of 20 per cent is 6 per cent, the grammar schools were doing no better than the comprehensive schools even if the latter took the full range of able pupils. Since they did not, the comprehensives were doing better; some of their rather less able pupils were evidently successful in obtaining two A-levels. The case of the last group is more remarkable: 35 per cent of 10 per cent is only 3.5 per cent, whilst 35 per cent of 15 per cent is 5.25 per cent. Thus these schools on average obtained at most 5.25 per cent successes and so did less well than the grammar schools.

In this example, we do not need 't' tests since we are comparing entire populations. If, however the figures arose from samples, the differences should be tested for significance. Assuming that the letter writer's figures were correct and applied to whole populations or to large samples, we may speculate on the cause of these differences. Is there a tendency perhaps, where entry to schools and universities is competitive, to encourage the brightest at the expense of the relatively less able? In grammar schools, independent schools and direct grant schools, the less able are in fact well above average for the whole population, but they may be referred to and treated as stupid and so become discouraged. Alternatively, or in addition, teachers may tend to teach classes at an average pace, so that those below average (a very high proportion) fall behind and so do not obtain the successes which their abilities merit. Thus, if the figures were correct, it might be worthwhile to make further enquiries to see whether some schools avoid this unfortunate effect.

Some Other Theoretical Distributions

So far, we have discussed the normal distribution and have seen how to use areas under the normal curve in studying populations or large samples. The 't' distribution has been introduced and the 't' distribution used in comparing the mean of a small sample with an expected value. Sometimes, in addition, variances of samples have to be compared. To test whether one sample is more variable than another, i.e. whether the variances in the two samples differ significantly, the *F-test* is employed.

The theoretical distribution, known as the *F-distribution*, is not even nearly normal for small samples and differs in shape depending on the relative sizes of the samples being compared. Three tables are commonly available showing the probability of obtaining different values of F for samples of different sizes; the three tables correspond with probability levels 0.05, 0.01 and 0.001.

Example 5

Scores for 25 pupils taking a history test have a standard deviation of 17, scores for 19 of these pupils who took a maths test had a standard deviation of 11. Do the variances differ significantly?

The variances are 17^2 and 11^2 respectively, i.e. 289 and 121.

$$F = \frac{\text{larger variance}}{\text{smaller variance}} = \frac{289}{121} = 2.4 \text{ (approx.)}$$

The significance of the F-ratio obtained is checked against the appropriate 'table value', this being dependent on the degrees of freedom (df) for each of the two variances. In the present example, there are 24 degrees of freedom for the larger variance (history, 25–1) and 18 for the smaller variance (mathematics, 19–1). Reference to Table 8.10, an abridged version of significant F-ratio values, in which the upper numbers of each pair are the figures for the 5 per cent level and the lower ones (in **bold** type) are those for the 1 per cent level, shows that the value F = 2.4 lies between the 5 per cent level (2.15) and the 1 per cent level (**3.00**) for 24 and 18 df values. This means that the null hypothesis (see the Glossary) that the variances do *not* differ is rejected. Their difference is significant; it is a difference which would occur by chance less frequently than 5 times in 100 times. Make sure to match up the degrees of freedom accurately, when reading from a table of F-values: the df for the larger variance (history) run *across* the Table, and the smaller one (mathematics), run *down* the Table.

Table 8.10: *F-ratio table values*

		1	2	16	20	24	30	40	←
Degrees of freedom smaller variance	1								Degrees of freedom larger variance
	2								
↓	17			2.29	2.23	2.19	2.15	2.11	
				3.27	**3.16**	**3.08**	**3.00**	**2.92**	
	18			2.25	2.19	2.15	2.11	2.09	
				3.19	**3.07**	**3.00**	**2.91**	**2.83**	
	19			2.21	2.15	2.11	2.07	2.02	
				3.12	**3.00**	**2.92**	**2.84**	**2.76**	
	24	3.40							
		5.61							

The F-test is analysis of variances. Frequently, a research worker will deal with more than two samples and so will wish to compare their means simultaneously. To take a simple example a psychologist might be interested in comparing attitudes of three different age groups of children towards learning science at school. A more complex comparison would be required if the purpose was to compare the performance of boys and girls aged 12, 14 and 16 years in problems at two different levels of abstraction. In a still more complex experiment, the purpose might be to compare performance of 5-year-olds on four different kinds of tests, using four different kinds of items. Numerous designs are possible, depending on the number of variables to be integrated, whether or not the experimenter is interested in all their interactions and, of course, the availability of subjects.

The first of these comparisons is quite easy to handle, but as additional complexities are introduced, it is advisable to look up possible designs of experiments in such well known texts as *Experimental Design* by Cochran and Cox (1957) or in rather less mathematical texts such as *Design and Analysis of Experiments in Psychology and Education* by Lindquist (1956). These enable a research worker to find the most economical design in order to study the effects of different variables and their interactions.

Sometimes, when it is not simple to make comparisons between groups, when the groups differ in size the χ^2 test is used. Are there significant differences between them in terms of the frequency of distribution? In such situations, the chi-square (the *chi* rhyming with 'my') test may well be useful. This helps us to test whether the differences in the *observed* and *expected* frequencies in the data from two or more groups are the product of a statistical accident or 'freak' or are the product of some underlying cause. Suppose, for example, the researcher had data on the career choices of a group of students, from different social classes (socio-economic groups). The chi-square test could be used to test the significance of the differences. The basic formula for χ^2 is:

$$\chi^2 = \sum \frac{(O - E)^2}{E}$$

Table 8.11 sets out the data, with the final column giving a coding for the figures. (The coding is to enable the reader to follow the formula which can be used, in a 2 × 2 Chi-square.)

The χ^2 distribution can be used with non-normal distributions and even with discrete variables. Thus it is a very useful and powerful test. Statistics relating to

Table 8.11: χ^2 distribution
Career Choice

		professional	non-professional	total	*formula guide*
social class	1,2	55	20	75	*a b a+b*
	3,4,5	27	68	95	*c d c+d*
	total	82	88	170	*a+c b+d* N

non-normal distribution are known as *non-parametric statistics*. The formula that can be applied in cases like this example, where there are two groups (*here* social classes 1, 2 and 3, 4, 5) and two categories of response (*here* professional and non-professional career choice) is as follows:

$$\chi^2 = \frac{(ad - bc)^2 \times N}{(a + b)(b + d)(c + d)(a + c)}$$

We then get the following:

$$\chi^2 = \frac{(55 \times 68 - 20 \times 27) \times (55 \times 68 - 20 \times 27) \times 170}{75 \times 88 \times 95 \times 82}$$

$$= \frac{174080000}{51414000} = 33.9 \text{ (approx.)}$$

For 1 degree of freedom (as is the case in 2×2 chi-square calculations), the probability of a value exceeding 10.83 is 0.001. Since 33.9 is much greater, its probability is small. This enables us to reject the null hypothesis (see the Glossary), that there is no difference in career choices between the social classes; the difference between the groups is therefore statistically highly significant.

Non-parametric Distribution and Tests

So far, we have considered distributions which are distributed normally or samples drawn from normal distributions. In some studies, skew, bi-modal, U-shaped or T-shaped distributions may be found and for this we may need different tests. For instance, in sociometric studies in which children say who they would like to sit next to, to work with or to play with, one or two children may prove popular. These are the 'stars'. The majority receive far fewer choices or even none at all. If we plot the distribution of frequencies against number of choices the distribution is *positively skewed*, i.e. the tail is towards the positive end, see Table 8.12 and Figure 8.5. In an easy class test in which nearly all children do well, the distribution is *negatively skewed*; the tail of the curve will then be to the negative end.

Table 8.12: Choice of friends: Distribution

No. of choices	0	1	2	3	4	5	6	7	8	9	10	11	12	13	14	15
Frequency		1	3	8	10	7	6	5	4	0	2	2	0	1	0	0	1

To compare scores in distributions of these kinds, it is more meaningful to obtain *median* scores than means and to obtain *deciles* or *percentiles* to compare performance than to obtain standard scores. The 'median' score is defined as the point on the scale of measurement above which are exactly half the measures and below which are the other half. It is defined as a point and not as a score or any particular measurement. It may be obtained accurately from a graph or by making a calculation. Similarly, the upper quartile (or 75th percentile) is the point above

Figure 8.5: Choice of friends: Distribution profile

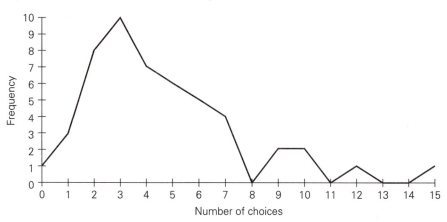

which are exactly a quarter of the measures, and the lower quartile is the point below which are exactly a quarter of the measures. These measures are suitable for use in comparing large samples, for example, of GCSE and A-level marks which often are, but need not be, normally distributed.

Example 6

Table 8.13 shows distributions of marks in pure mathematics and physics papers taken by some sixth form pupils. End points of intervals have been corrected so that the scale of marks becomes continuous. It is evident that marks in physics are poorer than those in pure mathematics. This suggests that either the physics paper was harder or that the candidates who took physics were less able than those who took pure mathematics. This is easy for an examiner to investigate as many candidates take both subjects. Here the candidates are about equal in calibre so the physics paper was evidently more difficult. Drawing cumulative frequency graphs for both samples by plotting cumulative percentages against the mark at the upper end of an interval gives the results shown in Table 8.13.

Table 8.13: Examination performance in 2 subjects

Mark	Pure Mathematics			Physics		
	Frequency	Cumulative	%	Frequency	Cumulative	%
89.5–100.5	20	5100	100.0	0	1700	100.0
79.5–89.5	120	5080	99.5	16	1700	100.0
69.5–79.5	390	4960	97.6	60	1684	99.0
59.5–69.5	950	4570	89.9	231	1624	95.5
49.5–59.5	1239	3620	71.1	337	1393	82.0
39.5–49.5	1221	2391	46.6	461	1056	62.1
29.5–39.5	810	1170	23.0	392	595	35.0
19.5–29.5	289	360	7.1	159	203	13.3
9.5–19.5	64	71	1.4	38	44	2.5
0.0–9.5	7	7	0.1	6	6	0.3
Total	5110			1700		

Figure 8.6: *Comparison of marks in pure mathematics and physics*

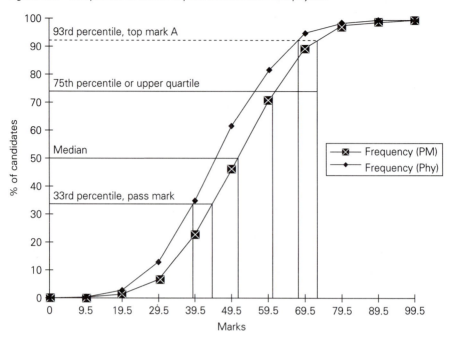

It is now possible to compare marks so that equal standards are required for pass marks and successive grades in the two subjects. If it is agreed to fail one third of candidates, the pass mark in pure mathematics is 45, and, in physics, is 38. If only the top 7 per cent are to receive A grades, the corresponding marks are 73 in pure mathematics, and 67 in physics. The median and upper quartile (75th percentile) are also marked on the graphs; the method is applicable if the distributions of marks deviate substantially from normal.

Non-parametric tests have been devised to provide tests of significance for distributions which are not normal. It may not be possible to specify the functional form of the population distributions but only that the accumulated distribution function is continuous. An alternative term for the tests is *distribution free*. The best known non-parametric test is the χ^2-test, but many other tests have been developed. In practice, such tests have the advantages of simplicity and wide application, but they have certain disadvantages as compared with parametric tests. The conclusions drawn are weaker and the use of parametric tests as approximations may give more information than the use of a suitable non-parametric test.

Here only two fairly common tests are mentioned: these are the Signs test and the Median test. The *Signs test* can be used for pairs of observations, for instance, for measures for the same sample on two occasions, when it is suspected that the population is changing. If the differences were due solely to chance we should expect that about half the differences were positive and half negative. This is like tossing coins, again. We want to know the probability of 4 negative differences (tails) among fifteen trials (tosses). We need the probability that this number is less than 4, i.e. the first three probabilities from the 15th line of Pascal's triangle:

$$^1/_2 \ 15 \ (1 + 15 + 105 + 455 + 1365) = 0.0592$$

Since the probability of four negative differences is greater than 5 per cent the two sets of observations do not differ significantly at this level, i.e. we accept the null hypothesis that the sets of observations do not differ.

Table 8.14:   Probability and frequency

Pair No.	1	2	3	4	5	6	7	8	9	10	11	12	13	14	15
y	34	28	29	45	26	27	24	15	15	27	23	31	20	35	20
x	33	36	50	41	37	41	39	21	20	37	21	18	29	38	27
d = y − x	−1	8	21	−4	11	14	15	6	5	10	−2	−13	9	3	7

The IQs of two remedial classes are as shown in Table 8.15. Do they differ significantly?

Table 8.15:   Inter-class comparison: IQ scores

IQ	
Class A	**Class B**
98	96
139	89
93	117
120	100
103	110
106	98
115	105
108	92
107	86
121	128
91	
118	
135	
123	
105	

When the IQs are put in order it is possible to find the overall median of the 25 scores, i.e. the 13th score. The first 13 are: 139, 135, 128, 123, 121, 120, 118, 117, 115, 110, 108, 107, 106. Thus the median is 106, see Table 8.16. The null hypothesis that IQs of the two classes do not differ is therefore accepted.

Table 8.16:   *Inter-class comparison: IQ distributions*

IQ scores	Class		totals
	A	B	
above 106	9	3	12
106 or below	6	7	13
totals	15	10	25

Using the same formula as we did for χ^2 in the example considered with Table 8.10,

$$\chi^2 = \frac{(ad - bc)^2 \times N}{(a + b)(b + d)(c + d)(a + c)}$$

we get:

$$\chi^2 = \frac{(63 - 18) \times (63 - 18) \times 25}{12 \times 13 \times 15 \times 10} = \frac{50625}{23400} = 2.16 \text{ (approx.)}$$

For one degree of freedom, χ^2 must be 3.84 or more to be significant at the 0.05 level.

Correlation Regression

So far in this chapter, we have looked at differences between scores, means or variances. However, in some investigations, social scientists are more interested in how far variables agree with each other. If so, they are likely to prepare contingency tables or to calculate a correlation coefficient between each pair of measures.

Table 8.17, for instance, is a *contingency table* showing the relationship between point scores obtained in students' three best A-levels (A = 5 points, B = 4, ... E = 1) with class of degree in physics, obtained three or four years later, from first class (I), upper second (II, 1) ... to pass (P) or fail (F) (King, 1973). It is obvious that, although there is a tendency for those who were well qualified initially to obtain better class degrees, there are quite numerous exceptions.

If however, all those obtaining over 11 points for A-levels had obtained first class degrees, those obtaining 11 points had obtained upper seconds, and so on, whilst those scoring less than 9 points initially had all obtained pass degrees or had failed or withdrawn, the table would have looked very different. On combining the P and F columns, 100 per cent would have appeared in each main diagonal space and all other entries would have been zero. The *correlation* would then have been perfect and would have been 1. Whilst in the extremely improbable event that those who began with the highest scores ended with the lowest and so on in reverse, the correlation would be perfect and negative and would then be −1.

Table 8.17: A-level performance and degree results

A-level points	Class of degree					Total %
	I & II$_{,1}$	II$_{,2}$	III	Pass	Fail	
over 11 pts	40	30	20	10	0	100
11 pts	20	30	25	18	7	100
9 or 10 pts	6	25	33	24	12	100
less than 9 pts	9	7	35	22	17	100

Figure 8.7: Correlating reading and reasoning test scores

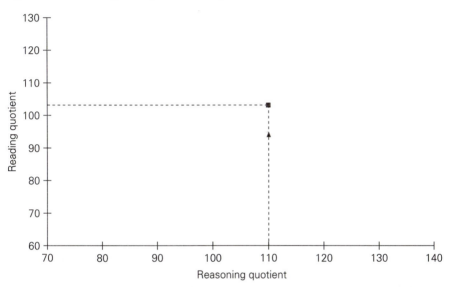

For Table 8.17, the correlation is 0.39 (it is calculated from frequencies, not from percentages); and this is exceptionally high as, on average, A-level results correlate about 0.2 with degree results.

Low correlations can occur simply because the range of abilities of the tested sample of students is very narrow. This is evident from consideration of a *scatter diagram*, see Figure 8.7. Tests of verbal reasoning and of reading quotients of a single child (A, B) say 110 and 95, can be shown by a point in a scatter diagram.

When all the children's scores are represented in this way, the result is a roughly elliptical scatter of points with a concentration along the main axis, see Figure 8.8. The narrower the ellipse, the higher the correlation. Here it is about 0.7. For *parallel forms* of the same test of reasoning, or of an achievement test, the correlation should be at least 0.8 and may be as high as 0.9 or 0.95 (for tests of personality or attitude, correlations of parallel tests or the same test on two occasions may be much lower than this). However, if only the average children are selected for consideration, say those who gained between 85 and 115 the points are

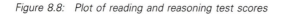
Figure 8.8: Plot of reading and reasoning test scores

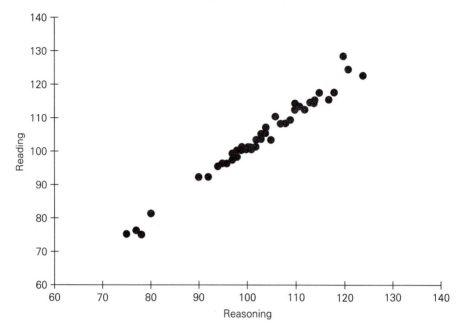

relatively more scattered, so the correlation for them is considerably lower, probably about 0.4 in this instance.

Since A-level candidates are already highly selected because they have all passed O-levels and have been chosen for the academic sixth form, they represent a fairly narrow range of ability; those who take degrees are probably of a still narrower ability range. This is one reason why correlations obtained between A-level and degree results are low. Other reasons may be that students who were coached at school do less well in university where they must think for themselves; distractions occur due to changing interests as the students mature; they may be bored with a course or be far more interested in university studies than those at school; or they may take a new subject entirely which was not available for study at A-level, so making their results difficult to predict.

Care is needed in interpreting correlations. A correlation of 0.9 between two variables does not necessarily imply a causal relationship between them. For example, the increase in violence portrayed in films/videos and on television probably correlates quite highly with the increased incidence of violent crime in real life. This does not mean that the one has been influenced by the other. It seems more likely that other variables are involved. A great deal of effort has been made to establish the 'commonsense' relationship by people who are convinced that it exists, but none of the results has stood up to inspection. Unfortunately, people wishing to prove a case will often cite high correlations as 'evidence' when the *real* causes must often be sought elsewhere.

We mention now that a number of different correlation coefficients are needed depending on the kinds of scores or measures and their distributions. If two sets of normally distributed scores have been obtained for the same sample, the *product moment correlation (r)* is calculated. When candidates are marked in order on two occasions or by two different judges, the *rank order correlation (p)* should be used. Where there is a range of normally distributed scores for one variable and only a dichotomy, e.g. pass–fail, for another variable (which is also normally distributed) the *tetrachoric correlation coefficient* is obtained. If both sets of scores for the sample are registered as pass–fail, although both variables are normally distributed, the *bi-serial correlation coefficient* should be calculated. Readers who are faced with the need to deal with data in these ways are advised to consult a text devoted to statistics.

Another important concept in studying relationships between variables is that of *regression*. If we take the average score, *y*, in an arithmetic test for all 7-year-olds, all 8-year-olds and so on to 14 years, and plot these scores against average age (*x*) we may obtain points which are roughly on a straight line, see Figure 8.9.

Figure 8.9: Age and arithmetic test performance

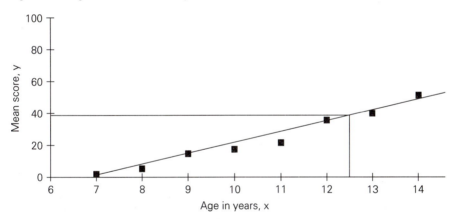

If so, it is possible to calculate the equation of the line which fits best, and this is called the regression line of *y* (mean score) on *x* (age). Given a child's age, e.g. 12$\frac{1}{2}$ the 'best estimate' of his or her score in the arithmetic test can be obtained from the regression line and is about 33. If all the separate points of the scatter diagram are entered, showing each child's score, the regression line is still the same, but the possibility of a substantial error in the estimate made from only one other measure is then more obvious.

Sometimes the regression line is curved. This happens when testing students under pressure, if they differ appreciably in level of anxiety. Those who are not anxious at all (often the extroverts) and those who are paralysed with anxiety (more likely the introverts) tend to do poorly, whereas students who experience just suffi-cient anxiety to be aroused to maximum effort, do best, see Figure 8.10.

Figure 8.10: Anxiety level scores and speeded test performance

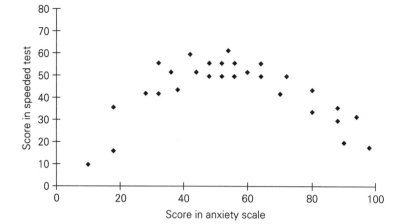

Since the test scores are clearly not normally distributed, the product moment correlation coefficient should not be calculated. Instead a coefficient M (eta) can be calculated to measure the degree of relationship.

When correlations have been obtained between a number of approximately normally distributed variables it is possible to detect relationships between them by *factor analysis* or to estimate scores in one variable from a *multiple regression equation* containing several other variables. If a table or matrix of correlations is obtained between, say, 20 variables of achievement in school, it may be possible to identify four or five factors which account for much of the difference between pupils, e.g. verbal and non-verbal reasoning abilities, verbal fluency, spatial imagination, numerical speed and accuracy. Attempts to predict success in various specialized studies might be made by using multiple regression equations based on a battery of tests to assess these factors and relevant personality factors. Again, readers whose interests have been aroused or whose research requires greater detail, should consult a specialist book on the subject.

The present chapter has sought to consider some basic statistical concepts and tools used in educational research. Within the confines of a single chapter, it has only been possible to scratch the surface. There are many specialist textbooks which offer advice on the detailed workings and the relative merits of particular techniques, see, for example, Keeves (1988), Linn (1989), Peers (1996). Finally, a word for those who consider themselves as limited, or even, non-mathematicians: computer technology! While considerable care needs to be taken in ensuring that the data collected are *accurately* recorded, computer software exists to perform calculations and to convert these, where required, into graphs.

Much use is made, in educational research and in other social science research, of SPSS (the Statistical Package for the Social Sciences). For those without access to SPSS, there are also more basic software packages, called spreadsheets, for example, Microsoft *Excel* or *Lotus 123*. These are widely available in software packages that come with PCs. If you have a computer, it is well worth looking to see what software is 'hidden' on your machine. Training courses in how to use the packages are useful, but it is well worth finding out what your computer can do, if so far your use of it has been confined to the mysteries of word-processing. It should also be pointed out that SPSS and *Excel* or *Lotus 123* all work on the same basic principles, and it is not difficult to apply what has been learned in one of them to the other. Moreover, it is also pretty easy to transfer data files from one spreadsheet to another. For example, some of the examples, including the graphs, used in the present chapter, were worked on a palm-top computer and transferred to a PC spreadsheet package, and then copied into a word-processing package, in seconds!

References

ANDERSON, G. (1994) *Fundamentals of Educational Research*, London: Falmer Press.

COCHRAN, W.G. and COX, G.M. (1957) *Experimental Designs*, 2nd edition, New York: Wiley.

KEEVES, J.P. (1988) (ed.) *Educational Research Methodology and Measurement: An International Handbook*, Oxford: Pergamon Press.

KING, W.H. (1973) 'A prediction from A-level performance of University degree performance', *Physics Education*, **8**, 2.

LINDQUIST, E.F. (1956) *Design and Analysis of Experiments in Psychology and Education*, Boston, MA: Houghton Mifflin.

LINN, R.L. (1989) (ed.) *Educational Measurement*, Washington, DC: Macmillan.

PEERS, I.S. (1996) *Statistical Analysis for Education and Psychology Researchers*, London: Falmer Press.

STORKEY, M. (1991) *London's Ethnic Minorities: One City Many Communities*, London: Research Centre.

Chapter 9

Educational Research and the Teacher

We are conscious that much of our exploration of perspectives and techniques in researching education has viewed the theatre from the outside. In so doing, there is one particular perspective on researching education that has not been as explicitly explored as would seem ideal. We believe that the relationship between the teacher and educational research needs exploring, because there ought to be a greater fusion between the two, if both teaching and researching are to achieve a more meaningful purpose. In and through that exploration, we want to bring together some of the points that we have made in the course of this book, which relate to educational research and the teacher, and without mention of which, our work would be incomplete.

Research and the Teacher

In Chapter 4, we briefly noted the general failure of researchers to interest teachers in their findings. Part, at least, of the problem arises from the differing perceptions by researchers and teachers of the nature and purposes of research. Most teachers would like to have immediate, and preferably straightforward solutions to their particular classroom problems. How, for example, to deal with a disturbed child? How to motivate children in the class to concentrate on their work? What is the most effective method of teaching a school subject? How to minimize disruptive behaviour? They look for practical advice on practical problems. Consciously or unconsciously, they make the same kind of demands as, say, an aircraft manufacturer who wants to improve the performance of the wing of a new aeroplane at 45,000 feet flying faster than the speed of sound whilst ensuring that it will perform properly at 110 miles an hour at zero feet when landing. The problem is passed to researchers who come up with solutions that are built into the design and tested in action. The success or failure of the research is quantifiable: either the new wing performs better than the old one, or it does not. If it does, the new wing is adopted by the company because it can be shown that the aeroplane flies faster, or is more manoeuvrable or more economical in flight or, preferably, all three. Unfortunately, educational research is not like that.

Educational research ultimately focuses on issues and problems related to learning and the social, emotional and personal development in the classroom. It cannot, however, answer the kinds of questions posed by teachers in the way that aeronautical research responds to the demands of the aeroplane manufacturer.

While the improved wing will function better wherever it is flown, the extent of the differences between two classrooms full of children and their teachers are such that what works for one will not necessarily work for the other. It is very exasperating for teachers to discover that the concerns of educational research do not seem to answer their needs. It might be added that it is not only teachers who have to face the fact that educational research does not supply information in a form that is immediately helpful to them; the same is largely true of educational managers and policy-makers. Morover, educational policies are often created by politicians, not on the basis of research findings, but arrived at as part of a wider dogma and imposed on teachers and schools in the heroic belief that they can be made to work. This approach underlies the 1988 Education Reform Act in the UK.

This Act imposed what might be described as the industrial/managerial approach to teaching. What is to be taught is prescribed and the students undergo Standard Attainment Tests (SATs), at ages 7, 11 and 14, to check that they are reaching the standards of performance expected of them. At the same time, schools are inspected at regular and frequent intervals to ensure that they are being properly managed and the teachers are performing their duties adequately. The nearest analogy to this process is that of a large industrial concern where raw materials (the children) arrive at the factory gates, are subjected to various prescribed processes (they are taught the National Curriculum) and the finished products are sent to market to realize their added value (the young people are sent out into the labour market to create wealth). It is not surprising that, to the best of our knowledge, few, if any, of the changes brought about by the Education Reform Act were based on research findings. (What is surprising is that the system bears many of the characteristics of a Stalinist command economy and yet it was imposed by a British Conservative administration committed to the notions of freedom and personal responsibility; but that is perhaps another story.)

Another problem is that basic, often highly theoretical, research seems to have little or nothing of value for the teacher in school. What Getzels (1969) had to say on the subject, despite this being 30 years ago, remains true:

> The fact is, basic research produces only tiny 'bits' of knowledge about an infinitely complex world. Given time, such incremental gains in knowledge may have some effect on practical situations, but schoolmen have long been aware that research findings usually have little practical bearing on the actual operation of schools.

Much research of this kind is not addressed to teachers, but to other researchers. In this respect, it resembles the work of researchers in, for example, particle physics. In the last 20 years, it has been established that protons and neutrons are not the elementary particles they were once thought to be, but are made up of smaller particles called 'quarks'. Moreover, these come in six different varieties: there are thought to be at least six 'flavours' which physicists call 'up', 'down', 'strange', 'charmed', 'bottom' and 'top', each of which has three 'colours' — red, green and blue. (These are, of course, merely labels: the particles can have no colour.) The point is that the research which led to these discoveries has, as yet, no practical application. The aeroplane manufacturer may have felt that the research was point-less and that the resources expended on it could have been better employed in solving some of the immediate and pressing problems he or she had to face. Such a judgment is not fair to the particle physicists. They were engaged in an intel-lectual exercise that was driven by the need to discover fundamental facts about the universe we all live in. The commercial worth of their discoveries formed no part of their terms of reference. Yet, who knows whether, 10, 20, or 100 years from now, their discoveries may result in inventions that change the nature of civiliza-tion, just as early work on genetic structures is changing ours today? Similarly, basic educational research that is being conducted now carries with it a potential for future change which cannot be foreseen. That it appears to have no immediate application for the teacher does not form the basis of a valid criticism for its conduct.

Another aspect of basic research is that it tends to produce findings that are mainly of interest to other researchers. This being so, accounts of the research are normally written with that audience in mind. This results in papers that are not easy for the non-specialists to read, however intelligent or otherwise well-educated they might be.

All things considered, teachers are more likely to find applied research, that is, research designed to address a practical problem or concern, of more interest than basic research. However, we suggested in earlier chapters that even applied research has had little effect on teachers and teaching. As with most failures of communication, the reasons for this are not one-sided. Part of the failure is the responsibility of the researchers and part lies with the teachers. We begin by sug-gesting where the researchers have failed the teachers.

If a study has as its objective the intention to address a problem faced by teachers, it is, by definition, a piece of applied research. Its findings should be accessible by the people whom it is designed to benefit. If they are not, the study might just as well not have been done. This has clear implications for the way the results are presented and where they are published. Research as an activity is often difficult. The researcher has often spent years in acquiring and developing the skills and knowledge necessary to conduct a research project successfully. Practical issues frequently make for great difficulty in its successful completion. Access to the sub-jects of the study, for example, can create problems with teachers, parents, head-teachers and school governors who seem to 'conspire' to keep the researcher away from the children. Given the many difficulties that may have had to be overcome during the research project (winning funding, accessing schools, data collection and meeting sponsors' deadlines), it might have been expected that researchers would have been eager to publish their findings for a wider audience. Yet, all too often, the researchers seem to spurn that opportunity, directing their reporting at fellow researchers in a manner suited to their needs, rather than at others, notably the teachers whose problems prompted the study.

Another reason why teachers may make less use of research findings than they might is to be found in the fact that they are often published in journals and similar publications that are not always easily available to teachers. Thus teachers remain unaware of many pieces of educational research that might well be of value to them. Researchers ought to remember that professional educators at all levels must have access to research findings if they are to be of use in schools.

It is perhaps ironic that, just as there may be an apparent divide between schoolteachers and university educational researchers, the closest links university education departments have with schools are through the teacher trainers. The latter, by virtue of their role in initial teacher education, find much of their time is taken up with the training and supervision of trainee teachers. This work involves providing training in the department and much time 'on the road' visiting trainees on school experience, quite apart from liaison work with the schools. This leaves them with little time to engage in research. Much of the research work, though not all, rests with the specialist researchers, who consequently have only limited time to 'teach'. They may only set foot in school when the collection of school-based data is unavoidable by other means! Some of them send out others to collect most of the data. The 'others' are typically contract researchers, who have employment for the length of their contract, unless funding can be found for a further project before the current one elapses. (An interesting view of the contract researcher can be found in Youngman, 1994.) Against which, it has to be said that data generated in schools take a considerable amount of time to process and analyse, once these have reached the research office.

Researchers are under considerable pressure to 'publish', to produce evidence of their research activity. Their output is subjected to scrutiny, under the UK University Research Assessment Exercise carried out every four years, — and rightly so. However, only research papers published in refereed research journals appear to have any impact on that assessment of researcher performance. This tends to require the writing of technical papers. For example, in a study conducted into the effects of a training programme on teaching reading, the focus in a technical paper may be on analyses of the theoretical literature, the data from the testing of the reading skills of groups of pupils in the control and treatment groups. The discipline requires the reporting of statistical analyses, perhaps that of pupil performance by gender, ethnicity, season-of-birth, IQ scores. That burden of proof requiring the recording of the narrowly defined and 'accurately' measured gains in pupils' reading skills is very different from what might be of immediate relevance to the practising teacher.

Although teachers would be interested in the results insofar as these reflected gains in pupils' performance, this would only need reporting in broad terms: say, that there were 'real' gains for pupils with low IQ scores especially. Their real interest would be in the 'practical' strategies/techniques emphasized or discussed in the training programme and whether they could use some in their classrooms. The theory part of the paper would probably be of little or no relevance, since it would be written for other researchers and well removed from the more basic nature of classroom theory developed by teachers from their experience and intuition, cross-fertilized by ideas gained from here and there. Moreover, the development of reading skills in pupils is only but part of the primary teacher's work, as compared to the researcher 'specializing' in reading theory and practice. Thus, the teacher should be seen as a very different audience from that targeted by the educational researcher through most professional research journals.

Turning now to teachers: what part have they played in the failure of communication that exists between them and researchers? One of the grounds of distrust of researchers by some teachers seems to have been the suspicion that the researcher was trying to dictate to the teacher what he or she should do. Traditionally, teachers have regarded themselves as autonomous; what happened in the classroom was a matter for them and the children. One benefit of the introduction of the National Curriculum in the UK has been the breakdown of this tradition. Teachers in schools have now to perceive themselves as members of teams, each with a part to play in the achievement of common objectives. This change may affect the extent to which research findings are adopted by teachers as well as the speed with which they penetrate to schools.

There is also the fact that teachers are essentially conservative in their practices. It is right that they should be cautious about changing their methods and approaches to teaching. Children are not guinea pigs. A primary school teacher will have the responsibility for a class of children for a year of their lives and it is his or her duty to provide them with the best education possible during that time. He or she will have an array of skills, knowledge and expertise which have been tried and tested and are known to produce acceptable results. If one or more of these is modified, rejected or replaced as a result of the teacher's being influenced by some research, the results may be better than those anticipated from the use of the old methods. However, the teacher's natural concern is that they might be worse, in which case he or she has failed those children. It is not surprising, therefore, that, professionally speaking, teachers tend to be conservative rather than radical in their approach, to the extent of being distrustful of new methods, however well researched. This tendency may be reinforced by the fact that many teachers are not trained to make judgments on the reliability of research findings.

The Teacher as Researcher

One of the most interesting and potentially valuable developments in recent years has been the growth in support of the idea of the teacher as researcher. The notion of the practitioner-as-researcher is well described in the educational literature. It has also been seen as 'an ideological movement aimed to bring a democratisation of educational research, with a move to get away from the assumption that only academics are legitimate generators of knowledge, towards a situation where it is acceptable for practitioners to research their own practice' (Titchen and Binnie, 1993). According to Carr and Kemmis (1986), the notion of the practitioner-as-researcher became popular when teachers were developing professional roles and were looking for opportunities to establish a research role in which they could explore and analyse their own practice. This type of research was regarded as more meaningful and relevant to classroom practice than that which was carried out by outside researchers and academics. Teachers were also beginning to adopt the 'accountability movement' which demanded a self-monitoring strategy to justify their practice and to examine critically the context in which practice takes place.

Elliott (1990) draws attention to the importance of teacher involvement in the research process, arguing that:

> ... educational research is a form of practical inquiry which fuses inquiry into practice. There can be no educational research if teachers play no important role in the process of articulating, analysing and hypothesising solutions to complex educational problems. The specialist inquiries of professional researchers should be viewed as subordinate to this fundamental process.

It is possible only to speculate why the idea of the teacher as researcher has attracted support. Perhaps it reflects the perception of the work of university researchers as being too distant from the realities of the classroom. Primary school teachers in the UK, for example, face the everyday problems of successfully motivating young children to learn how to read or gain an understanding of number. They might be forgiven for forming the view that much, if not most, of the work of educational researchers has little relevance to their most pressing needs. This feeling may have been intensified by the pressures to succeed brought about by the National Curriculum and its associated regimen of tests at the end of the designated key stages, and school inspections by the Office of Standards in Education (OFSTED) at regular and frequent intervals.

It might be worthwhile to consider the combined effects of these pressures. For each subject or subject area, every school now has a lead teacher responsible for the delivery of the curriculum. This inevitably results in the formation of teams of teachers working together to produce programmes of study calculated to provide the knowledge and skills expected in the pupils so that they perform well in the key stage tests. In determining the attainment levels of the pupils, the tests provide a measure of the effectiveness of the teaching strategies adopted. The teachers are then in a position to reflect on the degree of success their teaching has achieved and to devise improvements to their programmes accordingly.

This situation might be seen as one that was in keeping with the conditions for action research, as captured by Kemmis and McTaggart (1988):

> The linking of the terms 'action' and 'research' highlights the essential feature of the approach: trying out ideas in practice as a means of improvement and as a means of increasing knowledge of the curriculum, teaching and learning.

It is easy to criticize the procedure as it operates in practice in schools: that the process is not perceived by the participants as 'research'; that the formal posing of research questions is not undertaken; that variables are not identified; that the test at the end is not specifically designed to identify success or failure in the strategies adopted, and so on. Yet, what the teachers are engaged in is action research. Of all the approaches to researching education, it is the one most natural for teachers to take and the one most immediately beneficial to their professional concerns in the setting most accessible to them. If, as seems likely, increasing pressure is brought to bear on teachers to become more effective, the way forward is for them to see themselves as researchers as well as teachers and to adopt action research as part of their professional armoury. There is, after all, nothing magical or excessively difficult about action research. Certainly, anyone who has qualified as a teacher and can open up the world of learning to children and young people is perfectly capable of being a member of an action research team and making real contributions to the teaching/learning process.

Nor does it involve a great deal of extra work. After all, as has been seen, the essentials are already in place and teachers are, in a general sense, already engaged in it. All that is required is a more rigorous approach to their existing activity *and* a system that ensures the results of their work are published for the benefit of their colleagues nationally. The responsibility for this might well be taken over by the teaching unions as a joint enterprise. On a purely pragmatic level, the development of a research capacity would do much to enhance their claims to be professional associations representing serious practitioners engaged in work of national importance. The research undertaken by their members would provide them with much-needed ammunition to respond to ill-informed attacks on teachers and schools that have been such a feature of the last 15 or 20 years in the UK and show little sign of abating. It would also support their case in their traditional function of trying to gain improvements in salaries and conditions of work for their members.

Perhaps just as importantly, it would break down the traditional barriers between teachers and researchers. Despite the advances made over the years in educational research and the increased levels of training received by teachers, it is disappointing that the reluctance of the latter to make use of the findings of professional researchers has been slow to dissipate. It may be that this has been because there is no sense of ownership on the part of teachers. Researchers were seen as people inhabiting universities engaged in an esoteric activity which had little or no practical application in the classroom. Even worse, they have seen research politicized to provide policy-makers with ammunition to attack them and their schools. The development of the teacher as researcher would do much to break down the existing division between those who research and those who teach. It would help to generate that missing sense of ownership of the findings of the research community. Finally, and most importantly, it would result in the development and transmission of better teaching strategies and techniques: pupils and students would benefit.

These are not new ideas. Almost 20 years ago, Eggleston (1979) was writing:

> Constantly, teachers are regarded . . . as the objects of communication and consumers of research findings. While I would agree that it is our responsibility to write accounts of our researches and their implications in comprehensible prose which give teachers access to our minds, and share the hope that our research does yield usable findings, I am even more concerned that we think of teachers as professionals with whom, rather than on whom we do research. Effective teaching is more likely to be achieved when the teacher himself/herself is operating in reflective and empirical modes. Teachers operating in this way cease to be tiresome intervening variables and become self-conscious instruments of educational process.

It has to be said, however, that there is a long tradition of separating the functions of teaching and researching. Over 40 years ago, Lieberman (1956) was asserting that the teacher's job was to apply the educational findings of researchers who were responsible for generating them. In justifying his proposition, he pointed out that the average classroom teacher was always under the pressure of work and was unacquainted with the principles and techniques of research. He asserted that 'developing, testing and confirming knowledge is not something the practitioner can do as a hobby or in his spare moments at work. The discovery of new knowledge is a full time job', although he accepted that teachers might conduct some research in their own classrooms to obtain, for example, information about the attitudes of their pupils. However, this would not add to existing knowledge in the field.

Many social scientists supported this view. A number of early curriculum development projects viewed the teacher as a kind of technician who had learned certain techniques for transmitting knowledge, skills or habits and who existed to put into practice ideas that had been developed by others. The reader may take the view that this tendency has been resurrected in the National Curriculum. Others took a different stance. They saw classroom research by teachers as a method of encouraging them to become creative, rather than merely reproductive, professionals. This was a view which Stenhouse had strongly endorsed. His challenge to the previously held views on the curriculum and pedagogy cannot be overestimated. He pointed out the limitations of the behavioural objectives/outcomes model of the curriculum, and argued for direct teacher involvement in the educational research process, including curriculum design and development (Stenhouse, 1975). This, he did in the belief that teachers were not simply technicians who implemented educational theory but were professionals who generated theory based on their classroom practice. His writings and example gave a considerable impetus to the development of action research in the UK.

The debate stems from differing notions of what constitutes 'real' research and has to be placed in its historical context. Lieberman was arguing as a professional researcher who believed that the only real research was research conducted by using 'scientific' or experimental methods. Some years later, Gage (1963) and Van Dalen (1966) were pressing the case that all educational research need not be designed to add to our 'scientific' knowledge. In this, they were taking Corey's (1953) position who, in arguing for teacher participation in research, took the view that keeping educational research within the domain of the professional researcher was to take too limited a view of the teacher's role. He maintained that teachers made better decisions and were more effective practitioners if they conducted what he called 'action' research.

The Teacher Researcher and the Research Community

Hargreaves (1996) suggested that much educational research in the UK was irrelevant to classroom practice. He argued that the estimated £M50 spent on it was poor value for money in terms of improving the quality of education provided in schools. He went on to say that too much of it was concerned with fashionable methodological debate that was incomprehensible to any but those who were in the academic research community. These are powerful criticisms coming from a Professor of Education at the University of Cambridge Department of Education, particularly in the context of the concern of successive governments with school effectiveness. Moreover, Michael Bassey, in his Presidential Address to the British Educational Research Association in 1991, referred to 'too many research papers (being) expressed in clumsy English, overloaded with terminology that is familiar to few people, poorly structured, long-winded, and in general written from the perspective of the writer without concern for the reader' (Bassey, 1992).

As already seen, there is ample evidence to suggest that there has been, and still remains, a divide between teachers in schools and researchers in universities. Apportioning blame for this would be a futile exercise. The fact is that the world of education falls into two definable parts: on the one hand, there are university teachers who, as part of their contractual obligations, are expected to spend about half their working time engaged in research, and on the other, schoolteachers who are perceived, and perceive themselves, exclusively as purveyors of knowledge with no research function. This is mirrored in no other profession. For example, in medicine (a profession with which teachers frequently compare their own, and one used by Hargreaves in his speech), doctors and surgeons are not only expected to cure sick people but also to engage actively in research into ways of achieving their aims more effectively. This state of affairs carries with it two benefits and the two are arguably connected.

First, there is a greater interest in, and willingness to use, research findings for the greater good of patients. Second, there is the matter of professional morale: all are members of the same team engaged in a common enterprise. That is not to say that some medics are not engaged in some studies that are, apparently, tangential to the main purposes of medicine. They are, but the great majority of medical research programmes are directly concerned with how best to cure the sick and alleviate suffering. Most of the research is driven by the need to improve patient care. In a word, it is *applied* research, as we have defined it; it is research designed to solve an immediate and practical problem.

Earlier in this chapter, we looked to see how teachers could most easily and quickly become part of the research community and suggested that action research was the likely route. However, this will not, of itself, bridge the divide between them and those who work in university departments of education. If teachers are to become active as researchers, their interests and those of lecturers in university departments of education will have to be brought into closer alignment. This can only be brought about by university research programmes becoming increasingly focused on issues of concern to teachers in schools. It would clearly be disastrous if teacher researchers were to occupy the central ground in the search for increased school effectiveness, whilst university researchers pursued ever more arcane research objectives in some sort of peripheral intellectual world, out of touch with education's most pressing concerns.

There is much to be said for Eggleston's (1979) suggestion that teachers should play a major part in the research that has to do with making schools more effective. An important issue of both principle and practice is that they should do so as equal partners in the enterprise. To put it bluntly, it would be a self-defeating exercise if teachers were to be treated as private soldiers in research teams that were led as a matter of course by an officer class recruited from university departments of education. The fact has to be faced that present funding arrangements for research are controlled by the D*f*EE, the ESRC and, to a lesser extent, a number of charitable trusts.

These organizations appear to assume that only bids for research funds from university departments of education and similar bodies should be taken seriously. It is outside the scope of this book to make detailed suggestions as to how this situation should be changed. What is clear, however, is the need for change if teacher researchers are to become full members of the research community. Some funding will have to be made available to schools to make time for research activities by teachers. Few teachers would disagree with Lieberman's observation that they are always under pressure of work. However, if schools are to become more effective, there is likely to be some cost involved. In the next section we consider the value of such research in the education of children.

Moreover, other than research undertaken by the teachers themselves, it is all too infrequently the case that the teachers set the agenda or the terms of reference, even though UK teachers' professional associations do commission research on behalf of their membership. Such research might well relate to teachers' pay and work conditions in some shape or form, rather than being addressed at immediate issues in the individual classroom.

Much funded research conducted by researchers is aimed at meeting the criteria of those (experienced researchers), to whom proposals are referred for judgment as to their merits. Other research is funded to meet the specifications of the D*f*EE, or one of its agencies. The latter type of research typically seeks to evaluate the system or a particular part of the system, such as, for example, the evaluation of public examinations or national curriculum tests. This tends to be 'critical' in character with the objective being to determine whether the system is working satisfactorily, and, by implication, whether the teacher is doing his or her job 'properly'. What would be of greater use to teachers would be research aimed at helping them to improve their classroom performance, whether this related to presentation techniques, pupil behaviour, motivation, classroom organization, and so on.

The Value of School-based Research

There are (at least) two ways of considering the value of school-based research. A professional researcher might well assess its value in terms of its methodological rigour, the extent to which it builds on the body of existing knowledge and extends it, and its generalizability, that is, the extent to which its findings can be applied to wider populations. For much educational research, these are valid criteria. If they were to be applied to the majority of the action research conducted in classrooms, it has to be said, such research would fail to meet them. Are the criteria appropriate? We would argue that, in many cases, they are not. Before going any further, it would be as well for us to make our position clear.

In saying that these criteria are not applicable without modification to school-based research, we do not include formally conducted studies by researchers who may or may not be teachers, and which happen to take place in schools. Our immediate concern is with the situation of teacher-researchers conducting action research or formative evaluation research studies as members of a team in their workplace. It is that kind of research which, we would argue, is of most direct value to the teachers and the school in which they work.

If the research criteria traditionally used are to be modified or rejected, then the question arises, as to what is to take their place. Perhaps the best answer is to refer back to our earlier example of the research that might be undertaken to improve the performance of an aircraft's wing. If the new component works better than the existing one, it is adopted and everyone — the manufacturer, the airlines and the passengers — benefits from the improvement. Similarly, a group of teacher-researchers working in a primary school might, as a result of their shared, but informal observations, conclude that their pupils were not making satisfactory progress with learning how to write. They might consider that the pupils' handwriting was untidy, that letters were ill-formed or illegible, perhaps with frequent confusion of the letters 'b' and 'd', or any combination of these, or other possible faults.

Having agreed that significant improvement was desirable, the teachers might decide that it would be sensible to search the literature on the teaching of handwriting and review their own practices in the light of what was discovered. They would then have to agree on the teaching approaches and techniques to be adopted in their search for improvement. Before introducing these new practices, it would be wise to collect evidence of the children's present abilities and performance under controlled conditions to provide a baseline. This could be managed in the course of normal lessons and would have no ill-effects on the children's learning. They could then proceed with their new approach and compare the results with their baseline evidence at suitable intervals, say, after a term and after a year. They would then be in a position to measure the effectiveness of their work by a number of objective criteria, such as legibility, letter formation, letter confusion, speed and accuracy. (We would like to add 'tidiness' on the grounds that it is possible to arrive at a consensus about what constitutes a desirable level of tidiness but accept that it is not easy to arrive at an objective definition which would make it readily measurable.) They would then know, like the aircraft manufacturer, how and to what extent the new model performed better than its predecessor.

It is not unlikely that, in this process, they would discover new possibilities for improvement in their teaching which could be incorporated and tested in the same way. There is no time limit to the process. Ultimately, the teachers might feel that an effective limit had been reached in their search for improvement in this area and other identified needs required similar treatment at a higher level of priority.

We shall now consider what characterizes this example:

- The question, 'Is there a failure in the way that handwriting is taught and are there measures that can be adopted to improve matters?' was identified by teachers.
- It arose from their everyday professional activities.
- The research, development of new methods of instruction and their application in the classrooms were undertaken by the same group of teachers. They were all participants. There was no division of responsibility for the three phases with the result that all had an equal sense of ownership and commitment to its success.
- From its inception, the programme had, as its objective, the professional development of its participants, with the aim of making teaching and learning more effective.
- The programme had identifiable and measurable outcomes which would have a direct bearing on classroom practice.
- The teaching and the research components of the programme had a common purpose. It would be an example of 'research in action'.
- Another possible effect of the programme could be a change in the self-concept of the teachers from being artisans or technicians to being creative professionals.
- It is difficult to see how the whole process of identifying the problem, devising a potential solution and testing it in action in its natural environment could have been achieved other than by the teachers themselves.

Research of this kind is one of the most effective ways for teachers to do better what is expected of them. It is likely to sensitize them to the whole educational process so that it rapidly becomes part of their professional practice. By engaging in research, teachers can acquire a new perspective on the nature of their classroom problems and their resolution. It also provides a mechanism through which teachers and university researchers can be brought together in a common enterprise. In the example used above, the teachers might well have approached a local university department of education for assistance with the literature search, for technical advice and support from a member of staff interested in their enterprise. The important aspect of this association would be that the university member of staff would not be in a controlling position. He or she would be there to open up access to information and expertise which might otherwise be difficult for the teachers to find. By working with teachers as an equal, he or she would be in a position to be reminded of or learn from them the issues and problems that were of real concern to practising teachers in live situations. A channel of communication would be created between the school and the university through which could flow reminders that what happens in schools, the process of educating children and young people, must be the prime focus of educational research.

Referring again to Bassey's Presidential Address to BERA, in which he considered 'the relationship between educational research and the profession of teaching', we note the distinction he draws between the *reflective* and *expert*, the latter representing the traditional and the former the modern expectation of the professional:

The *expert professional* maintains a distance from the client. He or she is presumed to be able to understand the client's needs and is expected to solve the client's problems, with minimal involvement of the client. In return the expert expects unquestioning deference and respect from the client, as well as a substantial fee!

In total contrast, the *reflective professional* works with the client in trying to make sense of the client's needs and shares knowledge as needed to try to tackle the client's problems. He or she has no need of a facade to express professionalism. It is obvious from the purposeful interaction with the client. (Bassey, 1992)

If we are to improve the effectiveness of classroom research, it is essential that the research community involves teachers as partners in the research process. Both communities need to embrace this modern professionalism. If research and development work is to become relevant to educational advancement, professional researchers must understand the point of view of classroom practitioners. It should not be assumed that teachers are always right; however, research must try to understand the teacher's conceptions and misconceptions of the teaching–learning situation. In the last 20 years, the opinions of teachers seem to have changed with regard to the value of research findings. More teachers now regard research as a necessary professional activity. They seem to be willing to question their practices, provided that they are given positive help from those engaged in research and development.

To many of those reading this book who may well be professionals from the world of education, newly turning to the study of educational research, perhaps as part of their professional training or development, we would express the hope that you will play your part in the promotion of the partnership, that we and others advocate, between researchers and teachers. In so doing, we hope that you will come to find enjoyment and fulfilment in researching education.

References

BASSEY, M. (1992) 'BERA Presidential address in 1991', *British Educational Research Journal*, **18**, 1.

CARR, W. and KEMMIS, S. (1986) *Becoming Critical: Education, Knowledge and Action Research*, London: Falmer Press.

COREY, S.M. (1953) *Action Research to Improve School Practices*, New York: Teachers' College, Columbia University.

ELLIOTT, J. (1990) 'Educational research in crisis: Performance indicators, and the decline in excellence', *British Educational Research Journal*, **16**, 1.

EGGLESTON, J. (1979) 'The characteristics of educational research: Mapping the domain', *British Educational Research Journal*, **5**, 1, pp. 1–12.

GAGE, N.L. (1963) (ed.) *Handbook of Research on Teaching*, Chicago: Rand McNally.

GETZELS, J.W. (1969) 'A social psychology of education', in LINDZEY, G. and ARONSON, E. (eds) *The Handbook of Social Psychology*, 2nd edition, 5: Applied Social Psychology, London: Addison Wesley.

HARGREAVES, D.H. (1996) *Teaching as a Research-based Profession: Possibilities and Prospects*, Teacher Training Agency Annual Lecture, 1996.

LIEBERMAN, M. (1956) *Education as a Profession*, Englewood Cliffs, New Jersey: Prentice Hall.

KEMMIS, S. and McTAGGART, R. (1988) *The Action Research Planner*, Geelong: Deakin.

STENHOUSE, L. (1975) *An Introduction to Curriculum Research and Development*, London: Heinemann.

TITCHEN, A. and BINNIE, A. (1993) 'A unified action research strategy in Nursing', *Education Action Research*, **1**, 1.

VAN DALEN, D.B. (1966) *Understanding Educational Research*, New York: McGraw Hill.

YOUNGMAN, M. (1994) 'The career experiences of contract researchers in education', *Research Papers in Education Policy and Practice*, **9**, 3.

Glossary of Educational Research Terms

The terms included in this glossary are those often encountered in educational research reports and in the literature. This glossary is intended primarily for readers with limited knowledge of conducting research in education.

Accountability
Accountability in its simplest form means to hold some person or group accountable for certain behaviours or actions. Accountability is a relatively new concept in educational literature. The concept denotes that a person or persons who are given a task to perform should be responsible for the quality of the results of their performance.

Acculturation
The term implies a particular kind of cultural transmission; two culturally distinct groups come together in time and place, and, as a result, one of the groups (usually the smaller of the two) adopts some of the culturally defined characteristics of the other.

Achievement test
An instrument designed to measure the extent to which a student has attained certain concepts or skills in a given content area (e.g. reading or arithmetic), usually as a result of specific teaching.

Action research
Action research is undertaken by a person who is normally both the researcher and practitioner. Since this type of research is normally undertaken by practitioners, it calls for the researchers' involvement in the action process. For example, if the classroom teachers are involved in research activity, it is probably in the area of action or decision-oriented research. That is to say, the researchers seek to discover how and in what way(s) some aspect of their teaching is effective. Armed with this knowledge they can then make informed decisions whether to change their current practice.

Analysis of variance
To analyse the results of more than two groups, a test known as the 'F-Test' or analysis of variance is frequently used. This test is conceptually similar to the 't' test. It takes the total variance of a series of tests or variables into account and

analyses the aggregated variance along certain lines. This technique is useful in educational research, especially for comparing groups and at the same time allowing, for example, for the varying effect of different methods of teaching or treatments. Basically, this technique is a series of methods which allow the researcher to measure differences between scores or sets of scores.

Applied research
Applied research often refers to the extent to which research is directed towards the solution of an existing problem or is designed to provide information that is immediately useful. Much of the research conducted in education has as its goal immediate application of its results to solving a problem.

Attitude test
A test designed to assess an individual's feelings and tendencies toward action with respect to social objects, situation or people — for example, attitude toward ethnic minority groups. Attitude tests are relatively crude measuring instruments.

Audiences
An individual (e.g. teacher) or group (e.g. local education authority) that might use the research information produced by the investigator. For example, classroom teachers might be interested in finding a more effective way of teaching their subjects, and hence they might be the audience addressed by research through its findings.

Basic research
A type of research which is normally designed to extend the boundaries of existing knowledge in a particular discipline and the results may not necessarily be of immediate practical use. The findings of basic research are expected to add to our store of information, or of theoretical knowledge.

Battery of tests
A group of tests or sub-tests arranged to be administered together that measure different aspects of the same characteristic (e.g. questionnaire and projective type personality tests). Sometimes the term is loosely used for any group of tests administered together to the same sample.

Behavioural objectives
In many educational programmes goals are stated in a way that specify what the learner will be able to do after specific instruction, i.e. the learner's changed behaviour.

Behavioural validity
A method of assessing the quality of a psychological test by direct observation of actions associated with the measurable variable. For example, in order to ascertain

the validity of an attitude scale, the attitude as denoted by the test score is compared with observable behaviour in a corresponding situation.

Bias
The researchers' conscious or subconscious influence in the process of research design, data collection, analysis and interpretation of results can distort the conclusion of an investigation. Furthermore, their biases also operate in the selection of problems for research.

Biased sample
The outcome of a sampling procedure that systematically excludes certain kinds of individuals or sub-groups, or systematically under-represents certain kinds of people that should have been included in the study (see also, Random sample).

Case study
In a case study, a single case is studied in depth for a period of time and the results recorded. A case study may be of a person, a group, a family, a classroom, a town or a nation. The aim is often analytical rather than quantitative. A case study is normally part of descriptive research.

Checklists
Tools which are used for the collection of data about events, materials or people; certain characteristics are judged to be simply present or absent rather than rated along a continuum. For example, research articles can be evaluated by using a checklist which may contain questions such as, 'Is the problem clearly stated?'

Chi-square
A statistical technique appropriate for frequency based data is called the chi-square test. The analysis determines the probability that the frequencies observed in the study arise from some underlying cause and are not simply the result of chance.

Class interval
The range of scores treated within one group is called 'class interval'. For example, if the researcher had to treat all scores/values from 10 to 20 as one group, and from 21 to 30 as another group, these ranges would be called 'class intervals'.

Coefficient of correlation
A statistical measure of the degree of relationship between two sets of scores or measures for the same group of individuals. It does not imply that changes in one variable cause the changes in the other variable. It simply describes the patterns of variations. The correlation coefficient most frequently used in educational research is known as the Pearson 'r' or as the product-moment correlation. Coefficients of correlation can have values ranging from −1 (indicating inverse relationship), through 0 (showing no relationship) to +1 (positive relationship). As a general rule, the

rank-order correlation coefficient is preferred when the number of cases is small, (say 15 to 20).

Comparative studies
A type of research in which attempts are made to ascertain common factors or relationships among phenomena. Although studies of this type often employ statistical correlation to determine relationship, correlation is one of the ways of making comparisons.

Consumers of research
Those individuals or agencies that are interested in research findings. For example, a classroom teacher may be interested in finding a more effective way of teaching, parents may like to understand their children better and a local education authority may wish to know the impact of mother-tongue teaching on pupil learning for the purposes of educational planning.

Construct validity
It addresses itself to the problem of determining to what extent a test or research tool measures a particular, theoretically defined aspect of the relevant behaviour being studied.

Control group
A group of subjects or participants that is comparable (but not necessarily identical) to the experimental group, and which is not exposed to the experimental treatment or learning experience. The function of the control group is to indicate what would have happened to the experimental group if it had not been exposed to the experimental treatment.

Criteria
Standards of dimensions on which a research programme, outcome or process is to be judged or evaluated.

Criterion-referenced test
A type of test that attempts to assess performance in tasks on given criteria. The essential feature of a criterion-referenced test is that it intends to show specifically what the person can do rather than comparing one person with others. It contrasts with a norm-referenced test.

Cross-sectional studies
A method of research in which developmental trends are based upon comparisons of groups who differ in age at a given time.

'Culture-fair' tests
Tests that attempt to show that the test items or questions are equally difficult or easy for all groups or whose answers will not be determined by respondents' race, nationality, social class or cultural background.

Degree of freedom
This refers to the number of observations or scores minus the number of parameters that are being estimated. For example, in using N sample observations to estimate the mean of the population the degrees of freedom will be N-1.

Dependent variable
The variable that is affected or influenced by the experimental treatment is called the dependent variable.

Descriptive research
This type of research is primarily concerned with the nature and degree of existing situations or conditions. Descriptive research is often characterized by observational techniques which sometimes involve the collection of very large amounts of data. The researcher observes and records but does not interfere with the 'natural' situation.

Diagnostic test
A psychological test which is used to locate specific areas of weakness and to ascertain the nature of weaknesses rather than to assess the level of attainment.

Empirical research
This type of research is based on observation, case-study, experience of factual information rather than on reason, logic or theory alone.

Empirical validity
This kind of validity provides the evidence that a test score can be interpreted in a particular way because of the relationship between the test performance and behaviour in some other activity. In other words, empirical validity is based on the correlation of the test with a suitable criterion.

Evaluative research
This term is often used in curriculum development to refer to the procedures adopted to collect and analyse data concerning the effectiveness of a particular programme. However, this type of research can range from simple appraisal of particular aspects of social practice to complex educational investigations taking several years.

Evidence
The term is often used in research to refer to findings or results which may contribute to the consideration of a particular issue.

Experimental group
The group or groups exposed to a particular treatment or learning experience.

Experimental research
In this type of research, the investigator seeks to determine what can happen under a given set of situations or circumstances. It is usually conducted by controlling certain conditions in which the independent variable and dependent variable operate.

Face validity
It refers to a kind of validity that is established on the basis of a subjective evaluation or intuition. For example, a measuring device or tool appears to be a good measure of whatever one is trying to measure.

Factor analysis
An analysis of the correlation among tests or test items to find out what elements or characteristics they have in common is referred to as factor analysis. There are several methods of analysing the intercorrelations among a set of test scores or test items. Factor analysis is a sophisticated statistical technique for sorting out the correlations between variables.

Formative evaluation
Evaluation carried out at intermediate stages whilst changes can still be made to the course or programme of study is called process or formative evaluations.

Frequency distribution
A frequency distribution is a quicker way of tabulating a lot of scores. It shows the number of times each score occurs in a total list of the possible scores. As a rule the largest score is placed at the top of the distribution.

Generalization
This refers to the findings of research which can have applicability to other situations, contexts or settings. Generalization is supposed to be a major aim of educational research.

Group test
A test that may be administered to several individuals at the same time, possibly by one administrator.

Halo effect
This refers to the tendency to be influenced by one's general evaluation of the other individual on one striking dimension (e.g. ability) and to attribute to him or her, perhaps unfairly, other characteristics arising from the evaluation of that dimension.

Histogram
A graphic representation of examination mark or score distribution in column form instead of curve form is called the histogram. The histogram is sometimes referred to as a 'frequency graph'.

Historical research
This type of research is concerned with a critical description and analysis of past events mainly for the purpose of gaining a better understanding of the present. It may include comparative and evaluative elements of research, or be partly philosophical in its approach.

Hypothesis

An hypothesis is a tentative answer to the problem set out in the research. It is a guide to the researcher in that it delineates and often determines the procedures to be followed in studying the problem.

Independent variable

The experimental condition imposed in a study is referred to as the treatment. A treatment is a type of independent variable. An independent variable is a treatment only if it can be manipulated by the researcher.

Individual test

A test that is designed for administration to a single person rather than to a group of individuals.

Instrument

Any technique or tool that the researcher uses to determine a value in terms of quality or quantity is called an instrument, for example, a questionnaire, an interview schedule, attitude scale, or achievement test.

Interview

This is a method of obtaining data that normally involves face-to-face communication between the researcher and the respondent.

Interview schedule

A set of questions designed to elicit particular information. The questions may range from open-minded ones (e.g. semi-structured) which allow the respondents to express themselves freely, to those which limit answers to predetermined categories (e.g. structured), as utilized in the public opinion survey.

Item analysis

The procedures for selecting items to constitute psychological tests yielding scores which will satisfy prespecified conditions are called 'item analysis'. The term has been used loosely in the literature. However, it commonly refers to the determination of the difficulty index and discrimination index of a test item.

Lie scale

A set of items, comprising part of a larger set on a questionnaire, intended to identify those respondents whose responses are unreliable because of their tendency to create a 'good' image of themselves, i.e. deliberate attempts to fake their responses to questionnaire items.

Longitudinal research

In this type of research, data are collected on the same individuals at different points over a period of time.

Mean (Arithmetic mean)
This usually refers to the arithmetic mean when it is used in psychology and education. It is obtained by summing all the scores in a group and by dividing the number of cases in the group. Thus, it indicates the average score obtained by a group.

Median
This term is referred to the score value in a distribution of scores which marks the midpoint of the set of data. 50 per cent of the scores are above and 50 per cent are below it.

Mode
The score or the measurement value that occurs most often in a distribution is called the mode. The mode is easy to locate in a frequency distribution because it is merely the score value that has the largest frequency.

Model/Paradigm
The term 'model' is used in both the natural and social sciences. It indicates a close representation of certain aspects of complex phenomena designed by using objects or symbols which in some way resemble phenomena. A model is essentially an analogy which is useful in helping the researcher to think about phenomena. In recent years 'paradigm' has become an increasingly fashionable alternative.

N
The number of subjects in a particular study. Thus, when N equals one it is representative of a single case study.

NFER (National Foundation for Education Research)
The NFER is an independent body which was set up in the UK in 1947. Its main function is to conduct large-scale and long-term educational research. It has established a journal *Educational Research* and a Test Service and Agency from which information about a wide variety of tests and the tests themselves can be obtained. It is supported by the DfEE (Department for Education and Employment), LEA (Local Education Authorities) and teacher organizations.

Normal distribution
A distribution of test scores that in graphic form has a very specific bell-shaped appearance, called a normal distribution. The shape of the curve that can be drawn for these distributions is called a normal curve. The distribution has the same shape on either side of the centre point, the largest frequency of scores being located around the centre and the smaller frequencies of scores appearing at both tails of the distribution.

Norms
This refers to the levels of acceptable test performance based on response from a representative sample of a comparison group. Norms are descriptive of average,

typical or mediocre performance, and should not be treated as desirable levels of attainment of specified groups.

Norm-referenced test

A type of test in which an individual's performance (cognitive or affective) is compared with other individuals of similar age and background drawn from the same population. This is contrasted with criterion-referenced tests.

Null hypothesis

In research design it is quite common to formulate the hypothesis in a form known as the null hypothesis. This means that the researchers set out by assuming that the 'hunch' they have is not true. In other words, there is no likelihood of the hypothesis being significant. In order to test this, they state the research hypothesis that no difference between two things is expected.

Objective test

A test in which the markers always agree on correctness or incorrectness of the responses. The correct answer to each question is predetermined and is given in the test manual, which has to be followed exactly.

Observation

A research technique which utilizes direct contact between the researcher and the phenomena under investigation. The method is widely used in the study of child development (e.g. Piagetian studies). The major problem in observation is to assure that the behaviour is noted objectively and reliably.

Operational definition

In educational research, many terms cannot readily be defined, and hence researchers attempt to define them according to their use which is called operational definition.

Parameters

The value of a particular measure (such as the mean or standard deviation) assigned to population is called a parameter. In other words, if all scores of a defined population are available and the mean is calculated, the value obtained is a parameter of the population.

Personality assessment

A technique for the comprehensive appraisal of an individual's personality and the prediction of individual behaviour that utilizes a number of standardized instruments and techniques.

Phenomenological theories

A diverse class of theories, all sharing the assumption that subjective experiences are meaningful and reliable data for understanding an individual's personality. Other approaches related to such a view are humanistic, existential and experiential.

Projective techniques

Methods intended for the measurement of personality characteristics or traits that involve presentation of relatively unstructured stimuli to the respondent. The reason behind the use of such techniques is that deeper lying tendencies in an individual are not readily ascertainable through direct methods. Projective techniques vary in the degree to which the stimuli are unstructured such as ink blots (the Rorschach test), pictures (TAT), sentence completion, etc.

Population

The term population has a specific meaning to the researcher. It refers to the larger group from which a sample is selected for study. The sample participates in research and then inferences or generalizations are made about the population (also referred to as Universe). A population can be very small or very large. For example, all pupils aged 11–12 years in a particular school or Local Education Authority could be referred to as the population, dependent on the focus and scale of the research.

Quasi-experiment

Studies which involve non-manipulable independent variables are referred to as quasi-experiments. In this type of experiment, the conditions are taken as they are found in naturally occurring settings. For example, in a study in a natural setting, random assignment to experimental or control group status may be organized on the basis of normal teaching groups rather than individual pupils.

Random sample

A sample of the members of a given population is drawn in such a way that every member of that population has an equal chance of being selected, that is to say, the sampling technique eliminates the operation of bias in selection (see also biased sample).

Raw scores

The original scores obtained from a test are called raw scores.

Reliability

The term is commonly used in connection with a test or examination. The procedure is also used when using observational methods in order to ascertain at least a minimum degree of confidence in the data. Reliability refers to the extent to which a test or technique functions consistently and accurately by yielding the same results. A variety of statistical procedures exist to calculate a reliability estimate (e.g. test-re-test, split-halves).

Response sets

Any tendency causing an individual to give different responses to test items than he or she would when the same content is present in a different form is known as a response set. This is part of attitudinal factors which tend to introduce bias into self-report personality inventories. One such factor is social desirability, in which a respondent tends to agree with a test item that is generally considered to express a 'good' characteristic, and tends to disagree with less desirable items or questions.

Sample
A sample is a smaller number of elements selected from a population, assumed to be representative of that population.

Sampling error
An error which contributes to lack of representativeness of a sample. When researchers obtain measurement results from a sample of subjects and attempt to generalize to the total population they may make wrong generalizations because the sample chosen for the investigation was not perfectly representative of the population, from which it was drawn.

Self
The 'I' or 'me', of which the individual is aware in his or her thoughts, feelings, perceptions and actions. The self has a structure with various attributes and is subject to development and change as a result of interaction with others. The term 'self' should be distinguished from the terms 'identity', 'ego' and 'personality'. Briefly, the 'self' is just one element of the total personality of an individual.

Skewness
It refers to deviation of the shape of a frequency curve from a normal curve. A skewed curve, therefore, is a frequency curve that departs from the symmetrical shape either by having more cases on the right of the mean than on the left, or *vice versa*. In a skewed curve the values of the mean, median and mode are not identical.

Socialization
The process by which socially determined factors become influential in controlling or modifying the patterns of an individual's behaviour (e.g. parental influence, schooling).

Sociogram
A diagrammatic representation of the study of the interrelation patterns existing between people is called a sociogram. Thus, the relationships between an individual child and his or her friends can be shown by the use of personal sociograms.

Sociometry
A method of investigation which allows the researcher to study and plot the pattern of relationships between individuals in a group.

Standard deviation
In research studies, the investigator also wishes to know something about how the test scores are spread out. The standard deviation is a measure of the dispersion of

scores around the arithmetic mean. The more the scores cluster around the mean, the smaller is the standard deviation.

Standardized test
A test that has been tried out on a representative sample before publication to ensure that there is a standard to which persons taking the test can be compared. Such a test is accompanied by a manual which contains the directions and other conditions of administration, time limits, scoring scheme, normative information, and so forth.

Statistical significance (significance test)
The term is used when researchers report 'findings' rather than opinions. It is common practice for them to use phrases like 'significant at the 1 per cent level', 'significant at the 5 per cent level', 'not significant' (NS). This shows the degree of certainty with which one can trust the findings. For example, the 5 per cent level of significance implies that there is a probability of 0.05 that the obtained result is due to sampling error. The best known types of significance tests which have been developed in the social sciences are the 't' tests, the chi-square tests, and the F ratio tests.

Stereotype
The social perception of individuals in terms of their group membership rather than of their actual personal attributes is called stereotype. Such perceptions are often inaccurate for the person concerned, and may even be invalid for the group as a whole. However, once formed, stereotypes are difficult to change.

Subjects
The individuals who are studied in an experiment are known as subjects.

Survey research methods
These are normally employed to gather data from large numbers of people. There are many techniques of data collection that can be used in a process that is generally described as a survey.

Theory
In educational research, the term usually implies a set of formal statements describing and explaining the relationship between human behaviour and the factors that affect or explain it. A theory can range from the simple to the complicated.

Test-retest coefficient
This type of reliability estimation is obtained by administering the same test a second time after a short interval (say, two weeks) and correlating the two sets of test scores. This method is preferred for the measurement of traits that are theoretically expected to be relatively stable and consistent over time (e.g. intellectual and aptitude characteristics).

Trait

An enduring characteristic of the individual that is manifested in a consistent way of behaving in a wide variety of situations. Traits are of many types; some are broad in scope, some narrow, some on the surface and others are deep-seated.

't' test

The 't' test provides a method by which the means of the samples can be compared when it is assumed that the samples have been randomly selected and the scores are obtained from normally distributed populations.

Treatment

The experimental condition introduced in an educational study is referred to as the treatment. A treatment is a type of independent variable, that is to say, all experimental treatments are independent variables.

Triangulation

This is a process of corroborating judgments by drawing on evidence from more than one source — for example from interviews, questionnaires and observations.

True score

An individual's test score is affected by many floating variables that cannot be perfectly controlled. A true score is a hypothetical score, free of such influence.

Validity

In the field of educational measurement, validity refers to the degree to which a test, tool or technique measures what it is supposed to measure. No technique, tool or test possesses universal validity — it may be valid for use in one situation but invalid in another. Validity has different connotations for various kinds of tests, and accordingly, different kinds of validity (e.g. content, concurrent, predictive, construct) are appropriate for each.

Variable

This refers to a measurable or non-measurable characteristic of a population which varies from one individual to another. Age, gender, ability, personality characteristics are a few examples of human variables, and the researcher manipulates, controls or observes these characteristics.

Index

accountability 69, 70–1, 183, *193*
acculturation *193*
achievement test 58, 160, 173, *193*
Achilles, C. 66
action research
  application 47
  definition 12, 91–3, *193*
  role 64
  teachers' role 183–5, 188
Adelman, C. 36, 92
Altrichter, H. 93
American Educational Research
    Association (AERA) 58, 59
analysis of covariance (ANCOVA) 98, 103
analysis of variance 166–7, *193–4*
Anderson, G. 32, 45, 74, 87, 111, 114, 115, 161
anthropology 8, 10, 18, 86, 87
applied research
  definition 2, 11, *194*
  practical applications 39, 44–5
  role 47, 64
  support 68
  teachers' attitudes 180, 186
aptitude tests 62
Arnot, M. 67
Ary, D. 32
assumptions 4, 37, 51, 97, 135
Atkinson, G.B.J. 40
Atkinson, P. 86
attitude test 100, 133, 173, *194*
attitudes 4, 9, 10, 39, 65
audience 43, 47–50, 51, 180, *194*

Bagley, C. 39
Ball, S.J. 67
Barnes, J.A. 47
Barnes, J.B. 58, 75
Barzun, J. 75

baseline evaluation 90
basic (pure) research 11, 39, 44–5, 47, *194*
Bassey, M. 14, 67, 186, 189–90
battery of tests *194*
Beard, R.M. 61
Becker, H.S. 81
behavioural objectives 61, *194*
behavioural validity *194–5*
Bell, J. 112
BERA *see* British Educational Research
    Association
Berelson, B. 111
Best, J.W. 1, 6
bias *195*
  avoiding 76–7, 78, 87, 101, 102
  randomization 97
  researcher 38, 42, 76–7, 114, 128
  in sample 113, 118, *195*
  teachers 39
Binet, A. 59, 134
Binnie, A. 182
Black, P. 90
Blatchford, P. 66
Bloom, B.S. 35, 39
Borg, W.R. 86, 113, 114, 120, 142
Bouma, G.D. 40
Brehaut, W. 60
Brenner, M. 122
British Educational Research Association
    (BERA) 64, 67, 68, 127, 147–51, 186, 189
Brown, S. 69
Bruner, J.S. 31, 62
Bryman, A. 36
Buckingham, B.R. 59
Burgess, R.G. 89, 146
Burstall, C. 66
Burt, C. 59